P9-AEX-387

CRIME A DAY

Death by Electric Chair & Other Boyhood Pursuits

a memoir by

Joe DiBuduo

To Susan, one of my favorite teachers
Joe DiBuduo

Jaded Ibis Press
sustainable literature by digital means™
an imprint of Jaded Ibis Productions
Seattle • Hong Kong • Boston

Table of Contents

NAME DIBUDUO, JOSEPH
DOB: 01/2511940
SEX: M RACE: POB: CHELSEA MA MOTHER: MIRIAM
ATLAS FATHER: ANTONIO ADDRESS: 17 TUCKER ST DORCHESTER MA
ADULT APPEARANCES
THIS INFORMATION MAY CONTAIN CORI.
IT IS NOT SUPPORTED BY FINGERPRINTS'
PLEASE cHiir< iHni iHe NAMER EFERENcEBDE
LowM ATcHEST HEN AMEA NDD ArEo F BIRrHo F THE PERSON, COMMONWEALTH OF
    MASSACHUSETTS
CRIMINAL HISTORY SYSTEMS BOARD PCF: 00000099635 DOB:
01l25h940
"W A R N I N G T
,-. PERSONS COURT SUMMARY *"7
FORMAL NAME:
Page:01 ARRAIGNMENT:
ARGDATE:01/04/1961 PD:
OFF: A&B ON POLICE OFFICER DISP: I MO CMTD ARRAIGNMENT:
ARG DATE:02/01/1960 PD: OFF: LARCENY
OISP: 6MOC MTD ARRAIGNMENT:
ARGDATE:06/2011959 PD:
OFF: LARCENY ARRAIGNMENT:
ARG DATE:03/2611958 OFF: B&E NIGHT
DISP:1YR CMTD
DISP: 6MO SS PROB 5/201602 11160V OP 6MO CMTD COURT: BOSTON DISTRICT
COURT BRTGHTON DISTRICT COURT: BRIGHTON
DISTRICT PCF: 00000099635 SSN:0o0000o0o
DKT#: 1490a43ZZ A&B PO STATUS:C
WPD: DKT#: t490a42ZZ STATUS:C WPD:
DKT#: 1490a41ZZ STATUS:C WPD: DKT#:
1490a40ZZ B&E NT STATUS:C WPD:
COURT: SUFFOLK SUPERIOR

Introduction

I've often despised mainstream American society because of the abuse I endured in my youth. The police, the courts, the state institutions—they were all guilty. When I was growing up in the 1940s and 1950s, the Boston legal system incarcerated kids for "stubbornness," for ditching school, and for drinking. On account of misdemeanors like these, they sentenced poor kids to state institutions, to serve time right alongside guys who had committed far more serious crimes.

It seems many people associate Boston, Massachusetts with high culture, high class, and long history. The stories I heard in grammar school about Paul Revere, the Old North Church, Bunker Hill, and the Boston Tea Party, and expressions like, "Don't shoot until you see the whites of their eyes," are but a few of the adages and historical facts I learned as a schoolboy. Many events in my youth were equally historic but were rarely discussed outside the seedy Boston neighborhoods where they took place: tales of corrupt police officers and cynical judges, tough gangsters and endless brawls.

For years I never told anyone about my childhood transgressions. I just wanted to forget about them and the crimes I committed as a young adult. It hurt to remember. Then, at the age of 66, I enrolled in a creative writing class at a community college and began to record my memories. This catharsis relieved the burden of pain and shame I'd carried for decades. And though I'm proud that I survived

7

long enough to pen this memoir, I still feel like an outcast deep inside, because I don't think the same way as anyone I know. Maybe not like you, either. I hope this book will help you understand what it's like to be poor and live in an impoverished area.

Prologue

I grew up in Hano, also known as Hanoville, at the time one of the most impoverished neighborhoods in Boston. *Deprived* is a good word. I was deprived of educational toys and books, a fair education, and respectable role models other than my hardworking but absentee father. I also grew up without food, soap, and other basic needs that most Americans take for granted.

If you've never experienced stomach-wrenching hunger with no sign of rescue, or an excruciating toothache or earache with no access to medical intervention, then you may never understand what I'm about to tell you. You might think that my choices in life were caused by laziness, impulsivity or my inability to "pull myself up by my bootstraps." But, you'd be wrong. In order to accomplish that feat I would have needed to know which way was up. In Hano, there was no up; there was just Hano. No one I knew dreamed of a better world, a better place. Everyone I knew had a solution to every problem: Get drunk, and forget about it, or get drunk and fight about it. My beliefs took hold inside the hopelessness of Hano, and I was captivated by the dramas unfolding around me.

I grew up believing that the toughest guys in my neighborhood—those who fought the cops and resisted arrest—were heroes. By the time I was five years old, fighting the law had become my goal. My fantasy was to grow big enough to fight cops and beat them in a fair match. The 1931 movie *Public Enemy* was one of my childhood favorites. I often swaggered and grimaced in front of a mirror, repeating James Cagney's trademark line, "Come and get me, you dirty coppers!" The words became a metaphor for the criminal code of honor I longed to embrace. My environment only helped to reinforce my skewed viewpoint. In Hano, honor meant never ratting out a friend, never chickening out of a fight, and never refusing to share a drink or cigarette when you had one. My peers and I lived for today; we didn't consider consequences because we thought tomorrow would never come.

The Hano equivalent of a PhD or big sports award was serving time, and I was ambitious: I wanted my prison term, to be an ex-con and wear the label with pride. My ultimate goal was to rob a bank or store so I could get into a gunfight with police and go out in a blaze of glory. (I never imagined living to an age old enough that I'd need an education to survive.) I emulated the bad guys, never the white hats. When *I saw Kiss of Death* and watched Richard Widmark push a wheelchair-bound old woman down a flight of stairs and giggle as she rolled down them, I thought he was the best. That is, until I saw James Cagney standing atop an oil tank, shouting, "Made it, Ma! Top of the world!" right before the tank exploded.

Like most red-blooded American boys of the era, I also thrilled to images of the Wild West. Sometimes, after watching a Western, I'd think about becoming a cattle rustler, and when I got shot and died, I'd be just like movie cowboys who said goodbye to their friends and lovers while smoking their last cigarette. Every self-respecting cattle rustler was a tough guy who died with his boots on. Death before dishonor was a principle I deeply believed in and admired.

Anyway, death didn't deter me because it meant a release from the pain and hunger. Of course, I had no idea what dying was like; I just enjoyed thinking about the different ways I could go out. As I said, most scenarios involved violent gun battles against a swarm of law enforcement officers, or dying in the electric chair. In any case, I told myself, I'd go without a whimper—like a real man! Meanwhile, until the time came for my final shootout, I'd become a criminal to achieve one measure of respect in Hano. The other way would be by drinking as much as possible while becoming oblivious to the hard and hardened world where I lived.

I did accomplish my fair share of drinking and carousing, and I did come to fight the cops and commit some of the crimes I admired. At the age of twenty-two, I was well on my way to fulfilling my perceived destiny as an ex-convict. I had even volunteered for a tour of duty in Vietnam to learn how to kill, when a simple event in my life suddenly changed everything.

Taken Away

I'm told my life began in 1940, at 466 Broadway Street in Chelsea, a suburb bordering Boston. Miriam Atlas, my mother, was 25 at the time. A Jew, she converted to Catholicism when she married my father Antonio DiBuduo, a 52-year old immigrant from Naples, Italy. They wed in a civil ceremony because the Catholics would not allow my father, who was divorced, a church wedding.

I once found Mom's birth certificate with the name *Miriam Footnick* on it, but she beat the heck out of me for the discovery. Her family must have Anglicized the original surname, as did many Jews in the late 19th an early 20th centuries, to better fit into an increasingly anti-Semitic culture or to severe ties to the politically tumultuous homelands from which they emigrated. Her mother's family disowned her for marrying outside her faith, and my father's family was absent as well. Life as a "half-breed"—half-Jewish, half-Italian—was hard in an era when Hitler was exterminating anyone with Jewish blood.

Many residents in the rough Boston neighborhoods where I spent my early years held similar anti-Semitic views. Italians weren't much loved either, because Italy had sided with Germany in World War II. The racially mixed could usually choose one side or the other, but neither Catholics nor Jews wanted a religious mongrel in their midst. When I got old enough to be called *kike, dirty Jew,* or some other catchall slur, my identity as "half-breed" hit home. If it wasn't a

Jew-hating day, my good Irish Catholic neighbors would call me names like *greaseball, dago,* or *wop.* I soon realized the biggest asset to living with racial and religious intolerance in my neighborhood was learning how to fight.

The populace of Hano loved to fight, and to fight with a cop was the best fight anyone could have. No one ever claimed victory in these battles, but we never let the thought of losing stop us from trying. A cop fighter got a few free drinks to help relieve the pain of injuries from resisting arrest, and for a day or two he earned fame. Onlookers would count how many cops it took to subdue a combatant. (It usually took five or six officers, sometimes more, to put a Hano resident down.) As a consequence, police and emergency services avoided the area unless they absolutely had no choice.

We called our neighborhod "the slums" in those days. It consisted of two-flat and four-flat row houses, with a few single-family houses mixed in. The streets in Hano all ended at Braintree Street, at a seven-story building called "the box factory" by locals.

When most people discovered I lived in Hano, they'd take a step back as though our poverty was contagious. It seemed to be: I wasn't the only one in Hano who went hungry. Nor was I only kid with an unkempt house, or who dressed in tattered and dirty clothes. Our conditions were embarrassing but also the norm—until I learned to collect and cash in the empty soda bottles discarded by factory workers at lunchtime, and snitch baked goods from the local bakery at night, and swipe milk from the neighbors' porches early in the morning.

Before moving to Hano in 1944, we lived in an old boarded-up storefront apartment in South Boston, the rock bottom of Boston neighborhoods. Mostly large, poor Irish families lived there, and I never figured out how a hard-working Italian guy like my father ended up in a rundown neighborhood like "Southie." World War II was raging across Europe and the Pacific in 1944 and rationing was in effect, so I assumed that daily hunger was a normal state. I was four years old when Dad came home one sunny winter afternoon with a smile on his face and a big piece of meat wrapped in newspaper tucked under his arm.

My mother went ballistic. She took the haunch-shaped package and started hitting him with it. "I'm not eating horsemeat, you Italian bastard!" she screamed. "You have some nerve bringing this home."

Dad, a man of few words, remained silent.

Mom threw the package on the floor. I stared at it, shocked. I would have been happy to eat it, horsemeat or not. I eased out the front door with Tony, my six-year-old brother. We crossed the street to play war on an expanse of land where buildings once stood. It was now just a field littered with broken beer and wine bottles. The glass covering our neighborhood playground glittered in the sun's blinding rays like jewels tossed randomly over the earth.

"We're playing war," Tony said. "German planes are bombing us."

I knew people dived for cover when bombers attached, so I did the same. But when I landed a broken bottle lacerated my scalp. When I rubbed my hand over my head, it came away wet. Blood streamed down my face, just like a real war injury.

"They got me, Tony!" I cried.

"Better get you to the first aid station," Tony said, sticking with our war game. He took me by the hand and led me home. As soon as we walked in, our cat Minnie meowed her hunger whine. I held out my bloody hand and she licked it.

"I told you to watch Joey, not kill him," Mom screamed when she saw me. She grabbed her broom and started beating Tony with it. It seemed like she was always blaming Tony for things I did. I didn't understand why, but I was glad he got the beating and not me.

Mom washed my cuts off and told me I'd be fine.

Minnie followed me around the apartment, trying to lick my fingers.

After Mom finished with Tony's beating, he and I sat in our room listening to her argue with Dad about our apartment being a boarded-up store with just four rooms. He had plans to open the store and have my mother run it, but she wasn't having any part of it.

The next day my mother swept the kitchen floor while Tony and I played in the living room that she'd just finished cleaning.

"Watch this," Tony said. He tore a newspaper into little pieces and threw them into the air like confetti at a tickertape parade. I guessed he was trying to get even with Mom for smacking him with the broom, so I jumped in and helped.

Mom looked up from her sweeping. "You little bastards," she yelled. She raised the broom above her head, ready to beat us both, but we took off before she could catch us. We knew that if we ran she'd soon forget her anger, but if she caught us she'd spare no mercy.

This was my first recollection of what seems like hundreds of times Mom chased us with her trusty broom. Good thing we kids were faster than her.

* * * * *

A few days after I'd gashed open my forehead, there was a knock on the door. Dad wasn't home; it was just Mom, Tony, me, and my younger brother Bernard who would have been just a year old at the time, and taking a nap. Mom opened the door. A stout, stone-faced woman dressed as severely as her expression stood next to a small, dour-faced man wearing a dark suit. He brushed past my mother and grabbed Tony and me by our hands.

"Who the hell are you," said Mom, "and what do you think you're doing?"

"Child Welfare and Protection Agency," the man said. He showed her a badge and handed her a piece of paper. "Court order. Look at the bottom. Shows when you're due in court."

They dragged Tony and me out of the apartment while my mother's screams echoed in my ears. The welfare woman opened the door of a four-door black sedan. Well, in those days, most cars were painted black. The plush cloth seats seemed luxurious, and when the car moved I looked out the window, thrilled to be on my first car trip.

The man drove for a long time until finally we came to a large, secluded brick building surrounded by snow-covered hills full of trees. The car stopped and we got out. I didn't know what to think.

The building looked warm and clean, but a smell like a pail of dirty diapers permeated everything.

The man and woman handed Tony and me over to a young man apparently in charge of the facility. I thought of him as a keeper of kids, because I saw so many children milling around him. In my memory, the rooms and the kids and the staff merge into a dull gray blur.

That night we sat in a crowded dining room with about twenty round tables set with dishes, silverware, and napkins. Six kids were seated at each table. Tony and I sat side-by-side.

"Hey, we get to eat," Tony said.

I couldn't wait for the food to arrive. I anticipated mashed potatoes along with vegetables and meat. But a bowl of gooey green substance arrived instead. It looked like slimy snot when I twirled it around in the dish.

"I can't eat this," I told Tony. I looked around and saw other kids eating the slop, but I just couldn't.

"Me, either," Tony said.

My stomach ached from hunger and I wondered when we'd eat again. There were other meals, more edible than the first, and a couple just as bad. But just how much time we spent there remains a mystery to me. I don't recall missing my mom or dad, but I do remember being scared and confused at times. Having Tony there beside me was a comfort.

A few days after our arrival, Tony and I went out walking in the snow-covered hills surrounding the facility. It was great to see everything covered in white, and not have to watch out for broken glass and other trash littering the ground. I found a wooden ski longer than I was tall, the first I'd ever seen. Thrilled, I thought I'd found treasure and took it back to the building where Tony and I slept. But as soon as a counselor saw me carrying the ski, he took it away from me.

That night we had to take a bath. I stood in a line of about twenty boys, all around Tony's age. One by one they arrived at the tub where a counselor sat, and he took their dirty clothes. When they got out of the tub, he handed them clean ones. Then came my turn. After I undressed the counselor spanked me for not wearing under-wear. I didn't even know what underwear was. I'd never had any at home, and had no idea where to acquire any until the counselor gave me a pair.

* * * * *

My next memory is of Mom coming to take us away from the state-run home. I remember her holding our hands as we got off a streetcar at Union Square, a Boston neighborhood in the Allston dis-trict. We crossed a street and walked past a restaurant, two bars, a drug store, a Stop & Shop Supermarket, and a three-story brick building that housed a printing company on the first and second floors. At the corner of this building, Hano Street intersected with Cambridge Street. We turned down its steep slope and walked past empty lots and a park covered with asphalt. We were heading to our new apartment.

Tony and I wore sailor suits—dark blue outfits with white stripes, bell-bottom pants, and those little round white hats that sailors call "Dixie cups." I guess it was fashionable to dress kids in miniature uniforms during wartime. Some tough-looking older boys passed by and pointed at us.

"Look at the two sissies," one said, and they all hooted with laughter.

I got scared when the kids made fun of us because Mom and Tony didn't say a word. Showing up in this poor working-class neighborhood dressed like children of the privileged class was something I had a hard time living down. I can still hear the teasing I got for wearing that stupid uniform. But I can't blame Mom; she must have thought we were cute dressed like that. Her family was wealthy, so to her, even though we were poor and hungry, that mode of dress would have seemed perfectly normal. After marrying my father, she went from having anything she wanted to having nothing. She must have been bitter because her anger surfaced easily, and it seemed just about anything enraged her.

That day, our first in Hano, we continued walking past empty lots full of broken glass, just like those in Southie where we'd played. And except for a few other nationalities and Protestants, the population was the same: poor Irish immigrants. It all looked the same to me.

My mother took a shortcut through an alley that led from Hano Street to Blaine Street.

"This is where we'll be living from now on," she said. "Those son-of-bitches from social services said where we used to live wasn't fit. The judge returned you to us as soon as we found this place."

Mom pointed to a door with worn green paint, two brass number 3s, and a cracked glass window.

"33 Blaine Street. Remember your address so you don't get lost," she cautioned us. "Don't forget."

Blaine Street wouldn't be hard to remember, even though I'd never heard the name "Blaine" before. Everett Street ran parallel with Blaine at the rear of the building where we lived. Dorothy Muriel's Bakery was on Everett, a few doors up. One block over was Albany Carpet, a rug cleaning company that bordered an asphalt-covered park just two blocks from Hano Street. On Braintree Street stood the Metropolitan Transit Authority garage where the buses were stored and repaired.

On the opposite side of the street, Tony pointed to a mailbox in front of a single- family house. He took a moment to sound it out. "Fitz . . . Fitzgerald, that's the name on it."

Next to that was a row house with four flats. He read the names on the mailboxes: "McDonald, O'Brien, McIntyre, and Kelly."

"See," said Mom, "just like our old neighborhood. Everyone is Irish."

And so I began to feel more Irish than anything else. Later in life, my mom never sent any holiday cards other than for St Patrick's Day, so she probably felt the same way. She continued living in Irish neighborhoods until the day she died.

Yet even though I identified with the Irish culture of the other neighborhood kids, I still felt different. Somehow I knew I'd never fit in.

Weeks later, Tony and I asked about our cat Minnie. Dad took me back to South Boston to look for her. He told me the cat would be waiting at our old house. I didn't believe him because it had been a long time since we'd moved. Sure enough, though, Minnie was there waiting for us. We took her home to Hano.

Only Wimpy Boys Cry

"That's right, only wimpy boys cry."

I heard this remark a hundred times in the first month I lived in Hano. By then I didn't dare shed a tear, no matter what happened. I didn't want anybody to think me "a sissy." But inside, I wondered if I was different, because I didn't seem to share the mean streak of most boys I knew.

One day my Dad gave me two dollars to buy a new pair of sneakers. I bought them on my way to school, at a store that sold shoes and clothing. I put them on and threw the old worn and tattered ones in the garbage. Proud of myself, I told my first grade teacher, "I have new shoes."

She looked down at my feet. "Oh? Where are they?"

My heart sank as I realized my teacher didn't consider sneakers shoes. Her attitude surprised me because every kid in my neighborhood got sneakers when they shopped for shoes. I felt lucky to have them.

Lying in bed that night, an irrational fear overcame me, one that returned repeatedly over the years: I imagined someone chasing me (as often happened during my real adventures), and one of my shoes fell off. I couldn't go back and retrieve it without being caught. Where could I go with one shoe? I knew there wasn't any money to buy another pair. Visions of walking around with one bare foot raced through my mind. How everyone would laugh at me with one shoe off and one shoe on! I fell asleep and dreamed I had no shoes at all.

* * * * *

I knew I was soft-hearted because I never intentionally hurt any animal. I even sympathized with bugs—except for cockroaches, my mortal enemies. They seemed to follow me everywhere. I believed they'd eat me, if given the chance.

One night, hungry as usual, I went into our kitchen to see if there was possibly some food in the freezer or pantry. In those days, most ceiling lights had chains or strings attached as the on/off switch. As soon as I pulled it, the light came on and I saw roaches so numerous that they practically covered the ceiling. They scurried to hide, bumping into each another as they dashed across the ceiling. When they collided, they fell, raining down onto the kitchen floor and me. I ran for cover. After that, every time I saw a roach, I began to itch all over. I badly wished that my parents would get rid of the disgusting pests, but the price of an exterminator was way out of reach.

After the roaches had all scurried of, to hide in cracks and crevices, I came back into the kitchen. I turned on the gas stove burners to try to warm the room. Then I noticed them: roaches feasting on the greasy stovetop, forming lines in between the burners. One by one, they fled, jumping off the stove to escape from the heat from the flames. I stepped back and observed the orderly way they lined up and took turns jumping. It made me wonder if cockroaches had

23

minds like people, if they could scheme and plan. As many as there were, I feared, they just might overwhelm me one night.

* * * * *

On another of my nighttime forays to look for food in the kitchen, I pulled the chain on the ceiling fixture and the fixture shorted out. Electricity arced through the chain and wrapped around my arm. An outline of the little metal balls would remain on my skin for weeks. Right then, I knew what it meant when adults said, "burn in the electric chair."

The kitchen was at the rear of the apartment and held a table with two chairs. The table was always piled high with empty donut boxes, soda bottles, dirty dishes, glasses, and dirty pots and pans—a virtual paradise for roaches. Eventually, a dilapidated wringer washer joined the mess. My dad bought the washer on credit to help my mom with the laundry. The machine agitated the clothes, then Mom would crank the wet clothes through the manual wringer before hanging them on a line to dry. A week after she got the machine, the motor broke down. The washer sat in the kitchen for years, half-full of stinking water.

Eventually, a freezer joined the waste. It was another "luxury" that hadn't worked out. Dad had purchased it full of food, including some frozen strawberries. For a few weeks, I ate those strawberries straight from their containers, imagining it was strawberry ice cream melting in my mouth—and delighted that no roach had crawled over them. Once empty, though, the freezer never saw food again. Dad just couldn't afford to refill it.

It wasn't that we never had any food; we just never had enough to get full. Sometimes Dad would stop at a bakery after working all night and bring home loaves of French bread. When he did, we'd get up and eat our fill before the roaches got to them. Sometimes he would make a roast beef sandwich at work and bring it home. Though it was supposed to be his dinner, he'd share it with Tony, me, and anyone else who was awake in the apartment. Other times there would be no food at all for supper, and usually none the next day, either. So most of the time I didn't even think about being able to eat.

During the best times, Dad made pizza for dinner, or spaghetti. No sauce, no meat, but maybe Mom topped it with butter. If we had bread, we'd dampen it with water, spread sugar on top, and enjoy our sugar sandwiches. Even so, I don't remember us all sitting down to dinner together, as a family.

* * * * *

It seemed our family couldn't have been much poorer unless we'd been homeless—and I often thought homelessness might have been an improvement. Our apartment had three floors, with two bedrooms on the third floor and one bathroom on the second floor. (The toilet bowl in the bathroom was so soiled that my brother Tony used to use the bathroom at the nearest gas station.) The first floor had a living room, a dining room used as a third bedroom, a kitchen, and a small hall with a room at the end used for storage. The wood floors were littered with clumps of hardened dirt, next to impossible to clean off. My dad and I tried soaking these clumps with soapy water and scraping them with a tool made for cleaning floors, but we never succeeded in getting them clean. In a matter of days the floors were as dirty as before. Superman comics were popular at the time, and I used to daydream that Superman came and cleaned our home, as only a superhero could clean the dirt-encrusted floors and the refuse-strewn rooms and closets.

Our family grew during the years we lived in Hano. Tony is two years older than I am, and Bernard is two years younger. Marie came along six years after me, and Andy is eleven years younger. All the families we knew were poor, but our family was poorer than most. We didn't have a car, a furnace, a washing machine, a telephone, or a TV. We had hardly any blankets or clothes, and our washcloths, towels, sheets and pillowcases were rags. We didn't have hot water or heat, and the only soap in the house was usually brown laundry bar soap that barely cleaned, especially in cold water. There were no nail clippers, combs, hairbrushes, toothbrushes, or toothpaste in the house. My dad told me to use table salt on my finger and rub my gums and teeth with it. A trip to the dentist or the doctor was an unheard of luxury.

During the winter we had to leave the faucets trickling so the water pipes wouldn't freeze and burst. Thought there wasn't central heating, we did have a Franklin wood-burning stove. Boston winters were cold and long. Every night I'd stuff the stove full of wood, but no matter how much I used, the fire seemed to last only an hour or so. When I got a bit older I'd keep the fire burning for such a long time that the thick iron sides would turn white with heat, thus teaching me the meaning of "white hot." It was so hot that if I touched a stick of wood against the white metal, the stick burst into flames.

Other than the location, Hano was the same as Southie. In Hano, as in Southie, people seemed to know everyone in the neighborhood. During those hot and humid summer evenings, everyone sat on their stoops or front porches to chat with their neighbors. Staying indoors wasn't an option, because in those pre-air-conditioning days even an electric fan was an extravagance.

When I was still young most of the front steps of the apartments and houses were wooden. Later, the buildings' owners began to replace those old stoops with cement stairs. I'd wait for the workers to rip out the old wooden steps and then sift through the ground under them to find coins that had fallen from pockets over the years. My very first moneymaking scheme.

Not long after we moved to Hano, I contributed to filling the fields with broken glass by going on bottle-breaking sprees armed with empty wine and beer bottles left in the streets. The idea was to toss quart bottles as high as possible and watch them spin end over end, until they finally returned to earth, smashing when they hit ground. Then I'd throw rocks at the bigger shards until only tiny pieces remained. The crash and tinkle of breaking glass sent shivers of pleasure through my little body.

Breaking glass became so addictive that when there weren't any bottles to break around my house, I'd take a hike up to Union Square and dig through trash behind the Model Café and the Tavern, the two bars that dumped their empties in the alley. We kids called it "back of dance," though I never knew why. I could spend hours throwing bottles against the big boulders dotting the empty hills behind the bars. So habitual was this diversion that over the years, the broken glass covering the ground became ankle-deep.

When I turned nine or ten, I preferred to sleep in an abandoned car rather than at home. While out all night I observed delivery trucks early in the morning leaving foodstuff on people's doorsteps. The milkman would sometimes leave quarts of chocolate milk, eggs, and butter. Chocolate milk became my breakfast whenever I got up early enough. But it wasn't enough to satisfy my hunger. I had to find more food. I wished it wasn't against the rules to cry.

Her Trusty Broom

As I approached our apartment one summer day in 1946, I saw Mom gazing out the front window. Rivers of dried evaporated milk on the glass almost obscured her body, but I could still see the faraway look on her face as she scanned the street. She used evaporated milk to lighten her coffee, and because she could never find a can opener when she needed one, she'd smash open the can on the window latch. With every tin she pierced, the thick sweet liquid grew thicker and thicker on the pane.

Mom spent her days peering out at the world instead of cleaning or cooking. Our apartment had three windows, side by side, along one wall. The center window was a bay, protruding farther than the others. Mom chose to use the one next to the front door as the can opener, since the angle allowed her to view Blaine Street all the way to the end, where the box factory stood. She would lower the sash so that she had open space in front of her face as she stood there with her coffee and sour look, gazing outside.

Mom was a 220-pound woman. She told us her housedress was size fourteen—*and it takes a lot of woman to fill that size.* When I think of her now, I see her pockmarked face and, when she smiled, her remaining couple of teeth. Her eyes held a glimmer of kindness until she became angry. Then they glowed with an intense light that I thought revealed her mental instability.

When someone knocked on our door she'd yell, "My broom, where's my fucking broom?"

My brother and I would scurry around the apartment, searching for it. We'd hand it to her and she'd sweep her way to the front door, open it, and wave the broom back and forth as though she were industriously sweeping the floor all the time she talked to whoever stood beyond the threshold. Once she finished talking and the visitor left, she'd close the door and toss the broom away. Until later, when another knock at the door once again raised the cry, "My broom, where's my fucking broom?" In this way, she deceived everyone but us into believing how hard she worked to clean the apartment. But as I said, our house was a total wreck.

One time shortly after I'd seen her staring out the milky window, my friends Jimmy Connelly and Tommy Kelly were hanging out with me in the third-floor room I shared with my father.

"I'm going to get you, you little bastard!"

The words echoed up and down the hall as all 220 pounds of size-14 Mom stomped up the stairs banging her trusty broom against the wall to let me know she was carrying it. My friends hid under the table covered with a flowered oilcloth. What I had done I no longer recall, but it must have been bad to propel her up those steep stairs. Her broom may have been designed for sweeping, but she mostly used it as a baton for beating us kids.

The oilcloth covering Tommy and Jimmy moved across the floor like magic as they tried to sneak out of the room. Too late: The broom zeroed in and landed twenty blows before my mother understood their screams weren't mine.

I had tried to escape under the bed, but my head was sticking out.

"You little bastard," she yelled as each blow struck my immobile face. "I'll teach you!"

Despite my mother's aberrant ways, I know she loved me even as she swung her broomstick time and time again. Sometimes she would save the last bit of food for me rather than eat it herself, and she'd give me whatever money she had whenever I asked. The times she took us to buy treats —and sometimes banana splits at her favorite drugstore soda fountain — remain fond memories. But when the broom took control, my mother forgot about love.

Most bad memories have a way of disappearing, but some never go away. Today I think, *That's okay, Mom, I know you loved me. I know you only did it because I drove you insane.*

I can say that with confidence because now I know: If I'd had a kid like me, I would never consider beating him with a broomstick. I'd be tempted to use a baseball bat instead!

* * * * *

My mother spent money faster than Dad could earn it. She couldn't seem to understand or didn't want to accept that he didn't have unlimited income. Maybe the wealth of her family had blinded her to the realities of poverty: When we walked along Commonwealth Avenue, she'd often point out buildings and say, "My father built those."

When Dad got paid Mom would extract every last dime she could from him. Every payday, the same routine: My dad would hand her part of his pay and keep the rest to pay bills. Then she'd swear at him, pitch a tantrum, and throw the money he'd given her on the floor.

"Stick your goddamn money up your ass!" she'd shout. "It's not enough to do anything with."

As soon as she'd toss the bills and coins Tony and I would dive for them, but she was always ready with her broom to drive us away before we got our hands on any. Eventually, my dad would relent and give her the rest of his money. She'd go shopping for kosher corned beef, Kaiser rolls, potato salad, and comic books. Sometimes she'd spend practically his entire paycheck on junk.

Whatever food she bought lasted less than a day because Tony and I were conditioned to eat as much as possible whenever food appeared. Like I said, we never knew for certain when we'd eat again, and it seemed my belly was always empty.

One day my mother showed me a can and said, "Sears Roebuck and Company has come out with food you can cook in the can."

A perfect product for a woman who cared nothing for cooking or cleanliness! She wouldn't have to measure or mix ingredients, or wash a pot or pan. But she hadn't read instructions. She put the can on top of our oil stove without opening it first. A few minutes later, the can exploded, taking off like a red-hot rocket. It slammed into my shirtless back like a cannonball, directly between my shoulder blades.

Mom put a wet rag on the burn and told me to be quiet. I cried for hours afterwards anyway.

My mother knew how to cook if she felt like it, when there was food. She could make chicken noodle soup like no other. Sometimes she made spaghetti, and now and then she'd roast a chicken or turkey. Our breakfast, if we had one, was a doughnut and Pepsi, except for the few times I recall eggs frying in bacon grease and Mom burning bread on a gas burner in her attempt to make toast. Sometimes, too, she'd make mashed potatoes with chicken and corn for dinner. I can still picture her putting the butter and milk into the freshly boiled potatoes and mashing them with a fork.

One night as I sat in the living room watching Mom stare out that milk-stained window, I heard the ice cream truck's musical bells enticing the neighborhood kids to run outdoors. *Just like the Pied Piper in cartoons*, I thought. The ice cream man came around each day at the same time—right after people finished their dinners. Because I didn't have dinner most days, I grew hungrier the longer those bells rang. I'd dream about getting a drumstick, a sugar cone topped with vanilla ice cream and slathered with frozen chocolate and chopped peanuts.

"Mom," I said, "don't you have a nickel for ice cream?" "I don't have any fucking money," she said and turned around to look at me.

Behind my mom's foul mouth, I could hear she felt bad that she couldn't give me a lousy five cents.

Then, the ringing bells reminded me that I did have a nickel, one I'd been saving. I'd been reading a comic book, a story about a

1912 Liberty Head nickel that was supposed to be worth thousands. A few days later one came into my possession. I'd carried it around for months, not knowing how to cash it in. I dug it out of the watch pocket in my dungarees where I always kept it, and ran out the door, my taste buds demanding satisfaction.

"Give me a drumstick," I told the man in the white uniform.

The ice cream man took the nickel pinched tightly between my fingers. I hadn't wanted to let it go, but my stomach insisted I feed it with the ice cream clutched in my other hand.

He studied the nickel to be sure it wasn't a slug or wooden, then his eyes got big. I wondered if he knew how valuable it was.

I ripped the covering off the drumstick and bit a savory chunk of chocolate-coated ice cream off the cone. My taste buds and stomach thanked me with tingling pleasure as I sat down on our front stairs and let the ice cream melt in my mouth.

The next morning, Mom handed me a pillowcase. "Take this down to the cellar and fill it up with dirty clothes."

"What for?""Just do it," she said.

I ran out of the living room and through the hall to open the cellar door. The stink of damp, musty clothes hit me hard. I flicked the switch, but no light came on. Somebody had probably swiped the light bulb. We never had spare bulbs, so when one blew we'd take one that wasn't in use.

A cellar window at ground level let in a bit of light. I cautiously felt my way down the creaking stairs, expecting the Wolf man to jump out of the dark and grab hold of me. I made it to the bottom of the stairs without peeing my pants from fear. There was a huge pile of dirty clothes sitting near the bottom of the stairway. I began filling the bag.

The heap was the result of my mother's method of handling laundry. Her brother, Uncle Frank, would send us boxes of clothes from the department store he managed because he knew we'd have little to wear otherwise. But when our new clothes got dirty, Mom just threw them down the cellar stairs. When Tony or I needed a clean garment and asked her for one, we'd get the stock answer: "Go down to the cellar and find a clean dirty one." This never bothered me until I got a little older and figured out that wearing "clean dirty clothes" wasn't normal. Thus began my realization that I wasn't like other kids, that I didn't fit in with most people, not in my mind. I felt ashamed for being dirty all the time, but at the age of six, I didn't know what to do about it.I filled the bag and carried it up to my mother."Thanks, honey," she said, and gave me a hug.

I pulled away as fast as I could. I never wanted a hug or a kiss from her because she smelled so bad.

Mom noticed my revulsion. "Don't worry, Joey, after I win the Irish Sweepstakes and we're rich, we'll move to Commonwealth Avenue where all the apartments have steam heat and hot running water."

I dreamed right along with her because living without heat or hot water made it practically impossible to take a bath in the winter. If we had fifteen cents and the energy, we'd walk almost two miles to Brighton where there were public showers with hot water, but that didn't happen often.

One time I heated my own water on the oil stove in the kitchen. I poured the hot water into a pot not too heavy for me to carry and hauled it up to the bathtub on the second floor. I dumped it into the tub and returned to the kitchen for another load. By the time I carried the second pot up, the water in the tub was already ice cold. I gave up on bathing until spring came around.

In warmer weather, my family deemed a weekly bath sufficient. Evidently, though, my mother let those seven days turn into weeks because she always had body odor. I don't think she would have acted any differently if we'd had heat and hot water. I can't understand how my father could have sex with my mother smelling as she did. But he'd grown up on a farm in Italy and perhaps farmwomen had the same level of hygiene as my mother. Memories of her stink stay with me to this day. Because of her, I don't care how beautiful a woman is—the first thing I look for is cleanliness.

The day after I filled the bag with dirty clothes, I saw an old broken-down horse cloppety-clopping down our street, pulling a wagon piled high with old clothing.

The driver shouted as loud as he could to alert everybody: "Rags, rags!"

"Where's that fucking bag?" Mom demanded.

"What bag?"

"The one you filled with dirty clothes yesterday."

I pointed to a corner where she had thrown it. She grabbed it and went out to where the ragman stood by his wagon. She handed him the bag. He put it on a scale hanging from the sideboard. Three and a half pounds registered, and he handed my mom some change. She came through the door with a smile on her face, opening her hand to show me she had money. "Ice cream tonight," she said happily.

Tony and I rushed to the truck to get our ice cream.

The driver looked at me, and I looked at the beautiful new cowboy boots he wore. I figured he must have cashed in my valuable nickel. How I wished I could get a pair just like them! Then he put a drumstick in my hand and I forgot about everything else except how good it was going to taste.

Every day for a month Mom sent me to the cellar to fill the bag with dirty clothes to sell to the ragman, so we'd have money whenever the ice cream truck came around.

When the pile of dirty laundry disappeared, my mom sold all the clothes we weren't wearing. She scrounged and searched the house for anything she could sell. When the music drifted through the window and my mom didn't have money, I could see her sadness. I was sad too, so I found another way to feed my ice cream habit.

I began to wait all day for the sound of those tinny musical notes. Once I'd heard the cheerful signal, I rushed out the door. The truck was a smallish, pickup-like affair with a square refrigerated body. I knew the driver couldn't see the back or the door for retrieving ice cream. While all the kids with money lined up and bought their treats, I watched and waited. As the ice cream man drove slowly away, I hopped onto the rear bumper of the truck, opened the door of the refrigerated box, and threw out enough ice cream for Tony and me.

So, even with no money, I ate ice cream almost every evening that summer. I figured since I'd given him my 1912 nickel, he owed me.

Then one night I hopped on the bumper and discovered a padlock on the door. Summer was over.

* * * * *

If Mom had any money left after buying groceries—and despite our hunger—she'd sometimes buy a new hat at the millinery store. Women's hats were the rage in the 1940s. Many were creations made of straw, or felt adorned with feathers, flowers or even artificial fruit and leaves. I didn't understand why those silly hats were meant to be alluring, and I believed my mother liked them because they had lacy veils that covered her face and hid the pockmarks that childhood smallpox had given her.

Though she wore a fashionable hat on her head, Mom didn't seem to mind her bare feet. She went barefoot most of the time, and her feet became as dirty as our floors. I guess many people went barefoot at home then as they do now, but I recall her bare feet as a source of embarrassment.

I also remember Mom wearing a corset, a device that women used to pull in and hide body fat. The corset was made of a heavy fabric reinforced with solid whalebone strips, and eyelets on the backside with laces running through them. Corsets must have been sturdy because I watched my Aunt Lily yanking them as tight as she possibly could, trying to give my 220-pound mother the figure of a

100-pound woman. (Aunt Lily was my mom's only sibling who still spoke to her because she, too, had married outside the Jewish faith, to a man named Kelly.) I watched Mom inhale and try to make herself small around the waist and curvy on top, while Aunt Lily pulled on the laces to tighten them a bit more. I wondered how my mother could breathe while being bound up like that. A few years later, after she'd passed her mid-thirties, she seemed to have lost interest in her figure, and hats had gone out of style.

* * * * *

Sometimes my mother would take us and other neighborhood kids to "Sewer Beach," a level spot beside the Charles River about a mile from our house. It got its name from the slaughterhouse sewage that emptied there into the river. Mom liked to float on her back, and we'd hang onto her as if she was a rubber raft.

"Large snapping turtles live in the river," she said. "If you swim in the deep part, a snapper will grab you by the toe and drag you under water 'til you drown." She said this to of scare us from swimming in deep water.

When new kids moved into the neighborhood, my friends and I would convince them to walk to the river and then we'd ask them if they knew how to swim. We ganged up on anyone who said no and tossed them into a deep part of the river. It turned out that all the new kids could swim—they just didn't know it yet, because every single one ended up dog- paddling to shore.

One day, my friends and I were playing in the street. Old Man Fitzgerald, who lived across the street, always chased us kids away for making too much noise. To get even, I did what other kids in the neighborhood only talked about doing. I found a large pile of fresh dog shit, put it in a brown paper bag, set the bag afire, and set it in front of his door. Then I rang the doorbell, and ran and hid. I looked on as he answered the door and stomped out the fire. Of course, his shoes got covered with shit.

After that, to stay out of Old Man Fitzgerald's sight for a while, I walked to the Charles River to swim with Tony and our friends, Tommy and Ralphie. On the way home, we came across an apple tree where many ripe apples had fallen to the ground. They were soft and we threw them at passing cars to watch them splatter when they hit. We had a ball until one driver jammed on the brakes. A woman jumped out of the car and screamed, "I know you DiBuduos. I'll get you for this." She turned out to be Mrs. O'Donnell, clerk of the Brighton District Court where my older brother had appeared a few times, and where I would often appear in the future.

Another day, a couple of my buddies and I walked toward the Charles River for a swim, passing a yard where four men and three women stood.

"Hey, you kids come here," a man yelled.

I wondered if I should run and hide, but my fear subsided when I noticed that the faces of the people gathered around the big old tree seemed friendly.

I heard another man say, "You kids want some cherries?"

A long stepladder stood beside a tree. Seeing cherries growing there surprised me; before this I had never wondered where cherries came from.

The adults all looked at me and I first wanted to flee. But then they held out their hands filled with fruit from a tree that seemed to be proudly shedding its growth for that year. I'll never forget the old tree for giving me one of the warmest memories of my life. The kind owners gave us handful after handful of cherries. I gobbled them down and spit the seeds out before stuffing my mouth again. What a heavenly taste! To this day, I remember the sweetness and texture of those ripe cherries.

What impressed me the most about this family was that they appeared to be happy picking cherries and feeding them to us. Familial harmony wasn't a part of my life, and I envied them. I recall poignantly wishing that someday I'd have a happy family, too.

One-Eyed Italian Bastard

My father, Antonio DiBuduo, was born in 1888, in Barri, a little town near Naples, Italy. He served in the Italian Merchant Marines and jumped ship in New York City in the early 1900s. At that time, once you made it to the U.S., you usually stayed, and my dad became a citizen as quickly as possible. He spoke seven languages and English was one of them. He always wore a stocking cap, like Italian sailors. Men and boys always wore hats in the 1940s—fedoras, derbies, newsboy caps, stocking caps, and top hats.

My father's family baptismal records from Italy go back to the eighteenth century. I had ambiguous feelings about my ancestors when I first learned about these records. Those people may have been blood relatives, but Italian culture was foreign to me. Not being able to speak the language marked me as an outsider, and as with everything else in my life, I figured I'd never fit in.

I don't know how many brothers and sisters Dad had, but I do know that one brother became a priest, and another immigrated to Argentina and became successful in politics. I remember that uncle sending my father money. Other brothers sent him foreign currency too, some from Italy. Every time money arrived, my mother would yell, "This money is no fucking good! I can't spend it anywhere!" Had she considered exchanging it at the bank for U.S. currency? I'll never know.

Eventually, President Juan Peron appointed my uncle to a high government post in Argentina: Minister of Transportation. One day I came home from school and Tony was putting all his clothes into a box. "We're moving to Argentina. Dad's brother said he'd get us all good jobs there."Excited, I started packing what few clothes I had. Since my uncle always sent envelopes full of foreign money, I figured we'd have plenty to eat in South America. But the news of Peron's overthrow came before we could leave. I unpacked and never heard anything more about my uncle.

* * * * *

Who knows how much or how little influences what we become? I can see a number of incidents—some quite minor—that have stuck with me all these years, and may have contributed to my disrepute.

My father had one eye. As a small boy, I watched with fascination as Dad held open the empty left eye socket to put in his glass eye. A gray rope-like substance oozed around the socket. As he got older, he no longer wore the glass eye, and he looked like he had a perpetual squint.

"What happened to your eye?" I asked when I realized it was missing.

"Never trust your so-called friends," he answered cryptically, "because the only real friend you have is the money in your pocket."

I figured that he'd suffered betrayal by someone close, and the

43

result had cost him his eye. He'd had a whole other life before the one with Mom, and the details of it would remain as elusive as the story of his eye.

"He has seven other children," Mom said, "and his ex-wife's name is Victoria. They all got killed trying to climb over an electric fence."

When she told me this in 1945, I believed her without a doubt. So many people had died in the war, and I'd seen movie newsreels of battles in Italy. I had no reason to think she'd made up the story up. Not until recently, when my brother Bernie told me that he'd visited Dad's ex-wife and family in Worcester, Massachusetts when he was very young, and that he had to wait outside alone while Dad went in. Now, of course, I doubt Mom's story. But it's too late to try to meet any of my half-siblings; they're probably elderly by now, or have passed away.

At any rate, Dad was kind and loving toward me and my brothers and sister, and that was enough for me. I recall suffering several ear aches on many sleepless nights between the ages of seven to twelve. Sometimes Dad warmed up olive oil to squirt into my ear, which eased the pain. He always did his level best to provide for our family, though his best was rarely good enough in the financial sense.

* * * * *

When Tony and I were the only kids, we went on family outings. Sometimes we traveled to Revere Beach on the old trolley cars.

Constructed of wood painted red, the cars had wooden seats and leather hand-straps hanging from poles so that standing passengers could grip something. Each side of the car had a set of doors that opened by splitting in the center and sliding open, a process that fascinated me. A conductor stood near a glass fare meter in the middle of the trolley, with the doors on each side of him so he could observe the passengers arriving and departing. Riding these electric streetcars for a few hours to the shore and back was almost as much fun as riding the amusement park rides once we arrived.

After we got off the streetcar, we had to walk up a hill. A strong onshore breeze blew in our faces, bringing with it the scent of salty air and a chill. On one of our first trips to Revere Beach, we stopped at a tiny restaurant halfway up the hill. It felt good to step out of the wind and inhale the wonderful aromas of brewed coffee and grilled hamburgers. The sea air made food smell even better. The counters inside the restaurant were bolted to the wall, and red swivel stools were bolted to the floors. Tony and I sat on the stools and spun around and around.

"I want a Boston coffee," Mom said. "Do you kids want a cup of coffee?"

I'd never had a cup of coffee, so of course I wanted to drink whatever the grownups were having. I watched Mom dump lots of sugar into her Boston coffee (half milk, half coffee) and I did likewise. Looking back, that hot sweet brew was the best I ever had. After we'd drunk it all, we scaled the hill and I gazed across the ocean for the first time ever, astounded by the sight of water stretching out so

45

far that it met the sky.

The ocean side of the street at the top of the hill on Revere Beach had benches, a band shell, boulders, and a stretch of sand leading to the water. We put on our bathing suits and tiptoed into an ocean so cold I wondered why it wasn't ice. My feet and legs grew numb from standing in it. Mom and Dad ignored the cold. They walked away from shore until the water was deep enough to swim in, and they both dived in.

Blue with cold, I left the water. I gazed in awe at the carnival rides, roller coasters, and other amusements lining the street opposite the beach, and after Mom and Dad dried off they walked us across the street to the merry-go-round.

"Come on kids, I'll ride with you," Mom said. She grabbed Tony and me by the hand and pulled us down beside her on the merry-go-round bench. The ride was her favorite, and she took us on it every time we went to Revere Beach.

On another trip to the shore, we rode on a carnival ride made of individual cars that carried four people into a dark tunnel and exited five minutes later with everyone laughing uproariously. I wanted to find out what was so funny. I don't remember who I went with, but I must have begged hard enough to go, because I soon found myself climbing aboard, full of anticipation for what I thought would be a series of comic scenes. But darkness was all I saw.

Turn after turn in the darkness brought nothing but more darkness. Disappointed on the final turn, I could see the ride would soon end. The exit doors came into view, outlined by light leaking around the edges. I wondered why in the world everyone came out of the tunnel laughing, when suddenly, just before the car exited, a ragged dummy with a smile on its painted face popped out. I too came through the door laughing uproariously. Next to Mom's fake sweeping with the broom, this may have been my first experience with the comedy of deception.

I also enjoyed the Red Devil. Though not the tallest or most dramatic roller coaster on the beach, it was high enough to terrify me when it descended the steepest run because it looked like the low-hanging timbers would cut our heads off. I had nightmares about this roller coaster, but I rode on it every chance I got anyway. I was becoming a thrill-seeker.

Another time, we went to the circus. Mom bought Tony and I a toy: a monkey holding two small ladders. By moving the ladders back and forth, the monkey climbed to the top and down again. She also bought each of us a balloon and some Cracker Jacks. We wanted everything we saw, and she was as excited as we were. Then Dad told her he didn't have any more money. She didn't want to hear it. She began spouting angrily. Dad couldn't handle her rage and always gave in when he could. But that night he couldn't give her what she wanted.

I guess once my brothers and sister came along, it was too expensive to go anywhere. Mom squandered any money Dad earned. Minimum wage was seventy cents an hour, and Dad's take-home pay from the government job he held at the Marine Hospital came to forty dollars a week. Respected in our neighborhood for his hard work, Dad held two steady jobs and only came home to sleep, a unique situation in Hano. He'd also find extra work digging ditches and willingly do any dirty job that paid. I once saw him dig a ten-foot deep ditch with just a pick and shovel.

Despite his workload, my dad was continually trying to improve himself. I recall him taking me with him to the night school he attended, but I was so young that all I can remember is sparks flying all over the place. He wanted to learn to be an electrician but never succeeded. He did, however, finish a course that allowed him to get a so-called "engineer's license," a glorified name for a custodian who knew how to operate steam boilers.

He earned this license after he turned sixty-five.

* * * * *

When I was growing up, people had only two sets of clothing: one for work or everyday wear and one for Sunday. Even if Dad had owned more than one pair of socks or underwear at a time, he wouldn't have had a place to put them. With scarce closet space, there was nowhere to store anything. Where he hung his coat is where he stashed his stuff: cigarettes that he hadn't smoked, acquired free at the Marine Hospital; Parodi cigars that he broke up bit by bit to put in his pipe; and a bottle of Four Roses whiskey that he sipped to give his heart a boost. He'd hide under his mattress what little money he had to keep it safe from the likes of me and my brothers, who snitched any money we found.

Dad always smelled of Parodi — the dark brown tobacco rolled into his lumpy cigars. I imitated him, trying to smoke discarded pieces like cigars. They were so strong I got dizzy and wondered how Dad could stand smoking them.

I remember sitting in a dark, smoky room with my father and a group of talkative men who drank wine and smoked cigars—his many cousins who lived in Worcester, Massachusetts. This was the one and only time we went to visit them that I recall. I was five years old and don't have a clear memory of who was who, but I do remember the outhouse. My father took me by the hand, led me out the door and over a long wooden walkway to a small wooden building, like a shed. He opened the door and I saw a bench with a round hole in it.

"Where's the bathroom?" I asked.

"This is it," he said. "My cousins don't have indoor plumbing."

I sat on the bench and heard my waste dropping far below. I never imagined that anyone in the U.S. lived in primitive conditions like this. Not having heat and hot water at home wasn't so bad after all, I thought. What if I'd had to trek outside in the snow like Dad's cousins did every time they needed to use a bathroom?

When we returned to the house, someone had the bright idea of giving me a glass of wine. I don't remember how much I drank, but I did become intoxicated. They made a big deal of it and I became the center of attention. I could tell by the look on my father's face that he was proud of me. I wondered later how many times he regretted allowing me to get drunk that night.

I never really knew my dad well because he worked so much while we grew up. Even after he retired from the Marine Hospital and from tending boilers, with Social Security and a pension, he still sold newspapers on the street util he died at seventy-eight.

He taught me many things by example: Don't marry a woman thirty years younger than you; love your children unconditionally; and don't expect any rewards for working hard or being nice. The poor guy worked twice as hard as anyone I've ever known and was always kind, yet we treated him like a shadow.

* * * * *

"Anyone who's divorced is going to burn in hell for eternity," Sister Conception repeated for what seemed like the hundredth time. I attended religious training classes once a week at Saint Anthony's parish in Allston, and Sister was one of the nuns who taught there. According to her and the Church, divorced Catholics couldn't re-marry while both spouses lived, and my parents had originally married in a civil ceremony. But I never believed what they taught me in the religious training.

My disbelief started with what they said about Dad going to hell. I just couldn't comprehend a God who supposedly loved me but would send me to hell to burn for eternity if I didn't do what He wanted. Besides, divorce didn't mean anything to me. My father was a good man and worked hard to take care of us. He didn't drink like most other men in Hano, or beat his wife as they did. He brought his paycheck home instead of leaving it in the bar like so many of our neighbors. I interpreted what the nuns said to mean that no Catholic divorcees could ever enter heaven, and therefore a divorcee would burn in hell. If you left your husband or wife, it didn't matter how well you behaved. Divorced people were not welcome in heaven, unlike a married man who would be welcome, even if he beat his wife and kids.

All this contradictory blather made a nonbeliever out of me. How could a loving God punish someone who worked so hard and went to church every Sunday? Dad even tried to drag us kids with him. Going to church meant I had to kneel on a hard piece of wood while some guy in what looked like a dress performed the Catholic Mass in Latin, a language I didn't understand.

Sister Conception invited me to the convent and gave me a religious medal on a chain. Despite what she said about my father's divorce, I felt pleased because no one had been this kind to me before. Not one person outside of my family had ever given me anything. Even now, a feeling of appreciation for that nun's kindness remains with me, and I often think of her and thank her in my mind.

Sister Conception showed me around the building and the kitchen, where other nuns were busy baking bread. As I gazed around, I heard my mother's voice saying, "The convent walls are full of dead babies. The priests screw the nuns, and if they get pregnant, they put all the dead babies in the walls."

I checked the walls for any recently bricked-up areas, but didn't see anything suspicious.

I sensed that the parish priests didn't care for my family. When I turned eight, Tony and I watched as a priest married my parents in the church rectory. My father's ex-wife must have died, or maybe he received a dispensation from the Church in order to remarry. One of my father's brothers was a priest in Italy, and he may have been influential in the decision to allow my father and mother to be married in a Catholic ceremony. That day was one of the few times I remember my parents being happy together.

Hungry in Hano

The summer I was six, my mother's sister came to visit. Aunt Lillian and Mom sat together in front of the radio with a newly installed telephone sitting right next it. My mom had badgered my dad for months to have a private line installed so she could enter a contest called Dinner Winner, broadcast weekly over the radio. The announcer drew a phone number from those sent in the previous week. If the phone call was answered with "dinner winner" instead of hello, the person phoned would win a $25 voucher to buy a dinner, a generous sum in 1946.

While Mom and Aunt Lillian listened to the show, Tony and I wrestled on the floor, noisily knocking around each other and the furniture.

"Go out and play, you little bastards! I want to listen to him," Mom shouted, meaning the radio announcer, who she was not so secretly in love with.

Tony chased me out the door. I ran through the alley leading to Hano Street, where a guy stood yelling, "Watermelons! Get your fresh watermelons!" from the back of a flatbed truck piled high with glistening fruit. We turned around and ran home, hoping to get our mother to buy us one.

Tony rushed through the door and then stopped so suddenly that I bumped into him. When I saw why, I froze in my tracks too.

The phone went flying to the floor and my 220-pound mother and my 240-pound aunt were dancing and jumping around in circles.

"We won, we won, we won Dinner Winner!"

"There goes our watermelon," Tony said.

We left them dancing in the living room to go try to snatch a melon from the truck when no one was looking.

* * * * *

Radio was our main source of entertainment well into the mid-1950s, and Mom always had one blaring. I think that's how I learned to ignore the talk around me. As I listened, I developed definite tastes in music. I ignored the songs that were much too slow, like "Goodnight Irene Goodnight," "The Tennessee Waltz," and "Harbor Lights"—a few of many that annoyed me when they aired. I'd eagerly wait for Friday night so I could listen to some lively music. For a time, the only thing available like that was "The Irish Hour."

Later, as a young teen, I discovered rhythm and blues. Fats Domino came out with "Ain't That a Shame." Then came singles by The Drifters, The Platters, and others. It seemed that in the 1950s, almost all of the most popular groups were black. Black spiritual music was also fine with me, and I loved the emotion expressed in early soul music that seemed lacking in other music. Sometimes I'd wait until the wee hours of the morning to tune into a distant southern station that played country and western music. Then rock and roll came out and changed the music world forever.

But television held a special fascination for us while we were small. Tommy and Ralphie Livingston were the neighbors that Tony and I liked best. Their family had a TV, one of the first in the neighborhood. We went to the Livingstons' house almost every day after school to watch *Cecil the Seasick Sea Serpent*, *Howdy Doody*, and other kid shows. We always stayed through dinnertime, and Tony and I surreptitiously watched the Livingston family while we watched TV. Every night they each ate a plateful of food, something we only dreamed of. Our eyes followed every forkful from plate to Livingston mouth. I developed a vivid imagination while I pictured myself eating too.

One night after watching TV—and watching the Livingstons eat their dinner—I lay in bed with an empty stomach. A breeze carried the aroma of fresh baked bread, cakes, and pies through my open window, increasing my hunger a hundredfold. These delicious smells came from Dorothy Muriel's, a large commercial bakery located on Blaine Street near our apartment. Baking was done at night to prepare the morning shipment to market. The sweet, warm scent almost drove me insane. I couldn't remember when or what I had last eaten, and the fragrance of fresh-baked sweets compelled me to get out of bed.

"Tony, wake up." I shook my brother until he opened his eyes.

"Why are you waking me up in the middle of the night?"

"I'm starving. The smells from the bakery give me hunger pains. Let's go see if we can get some cookies or something."

"Get out of here. They're not going to give us anything." Tony rolled over and closed his eyes.

"Last night, I saw them rolling trays full of pies onto the loading dock out back when I walked by. We can take some stuff when no one is looking."

Tony's eyes got big when he heard about the trays of pies. He got dressed and we snuck out of the house. We went over to the Livingstons' place, and Tony threw pebbles at Tommy's window.

"Get dressed," he whispered when Tommy stuck his head out. "We're going to rob Dorothy Muriel's."

Tommy was ready in a minute. The three of us followed the scents to the back door of the bakery. Tony picked the lock and opened the door. We entered a dark garage where trucks sat at a loading dock, waiting to be filled with goods for delivery. Light from the windows in the bakery illuminated the back doors of the trucks. Every few minutes a man pushed a rack of shelves loaded with baked goodies next to the rear of a truck. The racks rolled on a platform the same height as the tailgates so that the baked goods could slide easily into the trucks at loading time.

We waited until the guy disappeared back through the door. Tony pushed me toward the stairs. "Go on, Joey," he said. "This was your idea, so you go get a tray of cookies."

My eyes beheld wonders: chocolate cakes, oatmeal cookies, and pies stacked by the dozens on shelves to be loaded for delivery.

I grabbed a tray of cookies off the rack and carried it down the steps to the floor of the garage where Tony and Tommy waited.

"I got mine," I said, "now you go and get some."

Tony and Tommy crept up the stairs to the loading dock and each grabbed a tray. Then we hurried out the door to the park across the street. I dived into my tray of cookies.

"Hold on," Tony said. "Let's share so we all have some of each."

Tony chowed down on the cookies, and Tommy ate pies and cookies. My hunger vanished after our tasty gourmet feast.

"What are we going to do with all that's left?" I asked.

"I can't bring any home," Tommy said. "Mom will know I stole it."

"Let's leave the rest on the park bench," Tony said, "where some hungry kid will find it."

So we left what we couldn't eat for others in the neighborhood who had no food. We made a habit of sharing from then on, and the food was always gone by sunrise. The bakery became a steady source of nourishment, and one of many ways I fed myself while growing up in Hano.

* * * * *

In spite of my nearly constant hunger, life in Hano was great for a six-year-old. I could do almost anything I wanted because my mom let us run wild. She did try, however, to get us to bed at a decent time. During the summers in the late 1940s, when it was time to sleep, my mom would stop whatever she was doing and say, "Bed-time."

"Okay," I'd agree, making Mom believe that I still listened to her. But I went upstairs to the third floor where I shared a room with my father. As he was always working, he never knew what I did.

Even at the age of five or six, I often climbed out the third floor window, shimmied down the drain spout, and met up with other "juvenile delinquents," as we liked to call ourselves. Our favorite game was running like a herd of wild stallions, clippetty-clopping throughout the neighborhood. We stomped the sides of empty tin cans to bend them in the center, causing the cans to grip like horseshoes. *Clippetty-clop, clippetty-clop!*

Once we finished waking people up with our racket, we'd have sword fights using metal garbage can covers for shields and sticks for swords. (I imagined myself a knight in the olden days.) When we tired of swordplay, we'd move on to rock fights.

Blaine Street had a vacant lot with overgrown weeds where we found rocks to throw. We chose sides and hunted each other, armed with pockets full of rocks. When I found someone, I threw a rock, aiming to hit my target. I never stopped to think what damage a fist-sized rock hurled through the air would do to another kid until one night, an egg-sized rock hit me in the head. A big lump swelled up on my cranium and it hurt like hell. After getting beaned, I learned my lesson and stopped participating in nighttime rock fights. It was a good thing my mother never noticed the bump on my head, or I would have had to think up a good lie.

During the day, the field on Blaine Street became our hunting ground for grasshoppers. One summer day Tommy and I waded through broken glass and growing weeds, looking to catch the insects.

"The flying ones are best," said Tommy, pointing to winged grasshoppers gliding from plant to plant. He caught one and squeezed it. Brown fluid oozed from the tiny body. "Look, they have Karo syrup for blood."

I didn't know what to think.

After hunting grasshoppers, we turned our attention to ants. Tommy had a pack of one-and-a-half-inch firecrackers. My stomach turned when Tommy squeezed the life from the bug. He stuck one into the top of an anthill and set it off. Ants exploded into the air.

Later the same week, Jimmy Bryant said, "Cats have nine lives."

"No they don't," I said.

"I'll show you!"

Jimmy caught a cat and took the frightened animal to the roof of a three-story building and threw it off. The cat hit the ground and staggered, too stunned to run. Jimmy's older brother Johnny caught the dazed cat and held it until Jimmy came down and carried it back up for another toss. Nine times the cat flew off the roof before it ran away, still alive.

I then firmly believed that cats had nine lives. So when Jimmy Connolly picked up a cat and threw it into a burning barrel to see if it had nine lives, I just stood there and watched. After the cat died my stomach churned every time I remembered how I didn't try to help the poor thing.

* * * * *

My brother Tony made friends with Jimmy Connolly soon after we moved to Hano. Our first summer there, Tony and I met up with Jimmy and his brother Dougie. One day Jimmy said, "Let's go down to the Coca-Cola bottling plant."

"Where's that?" Tony asked.

"It's close to the Charles River," said Dougie, "only a couple of miles. Once we climb the fence, we can drink all the Coke we want."

It sounded like a dream come true. But it was a long hike to the Charles River. The city of Cambridge and Harvard University were on the other side of the river from the plant. When we finished the hike, we found a wooded lot next to the fenced-in area where the Coca-Cola plant parked the delivery trucks. The fence had to be at least six feet high, with barbed wire strung along the top—not much different from other fences we'd climbed to get into places we weren't supposed to.

For shelter, we built a wall and a partial roof from fallen branches. Then all four of us climbed over the fence and snuck up to a window where we watched row after row of empty bottles passing by on a conveyer belt. I had never seen machinery like this before. The bottles went through a wash cycle, and further down the line they were filled with Coke. A machine stamped caps on six bottles at a time. All this was accomplished automatically; there wasn't a human in sight.

The next day we found trucks unlocked and loaded with Coca-Cola for delivery. We stuffed our pockets with as many eight-ounce bottles of Coke as we could carry. (Back then, Coke only came in eight-ounce glass bottles.) We climbed back over the fence to our fort and drank them.

I was in heaven, drinking as much tonic as I wanted. (In Boston we called pop or soda "tonic".) As we drank, we traded jokes and childish insults. Out of the blue, Dougie said, "Want a blowjob?"

"What's that?" I asked.

He demonstrated a blowjob by sticking an empty coke bottle in his mouth. I couldn't imagine why anybody would want to participate in something like that. I had no idea there was anything wrong with talking about this sexual act, so when I got home, I wanted to show off my newfound knowledge.

"Hey Mom, give me a blowjob," I shouted when I walked through the door.

"Where did you learn that?" Her eyes narrowed and flamed with an insane light as they always did when she got angry. "You little bastard," she said, reaching for her broom.

I ran away before she could hit me.

* * * * *

We had a dog I cared a great deal for, a mutt named Victory, the size of a large German shepherd. Victory was always hungry too, and I'd share my food with him whenever I had any. My mom had won the dog in a contest for growing the best garden in a Victory Gardens program in South Boston a few years before. This program encouraged city dwellers to grow their own food because of food rationing during World War II. Mom no longer kept a garden once we moved to Hano.

She often tied Victory to a light pole and told me, "Don't you dare untie him."

As soon as she told me not to, I went over and untied Victory. I held onto his leash and he took off running down the street, pulling me down and dragging me along behind him as if I were water skiing on my stomach. Victory ran a hundred yards, down to the end of Blaine Street and then stopped. I still held his leash, but blood poured from my scraped and bleeding chest, stomach, and arms. In excruciating pain, I limped home.

My mother took a long look at my bloodied body. "I told you not to untie him, you little bastard."

I tried to run, but with scraped arms and legs I couldn't outrun the broom. Mom added insult to injury.

Not long after this incident, Victory ran free and got hit by a car. Tony, two friends, and I put him in a cardboard box and carried him to a vet's office. Victory whimpered and writhed in pain. The vet gave him a shot. He relaxed and we thought him asleep, so we carried him back home in the box.

We didn't know the vet had euthanized him until my mother looked at him. "He's dead," she said.

I remember feeling sorrow, but can't remember crying. I had already learned that only wimpy boys cry.

Bursting with Curiosity

Like most boys everywhere, I was bursting with curiosity, ready to seek adventure at every opportunity. Sometimes I walked to the top of Hano Street where it turned into Union Square. It wasn't a square at all, but rather a circular-shaped intersection of streets with the Hanoville Veterans of World Wars Monument in the center. An eagle with its wings spread sat atop the round black-and-white marble column.

The slippery-smooth column was a challenge. I had tried to shimmy to the top a hundred times but never got past the plaque listing the names of local veterans who didn't come home. I wrapped my arms and legs around the column, scooted up and failed for the 101st time. Holding on with all the determination I could muster, I slid down the obelisk all the way to its base. That's where I saw a green insect with front legs folded as if in prayer. Rearing back, the bug turned its triangular head 180 degrees on a long neck to scan me with two large, jewel-like eyes.

Fascinated, I watched the bug pray. I couldn't get over this alien insect. Where did it come from? Where was it going? Was it really praying at this monument to the dead, or was I imagining things? Maybe, I thought, it was praying for a moth, cricket, or grasshopper to stroll by so it could have dinner. Afraid to touch it with my fingers, I poked at it with a small stick. As many times as I touched it, the bug refused to fly away. I didn't dare kill this creature because, in my mind, some spirit might have sent it to pray at this monument. When I grew bored with staring at it, I said goodbye and left it to pray or prey.

A bluff on the other side of the street—a mountain in my mind—grabbed my attention. One side had been leveled to make room for a gas station. Composed of solid rock, the bluff rose about a hundred feet above ground, its sheer wall almost a straight vertical drop from top to bottom. The summit called me to climb it.

Small, careful steps took me up to a height that brought scary thoughts of falling when I looked down. I raised one hand over my head while holding on for dear life with the other, grasping desperately for a dent, so I could climb another foot. Every inch of progress came with a prayer that I'd find another handhold. My first careful steps turned quickly into desperate fingertip and toetip grips on dirt-encrusted rock that could crumble and give way.

Halfway up and unable to find another grip, I decided going back down would be my best option. That is, until I discovered all the hand- and footholds I had used on the way up had become invisible. *Go up or go down*, I told myself, as fear turned my stomach. I pictured myself smashing into the ground. Desperation guided my fingers toward a dent above me. Inch-by-inch, fear by fear, I climbed to the top, praying all the while: *Please God, don't let me fall, and I promise never to do this again.*

As soon as I reached the top I forgot my fear and promise and ran down the hill to climb up again.

* * * * *

One summer morning, Tommy Livingston said, "Come on, I'll show you something."

"What is it?" I asked.

"Just follow me and I'll show you," he said.

Tommy and I were both six years old. His brother Ralphie was about the same age as Tony, two years older. We made a compatible foursome as we walked to the end of Blaine Street, where the seven-story box factory stood. Closed and empty on weekends, we figured we could play in the building if we could get into it.

We were looking for a way in when Tommy said, "Watch this."

He stuck a thin stick through a small gap in a set of double doors and raised the latch that held them closed. The door swung open. Inside, a bank of four freight elevators greeted us.

"Here's how you work these things." Tommy grabbed a wooden gate and lifted it up. It folded in two as he raised it, making room to load freight. Each elevator appeared to be six times the size of a regular passenger elevator.

"These things are exciting if you jump from one to another," he said.

I looked up the elevator shafts and saw steel beams with no solid walls in between.

"We can jump from the top of an elevator going down to the top of another going up, or step off onto a beam and let the elevator go by if we want. And this is how you make them go up and down."

Tommy pulled on the rope. Pulling one way made the elevator go up, pulling the other way made it go down, and stopping in the middle made the elevator stop. Almost like a car's transmission: Drive-Neutral-Reverse.

We stood on the elevator roofs and jumped from one to another as they passed each other, so if we were atop the one going down, we'd jump onto the top of the elevator going up. It was thrilling, and no one got hurt.

When we couldn't ride the elevators, we hopped aboard moving freight trains. I loved going behind the box factory to the railroad tracks and freight yard. The railroad called this place a switch yard. Freight trains shed and added boxcars, depending on their destinations. Diesel engines were the latest thing and hauled the longer freight trains. For moving box cars around the switch yard, steam engines were still used, the kind with cowcatchers attached to the front, just like in the movies. Crossing from one side to the other, I counted twenty sets of rails. This freight yard turned out to be a source of food, fun—and death.

The McIntyre boys, who lived across from us on Blaine Street and who played with us on our adventures and misadventures, were from a family of about fifteen, a fairly normal family size for Hano. (Some families had seventeen or more kids.) One of the McIntyre boys had fallen across the tracks while trying to hop a train, and that freight train had rolled over him. One of his brothers ran home carrying his head to show his mother, or so the story went.

I told my mother.

She said, "I don't want that to happen to you, so stay away from the railroad tracks."

Death didn't scare me then and dying didn't seem like a big deal. Heck, I always imagined I'd go out in a gun fight. But I did worry about going to the hell everyone said I was gunning for. I ignored my mother's advice as usual. How could a kid not hop on a moving freight train? I saw it as a fire-breathing, smoke-belching monster rolling toward me on shiny ribbons of steel. A thing I could vanquish only by climbing on its back and jumping from car to car to prove my courage.

A week or so after the McIntyre boy got killed, I stood waiting and listening as a huge black locomotive belched white puffs of steam and accelerated. Heavy iron wheels squealed and screeched as they rolled toward me on the steel rails.

My movie heroes did it, so I figured I too could climb aboard a moving train with ease. As the train went faster and faster, I ran alongside it, listening to the crunch of my feet in the loose gravel and the locomotive wheels screeching their unique song, metal on metal: wheel edges as sharp as a butcher's saw, waiting to catch my legs between them and the steel rails, leaving bloody stumps in their wake.

Thoughts about blood and gore didn't stop me from leaping through the air to grab the metal ladder rungs and board the moving train. I climbed to the top of the lurching car and jumped from one freight car roof to another, some higher, some lower than others. Just in time I turned and saw a bridge speeding toward me. So, *this* was how the monster wanted to vanquish me. I jumped down between cars to keep from being knocked off the top.

I rode that train for a quite a while. Once its velocity picked up to a good pace, I jumped off like the cowboys in the movies. But there weren't any trains going in the opposite direction, so I had a long walk home.

During that same winter I'd lie in bed (with every blanket and coat I could find piled high on top of me to keep out the cold of our unheated house) and I'd think about the switchyard and railroad tracks where McIntyre got run over by a freight train. I'd imagine his head still dripping blood as his brother carried it home to show their mother that he wouldn't be coming home to dinner ever again. Then I'd fall asleep and the recurring train dream would come: I would be walking along the railroad tracks and look up to see a train in the distance. I'd try to get out of the way, but my legs were always thigh-deep in mud. The train would keep coming, smoke belching, whistle blowing, wheels clacking louder and louder. In fear and dread, I'd try to run again, but my legs would remain stuck. The heat from the steam-driven engine would envelope me in a white cloud and I'd hear the squeal of brakes as the engineer tried to stop the train. In the dream, I'd struggle to get away before the train ran over me and someone had to carry my bloody head home to show my mother. Eventually, I'd force my legs to move and would wake up an instant before I died.

One night, dreaming in black and white as I usually did, I stood on the edge of a cliff. Twenty feet below, a slow-moving freight train rolled along, pulling open gondola cars. One of the cars was filled with hot molten metal from Harvey Steel that swished back and forth. Boiling bubbles burst as it passed beneath me, and I fell from the cliff. I knew then I was dreaming, and remembered hearing someone say that if a dreamer died in a dream, he'd die for real. I struggled to save myself but couldn't stop from falling into the burning hot liquid. But I emerged into a world of brilliant color, a vibrant butterfly that happily flew away.

When I woke up, I discovered the blankets and covers kicked away.

* * * * *

Jimmy Connolly, a kid Tony hung around with, pointed to a red brick smokestack built right beside the tracks. It rose at least one hundred feet into the air. Steel bars embedded in the brick made a ladder from the bottom to the top.

"If you go all the way to the top and look down, you'll get dizzy and fall off," he said.

I took the challenge and climbed to the top and didn't fall off or even get dizzy. After that, it wasn't a problem to climb the steel stanchions that supported the Everett Street Bridge.

I'd climb them from the ground up to the bridge, and from the surface of the bridge up the steel girders that rose in arched shapes thirty feet high above the road. After my initial climb, I made a ritual of climbing up and walking across the top of the steel arches every time I crossed the bridge.

Sometimes I'd walk up to Union Square where the streetcars ran. Hopping streetcars was more fun than riding trains. When one stopped, I'd hop on the back where I could stand on a coupling hitch. Streetcars ran on rails like the trains, but their power came from electric lines strung above the tracks. On the back of the street-car, a rod with a wheel rolled along the electric wire that provided power to the engine. When I wanted to get off, I would pull down on the spring-loaded guide rope attached to the bar going to the electric wire. Doing so caused the arm to come off the wire, and the spring would stand the arm straight up in the air. Stranded without power, the streetcar would stop. The driver would get out and curse me for stopping his vehicle. He'd have to spend a few minutes guiding the arm back onto the wire.

I was able to travel this way all over Allston and Brighton in my search for food and excitement—and I did all this before I knew how to tie my shoes!

Cute, Christmas, and First Crush

I rode a two-wheeler bike for the first time in Hano Park. I could barely reach the pedals of my friend Tommy's red Schwinn, but I didn't let that stop me. He stood behind me as I mounted the bike and held me upright while I put both feet on the pedals. There were no training wheels in those days, so Tommy ran and pushed me from behind while I pedaled as fast as I could, the bike wavering from side to side. If I pedaled fast enough I wouldn't tip over, but I always feared I couldn't stop safely at that speed.

Suddenly I realized Tommy had let go of the seat. I was doing it, riding a two- wheeler! I glided as far as I could and then managed to stop without falling. At that moment, I officially became a big kid because I could ride a two-wheeler. This felt nearly as thrilling as hopping a freight train. No more three-wheelers for me!

Lots of incidents in my life took place in that park, an asphalt area with a chain link fence surrounding it, seven or eight benches along the perimeter, one basketball hoop, and a shower pole hooked up to spray water through the fence in the summer.

One time I tried to take a short cut home from the park. I climbed over the fence and slipped. The ends of the wire at the top were sharp as razors, and one of the barbs penetrated my stomach and hooked itself under my ribs. I was too scared to cry even though the pain was severe. I didn't have the strength to lift my body. I hung on the fence for what seemed like hours, struggling to free myself. Panic set in. Norma Hill, an older girl, came along with a few of her friends and spotted me hanging from the fence. Two of them pushed up on my feet while Norma pulled the barbs from my stomach. What relief I felt when they set me on the ground! I hardly bled because the barbs that penetrated my skin had stopped blood from flowing through the lacerations. (I still have a scar that has moved from my stomach to just under my right ribs.) I never told anyone what happened because to get stuck atop a fence was a "sissy" thing to do.

Norma and her friends were members of a group of older girls who used to chase me and my friends through alleys. Once they caught any of us, they'd make us pull our pants down, then they'd be real quiet and stare for a long time before they'd let us pull our pants up. Their routine scared and embarrassed me. Until the girls helped me off the fence, I considered them the enemy.

A few weeks after rescuing me, Norma Hill said, "We took a vote who the cutest kid in the neighborhood is. You won."

I was speechless. This turned out to be one of the nicest things anyone had ever said about me. I'd never thought of myself as cute before.

* * * * *

It was 1946, I was six, Christmas had almost arrived, and I no longer believed in Santa Claus.

We never got much for Christmas, but my mom always took us

to the Boston Commons to see the giant tree and other decorations that we thought wondrous. The Commons was an open space downtown established in the pre-Revolutionary War days. (One particularly memorable year there was a Santa Claus with real live reindeer.) I was all eyes and ears as I watched the holiday shoppers headed for subway entrances located on the Commons. We always felt the spirit of the seasons even if we never got any presents.

But this holiday season was different. Mom had received a substantial gift from her brother, Frank. When we came home from the Commons, she got out her sales catalogues with colorful pictures of toys, something she often did even when we didn't have money. This year she promised us that our wishes would come true.

Tony and I went crazy, picking out almost every toy in the catalogues. Mom went shopping without us, promising that Santa was coming this year with all our expensive presents. We could hardly wait.

Two days before Christmas, my mother attended a social event in the neighborhood clubhouse. She took my two-year-old brother Bernie with her and left Tony to watch me. My father was working as always.

As soon as the coast was clear, Tony said, "Come on, Joe, let's find our presents."

I couldn't wait to see our new toys, so I followed Tony around and helped him search. We looked under all the beds, in the storage room, the pantry, and finally in my mother's closet, where we hit pay dirt.

Tony ripped open one of the wrapped packages and pulled something out. "Wow! Look!"

I had no idea what it was until he tore the gift wrapping away. It was a movie projector and films.

"Wow, Tony, Mom really got us one of the things I picked."

Tony industriously ripped open package after package. I saw a couple of boxed reels of cartoons. Back then, owning a projector and a screen to watch movies on was a luxury. Tony set it up, and we watched a few cartoons, but the camera soon became entangled with film.

"Maybe we better put it back," I said.

"No, I'll fix it," Tony said.

I watched as Tony pulled and tugged on the stuck film. He fixed it all right. It never worked again. We left the projector and torn up film on the floor and searched for more presents. Tony pulled out a large box and ripped the wrapping off. It was an electric train set.

"Wow!" I said, "I've always wanted one of those."

This was my dream come true. I imagined all the villages I'd build for the train to roar through.

"I'll set the train up," Tony said.

He did, and we watched the train make a few revolutions until something went drastically wrong. The engine began to smoke, wire connections sparked, and an acrid burning smell filled the room. Within fifteen minutes, smoke poured from inside its motor and its wheels would no longer turn.

"It's dead," Tony said. "Useless."

The floor was littered with torn-up wrapping paper, film pieces, broken tracks, and burnt connections. Tony and I made an excellent search and destroy team.

Mom came home, walked into the living room, and stopped cold. She gazed at the wreckage, speechless. I think she wanted to cry, but all she said was "Merry Christmas."

* * * * *

"Joey likes Jeannie," Mom teased in a singsong voice because she knew it embarrassed me. But it was true. Jeannie was one of a few little girls who lived in our neighborhood. I used to think about her all the time. Tony and I argued over whose girlfriend she was, and even though she probably didn't even know we existed, we fought over her anyway. The very first time I tied my shoes by myself, I ran out the door, hoping that Jeannie would see what I'd accomplished.

Not long after, I was initiated into the Hano arrestee fraternity. One night, Tommy Livingston and I climbed to the roof of a semi-trailer in a parking lot. From the top, we saw a hundred or so identical trailers. We found if we ran from the far end and jumped, we could land on the trailer parked next to the one we were on. We ran and jumped like little squirrels for a few hours and would probably have jumped for longer if someone hadn't called the cops on us.

The police arrived and yelled for us to come down. Scared out of my wits, I obeyed, something I wouldn't dream of doing in another year or two. Tommy came down, too. They put us in the back seat of a police car and spoke to dispatch on their two-way radio.

"Geez, I sure hope Jeannie doesn't hear them talking about me being arrested," I said, but secretly hoped that she would. The cops took us to Police Station #14, and my dad came and took me home. Now I could walk with my head held high. I'd been arrested, like all the tough guys from Hano.

My mom tried to find a way to blame Tony for my arrest. After the Christmas incident, her animosity seemed to increase, and she picked on him often. But he fought back whenever she attempted to beat him with her trusty broom.

One day, Tony and Mom got into it and started throwing empty milk bottles at one another. It didn't matter who'd started the fight because Tony never gave up. Mom's big brown eyes narrowed and blazed in anger. Tony's mirrored hers as he returned fire. Fortunately, they both missed their target, but the bottles shattered when they hit the wall and glass flew all over kitchen. It was a nasty scene, but I wasn't afraid. Violence was the norm at home and out on the streets. It seemed someone was always in a fight, whether it was with cops, drunks, neighbors, or family.

Tony and I fought about other things besides who Jeannie liked best. He was two years older, and every time he tried to make me do something we'd fight about it. One day I chased Tony out of the house and pushed him down in the street. I sat on his chest and punched his face left, right, right, left, beating the heck out of him while a crowd of neighborhood kids cheered me on. After I got worn out from hitting him, I ran into our house. He chased after me and beat the heck out of me.

Because Tony was bigger and stronger, I generally used whatever weapon I could find, including kitchen knives, to defend myself. This frightened Tony and he quit beating me up. He started punching our little brother Bernard instead.

I don't remember when Bernie was born. I was six at the time, and I'm a little more than two years older, so he must have come along before we moved from South Boston. My first memory of him is when Tony punched him in the nose and he cried, "My noise, my noise!"

I had to try it, so I punched Bernie in the nose too. Sure enough, again he cried, "My noise!"

* * * * *

Two days later, Tony came rushing into the house, so excited that Mom asked him what was going on.

"She's moving! There's a moving truck parked in front and they're loading all her furniture on it."

"Whose furniture?" Mom asked.

"Jeannie's."

My heart flip-flopped. Jeannie moving? It couldn't be true. I ran to her house and sure enough, men in work clothes were just closing the doors on a moving van full of furniture. I looked at the bare windows where Jeannie had lived. Her flowered bedroom curtains were gone. I knew then it was true.

Tony and I argued over which one of us was the saddest.

I think I was.

Grammar School Blues

When I was four or so, I heard my older brother Tony laughing his butt off.

"What's so funny?" I asked.

He held out a comic book. "When you learn how to read, then you'll know," he said.

It seemed like only a week or so later, I was suddenly reading. Whenever Mom spent Dad's paycheck every two weeks, she always bought *True Confessions* magazine for herself and comic books for Tony and me, even though we never had enough to eat. Later on, I'd read her magazines, as well. Sometimes I'd also find a *National Geographic*, though that didn't happen often. My favorite issues had articles about Africa and pictures of bare-breasted tribal women—quite a thrill back then.

One day, when I was about six, Tommy Livingston took me to the public library, located in a brick building above the stores in the business section of Allston. When we walked in, I couldn't believe all the books. Tommy showed me how he checked out books with his library card. I filled out an application for a card of my own. My handwriting was barely legible then (and still isn't now).

"Sorry," the librarian said, eyeing my dirty face and raggedy clothing." I think you better come back after you learn how to write."

Seeing all the books I could have read and then being denied access to them hurt me. I mistakenly thought they'd never give me a card after that first rejection. In hindsight, a library card might have changed my life, and the lack of it became one of my biggest regrets. (I was in my forties or fifties when I finally got my first library card.) If I could have read to my heart's content, I would have been better educated and probably chosen a different path.

Right about that time, I got a job selling papers. Between going to school and working at night, I no longer thought about the library. Another reason I began to avoid the library was because of its location in Allston's business district. Just a few years later, the police harassed me if I went anywhere near the area. By then, the only book I had was an old American history text I'd stolen from school and read over and over.

* * * * *

A few weeks after Jeannie moved away, I stopped worrying about her and started worrying about going to school. I wondered how I'd get along with the other kids. I didn't like competitive sports and didn't like to fight, but had often engaged in scraps. I figured it would be the same at school. I tried my best to fit in, but my big Jewish-Italian nose and my name made me a standout. Most of the Irish kids in Hano had pug noses, so I often got teased about mine.

My Uncle Frankie sent school clothes for Tony and me so we'd be dressed properly for our first day of school. We even took a bath the night before. The much-anticipated day dawned and my dad

walked me to Washington Allston Grammar School, about a half
mile from our apartment. Constructed of red brick, the two-story,
nineteenth-century building had massive windows about ten feet high
and four feet across. The teachers had to open and close the top
sashes of the classroom windows using an old-fashioned window pole,
a long wooden pole with a metal hook at the business end.

As if being an ethnic half-breed in an Irish school wasn't chal-
lenging enough, my dad was in his fifties when I was six. He always
looked old to me, with his one eye scrunched up in a perpetual
squint. Small in stature, he stood about five feet four, about the same
height as my mother, and walked with a limp, often complaining
about his legs hurting him. He wore his usual clothing that day—
gray work pants, a plaid shirt, his work boots, and his stocking cap.
Always kind to me, he wanted me to kiss him hello and goodbye, so I
squirmed and pulled away because he needed a shave and his whisk-
ers scratched my face.

When he left me I wanted to cry, but I knew better. I sat in the
classroom with a bunch of other kids, half of them sniveling. Even
some boys were crying. "What sissies," I thought.

The teacher, an agreeable-looking lady, stood up at her desk.
"Welcome children, you're now students at the Washington Allston
Grammar School."

My heart swelled. This was my first welcome anywhere.

She continued to speak in her melodic voice. "When I call
your name, please raise your hand." She ran her finger down the
attendance roll as she read. "Callahan, O' Brien, Mullins, Fitzpat-

rick . . ." all Irish names. When she got to DiBuduo, which she couldn't pronounce, the entire class looked my way and their giggles swept the room.

The teacher split the class into groups, and then showed us the wooden blocks, coloring books, and other toys we'd play with every day. *Hey*, I thought, *school isn't so bad after all.*

Of all the students, our teacher chose me to pick up the wooden blocks and other toys when school ended for the day. It was fun. I looked forward to school because the classroom was warm and clean, and the teacher treated me well.

Everything was fine, except that one of the teachers boiled cow's tongue for lunch every day and it stunk up the whole school. I only went to school for half a day in kindergarten, so it didn't bother me much then. But the next year, when I had to stay all day in first grade, I could barely stand the stink. I walked around with my fingers pinching my nostrils closed.

The stink didn't bother my grades though. I got a double promotion from first grade, skipping second grade and moving directly into third. (Tony was kept back that year and stayed in the second grade.) I really liked school. Once I started third grade, my teacher offered a prize for the winner of a daily math or spelling quiz. I won every time and I was thrilled with the coloring book, crayons, and other useful things. I couldn't wait to get to school every day to claim them. Before long, the teacher started offering two prizes, one for me and one for the runner-up.

One day my good fortune ended. I don't know whether it was

because I kept winning, or because someone believed that my being a grade ahead of my older brother would adversely affect him. I was put back in second grade, and Tony advanced into third. From that day on, I hated school. I clearly remember looking out the window and counting the long years I had left before I turned sixteen and could quit.

Not long after I was put back a grade, while on my way to school I detoured into a field. I crawled between a set of rear wheels of one of the parked trailer trucks and spent the entire day huddled there, cold and hungry—but happy not to be in class.

After my first time ditching class, it was easy to skip school over and over again. The truant officer came to my house. After that, my dad dragged me to school and watched me go in the front door. I'd go down the hall and out the back door.

My poor father tried his best, but I couldn't overcome my dislike of the situation. Maybe it was disappointment for being put back a grade when I was clearly the smartest kid in third grade. All the work assigned to me in second grade was too easy. Nothing could have been more boring than watching the minute hand move around the clock. I never got bad marks, other than for attendance, conduct, and effort.

Another thing I hated about school was that I never had underwear (and didn't like to wear it anyway), so when the teacher called my name, I had to stand beside my desk with an erection that looked like a tent pole in my pants. Pushing the "Under Thunder" between my legs worked for a minute or two, but it was so strong it would soon break free. The tent would take shape and it seemed like its all-seeing pole eye tried to bore through my pant leg. This went on during all the years I attended Washington Allston School.

Another irritation: My nose constantly ran and I never had a handkerchief or tissues to wipe it. Sucking it in became useless because there was just too much to inhale. Using my sleeves wasn't an option, because they were already full of snot. I couldn't bring tissue from home because there we used newspapers or magazine pages to wipe our butts. I needed permission to go to the school bathroom to get tissue, but I was too embarrassed to ask. So I used a textbook page to wipe my nose.

At home, washing with cold water caused my hands to chap, so they always looked dirty. One day, my first grade teacher handed me a bar of soap and said, "Give this to your mother."

I eagerly rushed home with my wonderful gift. But when I showed my mother, her face darkened. "Is this some kind of joke?"

I froze.

From her point of view, we didn't need soap, or else she thought me clean enough to go to school.

I got out of the way in case the broom came out.

When I didn't skip school, my teachers usually gave me a job to get me out of the classroom. I never intended to be troublesome, but to ease my boredom, I found ways to entertain myself that my teachers didn't approve of, like throwing spitballs or carving my name into the wooden desktop with my Boy Scout knife.

Lunch times only reinforced my hunger. Students were supposed to have a bag lunch, but I didn't. I yearned to capture a nibble from a sandwich thick with meat or get a swallow of chocolate milk from someone. How could they all sit and eat while I watched their gluttonous lips wrap around fare I could only dream of? With every bite, their eyes gleamed, sure no one would ever take a bite from their lunch. If I had my way, I would have changed that. Not one ever thought to share their lunch with me. I wondered if anyone even knew I wanted a taste. Big or small, it didn't matter. I closed my eyes, imagining a bite of sandwich and a swallow of chocolate milk that lasted forever. The sandwich probably tasted better in my mind than if someone had actually shared it.

School showed me it wasn't just my nationality and nose that were different from the other students. My clothing, my habits, my thoughts, and my behavior were all different. I refused to be intimidated by authority figures or other students. Lucky for me that I was big for my age. I didn't get pushed around, nor did I push around anyone. I just never fit the mold.

"Little Nigger" Paperboy

As a kid, I never meticulously planned crimes, but when the opportunity came along, I'd impulsively steal stuff. I'd learned from my Hano peers that stealing wasn't a sin if you really needed something.

I went out every evening to the depot where the train dropped bundles of an evening newspaper, *The Daily Record,* from the baggage car. This newspaper had several different editions and the first one, called the home edition, came out about 6 p.m. All the boys who sold papers for Red, our supervisor, had to help carry the thirty-pound bundles from the depot up to the corner about a half-mile away where he stood all night hawking papers to cars and passers-by. When I hoisted a bundle to my shoulder, it seemed to get heavier with every step. At age six, I could hardly carry it all the way to the corner, but if I couldn't carry the papers, Red wouldn't allow me to sell them.

Red gave each paperboy twenty-five papers to take to the bars and restaurants in the areas he assigned us. The streetcar drivers let newsboys ride for free, and we travelled all over Allston and Brighton. I tucked my lot under my arm and headed for my assigned area every evening. Before long, my side turned black from the newsprint and I wore the same clothes to school the next day. Newsboys traditionally carried the papers under one arm, not in a bag that would have protected our clothing. I wasn't one to break that tradition!

The Daily Record had a sister paper, *The Morning American*. Both were tabloids and easier to carry than a broadsheet like the *Boston Herald*, a publication with a larger circulation and one that I'd deliver later.

The *Record's* first edition was only purchased by people interested in the news or ads. The next edition, *Seventh Race*, had racing results and the pari-mutuel betting figures used to configure the daily number. Playing the numbers was a precursor to today's lottery. There were four rows of numbers, each with the sum of money bet that day. To get the winning numbers, you'd use the last digit of each row. The first three were the regular numbers. Some people played four numbers, the last digit in all four rows of numbers, played for a much bigger payoff. Those numbers lined up would be the winning number, called the nigger pool, a name possibly inspired because gambling on the numbers started in Harlem. Three numbers paid over a hundred dollars for twenty-five cents. I always played 308 and this combination would appear a few times a year, but only on the days I didn't play.

Seventh Race came out around 9 p.m. and sold better than other editions in all the taverns, where everyone wanted to check their numbers. After 9 p.m. I always heard, "Hey kid, what's the number?" And I always gave it out. I could have said, "Buy a paper and find out," but more than likely, someone would have kicked my ass for being a wise guy.

The final edition came out around 11 p.m. and contained all the day's racing results. I always stuck around to sell it. The taverns closed at 1 a.m., and the cafés at 2 a.m., when my workday ended.

Most other students at my school dressed well and looked scrubbed clean and rested. Because of my job, I went to school late with dark circles under my eyes and dressed in newsprint-stained clothing. I owned no decent clothes unless my uncle Frank had recently sent some. Even when he did, Mom never washed them, so they soon ended up in the rag pile.

One night, the janitor from my school saw me selling papers after midnight and he told the school principal about it. He called me into his office to ask me what I was doing out so late.

"Selling papers," I said.

"Yeah, I know that," he said, studying me. "But you need a license to be a newsboy and you have to be at least seven years old to get one."

"I'll be seven next year," I said.

He shrugged and that was the end of it. I went on selling papers late at night. Eventually, I started to sneak out of school just before lunch to a nearby restaurant to buy a sandwich and chocolate milk with the money I earned. I didn't have to sit there any longer with nothing to eat.

Hanging around bars and restaurants until the early morning hours wasn't exactly safe for a six-year-old kid, but I needed to earn money somehow. I did get to see my first naked woman when I walked into the One Gentleman Pub and went toward the stage yelling, "*Record, Record*, get your *Daily Record*." When I looked up, I stopped dead in my tracks. An undressed woman cavorted onstage.

Even at a young age, I was fascinated by her body. I must have stood there for five minutes before I felt a hand on my shoulder pushing me toward the door.

After ogling the nude burlesque dancer, I headed to the One Gentleman Pub every chance I got to sell papers. I never got to see her again, but I learned how to steal a bit of change from my customers. I'd set my papers on the bar or table when someone purchased a paper and I made change for them. I'd pick up the stack of newspapers and scoop a few pennies or a nickel up with them. I soon started to do this in all the bars where I sold papers. Some waitresses got wise and didn't want me in their clubs because they were afraid I'd steal tips. I never did, but I can see why they thought I would.

I don't know if my father even knew that Tony and I were newspaper boys because he was always gone. My mother had no objections, though. She allowed us to stay out as late as we wanted as long as we brought home a hot dog and a coffee for her.

Once we finished selling papers for the night, Tony and I would head for the diner. As soon as I walked through the door, I'd run to the pinball machine before anyone else started playing. I'd drop a nickel into the slot and watch the machine spring to life. Lights flashed, wheels swirled, and the odds lit up at twenty to one. If I got five balls in the pockets that lined up horizontally, vertically, or diagonally, I'd win twenty games. I dropped another nickel in and the odds jumped so I'd get forty games for the five in a row. The odds jumped with each coin deposited up to one hundred games for five in a row. One hundred games could be exchanged for five dollars.

I knew it was almost impossible to line up five balls in a row, but my stubbornness wouldn't let me quit trying until practically all my money was gone. To win five dollars would be winning a small fortune. I couldn't remember ever having had that much money.

When I finished playing, Tony would try his luck, but his usually wasn't any better than mine. We ate hot dogs and drank coffee while we played. When both of us ran out of money, we'd head home carrying Mom's hot dog and coffee in a paper sack. The next night, we'd do it all over again. The months passed quickly.

* * * * *

One night when I was eight years old, I went into Bickford's Restaurant, located almost directly behind Red's paper stand, to wait with the other paperboys for the next edition of *The Daily Record*. We sat at tables to keep warm while waiting for the delivery truck. Being brats, we loosened the tops of the sugar, salt, and pepper shakers, so when someone used them, they'd dump the entire contents onto their food.

One night, I walked to the counter and ordered a cup of tea for a nickel and a fried egg sandwich for fifteen cents. I stood waiting for my order when a drunken man, who easily weighed over two hundred pounds, turned and looked at me.

"Stop that damn banging," the drunk screamed at me.

Another person banged a coin on the counter, and the drunk got agitated. The banging didn't stop.

"I said, stop banging," the drunk yelled again.

I cast him a look that said, *Why are you yelling at me?*

He definitely thought me the guilty one, because he hauled off and punched me in the face. I just stood there, dumbfounded. The pain came later. Someone got upset that a grown man had punched a kid and they called the cops.

When the police came, one looked at me and shrugged. "It's only a DiBuduo."

I felt like dirt. It was as if they wanted to give the drunk a medal, while I thought they'd arrest him.

The police held my brother and me in disdain, and they knew my family was powerless to do anything about their abuse. Animosity developed between the police and my family when Tony acquired a corner where he sold newspapers. He did very well and started earning as much as our father. In those days, policemen got a lot of perks, and when too many of them asked Tony for free newspapers, he decided he couldn't give away papers and stay in business. So he told them, "No more free papers." The cops then began picking on me. Tony soon lost his position. He came back to work with me, selling papers for Red, who owned a different corner.

* * * * *

When I was seven, my buddy Tommy Livingston got a job delivering the *Daily Herald*, one of Boston's morning newspapers. This was a better position than my working all night, so I wanted to give it a try. I helped him deliver papers for a while so I'd know how to do it. Then I could get a paper route of my own. Tommy took me into the office where he picked up his papers every day and introduced me to his boss, Pat Ryan. The big, redheaded, cigar-smoking guy looked at me and brusquely said, "I'm tellin' you right now—I'll give you a job, but if you don't collect your bills every week, you're gone."

I delivered the *Daily Herald* every morning for about six months. I had to go to the office, pick up the papers, and then take them to apartment buildings. In order to drop the paper in front of the apartment doors of the subscribers, I had to get through the locked door in the vestibule. We weren't supposed to ring any bells to get buzzed into the buildings, so I'd open the vestibule doors with keys of my own. I found that most vestibule door locks would open with almost any key that fit inside the lock. I'd ring the buzzer when I collected bills one day a week. I looked forward to doing it, because I usually made three or four dollars in tips, more than my pay for delivering papers.

One snowy Sunday, the papers were so heavy I couldn't lift the canvas bag. Pat normally drove the kids to wherever their routes began on Sunday, but on this day he said to me, "Get to your route any way you can," though he still gave the other delivery boys a ride.

My heart sank. The snow was deep and I knew it would be hard. I dragged the paper bag through the snow for about a mile until I reached the first apartment building where I had deliveries to make. I let myself into the hallway and felt the heavenly heat hit my face as I stomped around to try to thaw my frozen hands and feet.

The wet snow had soaked the newspapers completely through. I delivered every soaked paper there and the other locations and I never went back to the office again.

When I didn't return to work, Pat told Tommy, "One thing about that little nigger, he always collected his bills."

His comment showed me exactly what he thought of me, probably the reason why he wouldn't drive me to my route like he did the others. Evidently, my filthy clothes repulsed him. After hearing his remark, I was happy I'd quit. But I needed money in order to eat, and I'd quit my other job selling papers when I took the job with Tommy. I had to find another way to earn money.

Scrounging Bottles, Fishing Cars, and Poker Pranks

A few months went by and spring filled the air. Workers from the box factory sat outside on the stairs, enjoying the sun's warmth while they ate lunch. When they finished eating and returned to work, they left their empty tonic (soda pop) bottles. I gathered them up because they were worth two cents each.

I took my bottles into Harry's, the neighborhood store where Hano residents purchased oil for their cooking and heating stoves, and milk, canned goods, grocery staples, and cigarettes. For five bottles, I got eight cents and could buy a Pepsi and two pieces of penny candy.

Once I figured out that tonic bottles were valuable, I'd collect empties, scouring construction and factory sites around Hano, wherever workers left them laying around after breaks or lunch. This source of cash enabled me to buy my daily Pepsi and donuts. Beer bottles weren't reused, but if they had been, I wouldn't have broken so many and could have made a fortune because there were always hundreds of them laying around Hano.

After I'd learned to read, I would scrounge all day to accumulate fifteen cents. Once I'd reached my goal, I'd go to Friendly's Pharmacy in Union Square where people from nearby neighborhoods also shopped. For me it was a treat to be in a place with a soda fountain, a pinball machine, and a row of public telephone booths.

When I ordered my milkshake, I'd watch in anticipation as the soda jerk pumped milk and poured vanilla flavoring into the metal tumbler and placed it on the electric mixer. After he whipped the milk mixture for a minute, he'd place a glass in front of me and pour the frothy shake into it. The soda jerk always left the tumbler on the counter so I could empty the rest into my glass. I'd stare at the shake awhile, imagining how good it would taste. I knew it would be gone in a matter of seconds. After not eating all day, the shake wouldn't make much of a dent in my hunger, and I always wished I had thirty cents so I could order a frappe—a milk shake with ice cream in it. These were tastier and more filling.

Afterward I'd head for the magazine rack where the comic books were displayed on the bottom shelf. Other than the ones my mom bought every now and then, this was the only way I could read them. I was thrilled to pick up *The Shadow* and read the subtitle, *Who knows what evil lurks in the hearts of men?* I knew the Shadow knew, and he was but one of my super friends. There was als Kal-El, who came to Earth from Krypton to become Superboy and Superman.

And I read how Batman and Robin waited in Gotham to see a bat signal appear in the sky before driving the Batmobile to the scene of crimes perpetrated by villains like the Joker.

The Green Hornet became another favorite, a vigilante who fought crime with his partner Kato from the supercar, "Black Beauty." I also listened to the Green Hornet on the radio, and he promised me a magic ring that never arrived. I often thought that if I'd gotten that ring, I'd have fought crime instead of committing crimes.

If that ring had ever arrived, I might have thought for myself instead of buying into the bizarre mentality of Hano, where it was considered "a crime" to do anything good or right. So, bad guys Lex Luthor, General Zod, Metallo, and of course, Bizarro gradually became my heroes instead. The tough life in Hano mocked any imitation of the crime-fighting heroes emulated by so many other little boys across America.

As I got older, I became an icon to some of the younger kids in Hano. I wore black, fought the cops, took what I wanted, and drank and scrapped almost every day. Someone should have written a comic book about my adventures: *Crooked Joe* would have been a fine name.

* * * * *

Collecting bottles eventually became difficult because other kids saw me cashing them in, and they began to scrounge for them, too. So I turned to "fishing cars."

In the 1940s and '50s, cars had small, triangular windows used to direct airflow inside. These were in front of the roll-up windows, and thieves often jimmied these. I walked around all day looking for anything of value inside a car. When I saw any item of interest, I'd pull out my trusty screwdriver and pry open the car's wing window until the latch broke. I'd reach my hand through the small opening to unlock the door and steal whatever I wanted. I could usually sell most anything I ripped off.

One time I opened the door of a car stacked full of boxes while Tommy Kelly kept watch. He came and shook my shoulder. "Someone's coming," he said. Let's go."

Enthralled with all the loot, I ignored him.

Suddenly, two rough hands grabbed me and pulled me from the car. "What the heck do you think you're doing?" asked a man towering over me. His fierce-looking face had a scar running across it. I tried not to show my fear and didn't reply; I didn't know what to say.

He stared at me for a few minutes as though making up his mind. I waited for him to slap the heck out of me or call the cops. But he just said, "Go on kid, get out of here and don't let me catch you again or I'll kick your ass."

It was "nice" of him to let me go. Getting caught didn't stop me from fishing cars, but it did make me more cautious. A few weeks later, as I sat in Sam's store eating my breakfast of Pepsi and donuts, Franny Burns said, "I'll give five bucks for a set of spinners."

Spinners were hubcaps that covered the entire wheel with a bar across them, considered cool back then. They were only used on the front wheels because a sharp car had fender skirts covering the rear wheels.

I finished my breakfast and, armed with my screwdriver, I went out hunting for a parked car with a set of spinners. I also kept an eye out for fox tails attached to antennas. If I found one, I'd break off the antenna. Fox tails were worth as much as a set of spinners, but both were rare in my neighborhood, so I had to look for them elsewhere.

I'd sold a few sets of spinners in the past, but finally gave up trying to steal a set for Franny because they were just too hard to find.

* * * * *

I still needed a way to earn money. I tried selling ice cream at Irish "football" games ("soccer" in today's USA parlance). I carried a portable cooler—an insulated box with a shoulder strap. I tried this for several weeks but never did well because I was embarrassed to walk around yelling, "Ice cream! Get your ice cream here!" So I just walked around and sold to anyone who approached me or waved me over.

Hano boys found all sorts of ways to make money. In the summer of 1948 when I was eight, older kids in my neighborhood used to play poker on the back porch of the Hano Street clubhouse. The porch stood four feet above the ground and was big enough for eight kids to play cards. I'd stand on the ground along with some other brats and watch the players, enjoying their antics. They grabbed their dealt cards and held them tight, squeezed them slowly apart, peering at them one by one, their faces reacting as they scoped the cards.

Some of the players were good actors and their faces showed joy when they should have shown despair. I knew this because I'd walk around looking at everyone's cards and saw who held the best hand. Sometimes the good actors would scare the best hand into dropping out when they raised.

All the card players wore Wrangler dungarees. These were one dollar cheaper than Lee's. Cuffs were fashionable, and every kid had turned the bottom of their pants legs up into a cuff. Once the cards were dealt, the players intently watched each other to see if anybody cheated or tried to skim the pot. While they were distracted, I watched my friend Jimmy Bryant put a lit cigarette butt in Franny Burns' cuff. Before long, smoke began to rise from the cuff while Franny eyed the other players. He didn't notice his jeans smoldering until sparks touched his skin. He jumped up to slap out the sparks. Everyone laughed, and no one got mad at the hole burned into the bottom of Franny's jeans. All the players watched amusement— except George McDonald who reached into the pot and took out some money while everyone was distracted by the fire in Franny's jeans. The players only made nickel and dime bets, but it added up to big money at the time, and I figured that when George stole money from the ante, he had at least three or four bucks in his hand.

Joe Sutton played every time a game went on. An overweight freckled redhead, he was a little older and smarter than the other kids. "Sucker," he'd say to the loser when he won after raising the pot.

No one got mad at Joe, but they did get even. He suffered from epilepsy, and when he won a big pot his eyes would roll up, then he'd shake all over, lose consciousness, fall to the ground, and go into spasms. One of the older kids would stuff a spoon or a stick in his mouth because in those days people believed epileptics would swallow their tongues during seizures. While Joe Sutton endured this, the other players took his winnings and changed the cards he held.

On one particular, humid, summer day, Joe slowly built his stake until he'd almost cleaned everyone out. Dealt four aces, Joe bet all he had, then his eyes rolled up as he fell and trembled on the ground. Someone stuck a spoon in his mouth and spittle ran until he almost choked. After a few minutes of thrashing around like he was swimming on the ground, his eyes flickered, and he became aware of his surroundings again.

Joe stood and looked at where he had sat. His dealt cards lay there, and only a few coins were left scattered on the floor where the boys anted their bets.

"How much was in the pot, and how much did I bet?" Joe asked. "Who won the last hand? Where did my money go?"

What he remembered was how he had to sell flowers to pay for a display case he had broken during a seizure, and how he used the money he had earned so far to play in this game. He remembered how much he needed and saw he had a long way to go.

He picked up his cards and saw four kings. "I remember, I remember, I had the winning hand!" he shouted. He bet all that he had left lying on the floor.

"I'm going to raise," Franny Burns said, and threw a twenty into the pot.

"I'll double that," Joe reached into his wallet and dug out two twenties he had folded up and tucked into a corner. A look of satisfaction washed over his face.

"Double you back," Franny said and dug money from his shoe and threw it into the pot.

Joe Sutton reached into his underwear and pulled out a fifty. "That's half of what I need to pay my debt, but I'm so sure I have the best hand that I'm willing to bet every dime."

"I don't have that much," Franny said.

Joe reached for the pot. "You lose."

"Hold on," said Franny. "I'll get the money." He showed his hand to those with money, and they invested. He put up another fifty. "Okay, Joe. I call."

"Read 'em and weep," Joe laid down his four kings and reached for the pot.

"Hold on there, buddy, I've got you beat."

Franny threw four aces on the boards, the same aces Joe held before he'd passed out. But Joe now remembered. "Hey, those were my cards. You changed my hand."

"Prove it." Franny gave everyone a warning look. We knew if we told the truth, there'd be hell to pay.

"Come on guys," said Joe, "you all know he took my cards. I really need the money to pay for damage I've done, so won't anyone tell the truth?"

"I will," I said.

Franny stared hard at me, and before I could say another word Tony took me home.

* * * * *

When I wasn't working, climbing mountains, breaking bottles, hopping trains and streetcars, or playing poker, I'd hang around Harry's store. In addition to being the place where I cashed in the soda bottles, the store was where my family had a credit account, like most families in Hano.

Harry sold sandwiches, and brewed coffee in glass quart milk bottles with lids on them. My mom got a bottle of coffee every day, and she'd get Pepsi's and donuts on credit, too. She spent her money on frivolous things before paying any bills—so she paid bills late or not at all. She'd let Harry's bill go, and his wife Frieda often came knocking on our door.

Harry died and a guy named Sam took over the business. Sam cut off Mom's line of credit, which made her very unhappy because now she had to perk her own coffee. I loved to stand at the stove and watch the bubbles through the glass top get darker and darker the longer the coffee brewed.

Not long after Sam took over, he caught me stealing an ice cream bar and banned me from his store. The store burned down and Sam moved to a new location one block away, into a vacant store that used to be called "Moe's." After the move, I was no longer banned, but I got arrested for doing something not connected to the store.

By the time I was ten, I was always getting arrested for one thing or another. This time a cop searched me and took everything from my pockets: a few keys, some change, and a jackknife. I wore an Eisenhower jacket with many pockets, and he searched through every one until he discovered a picture of a nude woman in the top pocket.

"Where'd you get this obscene photo?" he asked.

I didn't remember where I had gotten it or even why I had the picture. Today the photo would not be considered pornographic, but in 1950s Boston a photo of a naked woman was a big deal.

"I found it in Sam's store," I said.

The policeman released me to my father, but I had to go to juvenile court for possessing obscene material. This was the first and only court date when my mother ever appeared with me. Mrs. O'Donnell, the clerk of the Brighton District Court (and my nemesis), must have had the day off because she wasn't in the courtroom. The judge showed my mother the picture the police took from me. She literally blushed when she saw it, the one and only time I ever saw her turn red.

Intuitively, I knew Sam had paid the cops off so they wouldn't harass him about the photo. (Maybe that's why Mrs. O'Donnell hadn't been present.) I hadn't intended to make trouble for Sam, but I did. And I knew Sam would probably hate my guts from then on.

The judge released me to my mother's custody.

Pin Boy and Pinball Schemes

I turned ten in 1950 and got a job as a pin boy, setting up pins for games of candlepins. Candlepins is a bowling variation played primarily in the Canadian Maritime Provinces and New England states of Maine, Massachusetts, Vermont and New Hampshire. The candlepins were 15.75" tall, almost three inches in diameter at the center, and had identical ends. A game consisted of ten frames, with three balls to a frame—but some people cheated and threw four balls.

I started off with only one lane to set up pins. I sat beside the alley while the bowler threw three balls and tried to knock down all ten pins. If players knocked them down with one ball (strike) or two balls (spare), I'd jump down into the alley where the pins and balls fell into a recessed area about eighteen inches deep, located behind the end of the wooden lane. I picked up the balls and put them on the return, sending them rolling back where the bowlers waited. Then I'd hurry to line all the pins down across the back of the alley, grabbing one with each hand to set them on the painted circles, starting with the number one pin and working my way toward the back. The pins had to be set down carefully because the ends hit by thrown balls were dented and made it difficult to stand them up. Sometimes I'd get all pins set up and one would fall over, knocking down other pins, and I'd have to start over again.

Unlike regular bowling, candlepin bowling uses small balls that are thrown as hard as possible. The sound of balls smashing into pins is almost deafening at the end of the alleys. I hated waiting each time for players to throw all the balls before I could set up the pins again, and it took a long time to finish a game. I begged the bowling alley manager to give me two lanes to set up, like the experienced pin boys. For every game bowled (ten frames unless a spare or strike during the last one; then it would be 11 Or 12 frames), I received eight cents. By setting up two alleys, I could double my earnings.

"Okay," said Harry, the bowling alley manager, "but if you're not fast enough and make the bowlers wait to play, I'll put you back on one alley."

Harry seemed like a good guy. But I knew he was serious, so I hustled to get the ten pins standing. I'd get one alley ready and as soon as I finished, the next one would usually be ready to set up. When it wasn't ready, I had to sit on the thin alley divider. Sometimes the balls or pins hit me as I waited for the next round. And often, while concentrating on getting pins to stay up, I'd get hit by a flying ball or pin from the next alley. Bowlers sometimes became impatient and lobbed the ball before I jumped out of the pit. Or they had a bet going on who'd hit the pin-boy first. I knew to duck whenever loose pins lay on the alley. There was really nowhere to hide; all I could do was cover my head with my arms when I saw a pin or ball flying my way. I spent half my time dodging them, but despite the danger and annoyance, it was the best way to earn money at my age.

My pay came to less than one cent every time I jumped down in the alley, risking life and limb. Sometimes I'd have to search one or two lanes over for a pin that had flown and landed there. I made about three dollars a night, some of which was tips: a nickel or dime from each bowler.

The bowling alley closed at midnight, and I made it to the diner by 1 a.m. to eat and play pinball. The grilled hot dog with mustard, relish, and onions would often be the first thing I'd eaten all day. (I continued bringing my mom her nightly hot dog and coffee. When I got home, she'd be sleeping in the bed placed in the room that should have been our dining room. My little brother Bernard slept with her. I'd hold the cardboard container of coffee under her nose, and the smell would wake her. She'd offer me her toothless grin and her eyes would light up at the sight of coffee and food.)

The diner's pinball machine that I wasted my money on was a payoff machine. It cost a nickel a game, and the more nickels deposited, the higher the payoff odds. There were bumpers and holes for the balls to fall into, but no flippers. If five balls fell into holes side by side, the prize was five dollars. But without flippers, getting five in a row was practically impossible, until I figured all I needed was a little help. One night there were five of us standing around the machine watching a game, waiting for our turn to play. The diner counterman paid winners, and he was always so busy that he didn't give the game or players his attention.

I took a corkscrew with a wooden handle from my jacket pocket, acquired just for this purpose. I jammed the corkscrew into the wooden side of the pinball machine and started twisting it, using it as a drill. Soon I'd drilled a hole the diameter of the corkscrew, but hit a metal barrier placed around the inside perimeter of the machine to stop people from doing exactly what I intended.

"Anybody got an ice pick?" I asked.

Two boys standing around pulled ice picks from their pockets. (In those days, a lot of kids carried ice picks as weapons.) I used the pick to punch through the metal strip.

When I played this pinball machine, I was usually able to line up four balls side by side during a game. Getting the fifth one had always been a problem, but now when I needed one more number to make five in a row, I'd stick a metal clothes hanger wire through the hole and press down the button in the empty fifth hole. This not only worked on the payoff machines, but also on the games I used for recreation. A high score was always needed to win free games, so with a hole and a wire I got as many as I wanted. The pinball machines we played for recreation were exciting. Every time a ball scored, it would set off sound effects and flashing lights, and when players won a game, a loud clacking noise let everyone in hearing distance know a "pinball wizard" had triumphed.

I never thought there was anything wrong with cheating the game. Once I drilled a hole in a payoff machine in a bowling alley located in the basement of a commercial building. When I put in the wire, sparks flew. I continued to play while smoke poured from the machine. Some component had short-circuited. Through the smoke, I saw the game counter had one hundred games on it. I walked over to the counter where a guy with tattoos all over his arms sat at a cash register.

"Can I get my five dollars for the hundred games I have on your machine?" I asked.

"Tattoos" must have weighed three hundred pounds. He waddled over to make sure I'd won a hundred games. "Get out of here before I kick your ass," he said when he saw the smoking machine.

"What about my five dollars?"

One look at his face told me I'd better scram.

That was the beginning of the end of this money-making scheme. When the guys who owned the machines came to service them, they discovered the holes. After that, the machines were watched too closely to manipulate them.

* * * * *

Not only did I lose the pinball money, but the candlepins bowling alley closed for the summer because there was no air conditioning and no one bowled during hot weather.

Jimmy Bryant said, "Fuck working. I know how we can make some money."

"How?" I asked.

"The public pool opens on Memorial Day. We can go there and take all the bikes we want."

"But I already have a bike." I had put one together from parts of bikes that we'd stolen. Kids from Hano often stole bikes to ride home from wherever they happened to be, then dumped the bikes in an empty field when they were done with them.

"Don't be a dummy," Jimmy said. "You know how paperboys all need a bike? We can sell them cheaper than they can get them anywhere else."

Jimmy was one tough kid, and I usually went along with whatever he wanted to do. (As we got older, we thought we were the two toughest guys in Hano. Of course, deep down I knew it wasn't true, but it was fun to talk tough like our matinee idols.) We took a bus to the swimming pool and walked around the building, checking out the bike racks and scores of unlocked bikes. I grabbed a red Schwinn. Jimmy got a green one with white stripes, a horn, a basket, and streamers on the rubber handgrips.

We rode the bikes to Hano and exchanged seats and handgrips to disguise them. We went around asking paperboys if they wanted to buy a bike cheap. A lot of them didn't have the eight dollars we were charging, so we let them make weekly payments. Those didn't turn out to be such a good deal for the paperboys.

Jimmy decided to keep collecting every week. Protection, he said, so their bike wouldn't get stolen. We made pretty good money for a few months. There were only so many paperboys to sell bikes to, and the ones we had sold to eventually revolted and quit paying the protection money.

* * * * *

I didn't have a source of income until the day I went into the

Rexall drug store, where four phone booths stood against a wall, right behind the pinball machine.

If people from Hano had a phone, it was considered a luxury. Even if they owned one, they used pay phones because most could only afford a party line at home. If you wanted to make a call and picked up the receiver, you could hear your neighbors talking on the line. Some of the old women spent their days eavesdropping on these lines, so when you wanted complete privacy you used a pay phone.

Pay phone calls were a nickel. One hot summer day I tried calling someone and didn't get an answer. I hung up and waited for my coin to come down the return slot. It didn't. At that time, pay phones didn't have those little doors on the change slots, so I was able to stick my finger up the return. I discovered it was stuffed with paper. I worked the paper loose with my finger and sixty cents came rolling down the coin return slot.

From that day on, I stuffed the coin returns on every pay phone in every phone booth I could find. I'd go back to each one in the evening to collect, sticking my finger up the coin return slot and jiggling the paper up and down until the weight of the coins knocked it loose and both paper and coins slid down. For a kid, it was like hitting a jackpot on a slot machine! I made much more money stealing phone change than anything I had attempted so far. I did this for a few months, until the phone company began to install hinged doors on the coin returns, making it impossible to stuff them.

* * * * *

Around this time Jimmy Bryant became my best friend. We started doing almost everything together. I couldn't believe a kid half my size could be so tough. Jimmy never lost a fight except, as the years went by, he couldn't beat me because I learned all his tricks and knew what he'd do in a fight. He wanted to grow up to be a collector for loan sharks. He fantasized about breaking legs and wrecking homes when he went to collect. (I thought about him years later when I was offered that exact job.)

Jimmy had sixteen brothers and sisters. It was hard for me to believe, but his family was even poorer than mine. His father had the Irish curse: He spent any money he earned at the tavern. One of Jimmy's brothers and one of his sisters were albinos. Sometimes I'd run around with Johnny, the albino brother. One day he was so hungry that I went home where my mother was cooking a pot of beef stew (only because my father sometimes went grocery shopping to prevent her from spending all his money). When she wasn't looking, I took her wooden soup spoon and scooped out a hunk of meat. I stuck it in my pocket and went outside to gave it to Johnny. He devoured it like a hungry dog. There were countless hungry, delinquent kids like us in Hano.

I didn't always think about food, though. When I was ten, my biggest wish was to get a pump action BB gun, advertised in all the comic books for $4.99. If I would've saved some of my money, I could have bought it. By the time I chipped in for my mother's hot dog and coffee, paid for my lunch at school, and played some games on the pay-off pinball machine, there was never any money left to save.

I found a kid selling a muzzle loading BB gun for $3. I made payments of $1 for three nights and brought it home. It didn't shoot straight, so I practiced in the bedroom that I shared with my father. I didn't have any targets, but my dad had photos hanging on the walls, pictures of himself as a handsome young man with curly black hair and a straight patrician nose.

When I shot BBs into the plastered walls of the bedroom, they stuck, half in and half out. I began using the pictures of my father as targets. He came home and saw every picture of himself riddled with copper BBs.

"Why did you do that, Joey?" he asked. He wasn't angry, but I could see he was hurt.

I didn't know what to say. I guessed they were just convenient to shoot at. Today I thoroughly regret shooting up his pictures because the only surviving one is a blurry snapshot of him taken with my mother in the kitchen, in which he held my niece Dawn when she was a baby.

Around this time, Johnny Bryant was walking close to Hano Park when a BB hit him in his eye. He already had vision problems from albinism, and I thought he might go blind. I didn't want to shoot my BB gun after that happened. Because my Dad only had one eye, I may have subconsciously related the two incidents.

* * * * *

My next project involved an electric drill. I was fascinated to think I could penetrate metal with a tiny drill bit. The bed we slept in had a metal headboard and footboard. I drilled holes in them until I could smell drill motor burning. By the end of the first day of owning that drill, the headboard had more holes in it than Swiss cheese.

When my Dad came home and noticed the bed, he was upset. "Why'd you do that, Joey?" he asked.

Again, I had no answer.

I didn't think about drilling holes in the headboard and footboard being right or wrong; I just loved watching the bit going through metal.

Saint Elizabeth's and the Stolen Baby

When I was eleven years old, my father took me with him to Saint Elizabeth's Hospital in Brighton where my mother was due to deliver her fifth baby. I sat in the hallway outside the delivery room with Dad, waiting for the baby to be born. I watched my father stoically sitting in the same spot where he'd probably sat four times before. From behind swinging double doors came shrieks of pain that echoed up and down the dingy hallway with damaged yellow tile floors and walls painted puke green.

Suddenly, the shrieking stopped and a woman wearing white burst through the doors carrying a swaddled bundle. Sixty-five and still spry, my father jumped up to see if he had another boy or a girl.

"Not yours," said the angel of mercy as she hurried down the hall. An astonished look came over my father's face. Before long another nurse pushed through those same double doors carrying a baby boy.

My father put on a smile. "I'll call him Andrew," he said to no one in particular, holding his arms out to receive his newborn.

When we went in to see my mother, she screamed, "I had two babies, not one! The dirty bastards stole one!"

My dad didn't know what to say.

The doctor looked at my father with sympathy in his eyes. "We gave her a shot to ease the pain, and she probably believes what she dreamed is real."

"Like hell," she said, "I had twins before. I know what it's like, so give me back my baby."

"Calm down, missus, or we'll have to send you someplace for the insane," the doctor said.

My mother complained about her stolen baby for years, but no one paid her any heed.

My brother Tony had a twin who died during birth, so it was quite possible that Mom did have twins once again. I wondered if Elizabeth, the hospital's namesake and the mother of John the Baptist, would have approved of the deceit used to remove this child from an impoverished mother's life.

Now that my brother Andy is gone, I often wonder if I have another brother out there. I believed my mother's claim then, and I believe to this day that the doctor and nurses at St. Elizabeth's kidnapped Andy's twin.

Dispy

I'll do the deed today, I thought, *make old Miss Curran jump.*

Sixth grade had become even more boring than fifth grade, so I took some firecrackers to school. When Miss Curran had her back turned, I went into the cloakroom behind her desk, took the package of inch-and-a-half firecrackers from my pocket and lit them. I saw expressions of amazement and horror on my classmates' faces, but not one of them warned Miss Curran. When the fuses sputtered with smoke and sparks, I threw the entire package under her desk.

I laughed with joy as loud explosions broke the silence. Miss Curran jumped and screamed, sending her wig flying. I burst out the door and ran a half mile to the Andrew Jackson School, where Tony attended "special" class. I snuck through the hallways until I found his classroom. When I peered through the door's window, I couldn't believe what was going on in there: Students were throwing things at one another and making loud noises. It looked like a riot. For the first time I understood that "special" class meant "retarded" class.

I had more tiny red explosives in my pocket. I lit a bunch and threw them into the hallway. A man with anger written all over his face came running from the principal's office.

"Come here," he yelled.

I ran from the school with him pursuing me, but I got away.

The truant officer came to my house the next day. "Joe has

116

been transferred to the Gertrude M. Godvin School," he told my mom.

"Why, what did he do now?"

The officer told her about the firecrackers.

"How is he supposed to get to Roxbury to attend school?" she asked.

"He can take a bus, or walk," said the officer. "I don't care. But if he doesn't go, he'll be sent away."

His words didn't scare me. I only wanted to have fun and had no intent of causing any harm. I guess the deciding factor was my not conceding that my behavior was unacceptable to my teachers. Those moviemakers who made the gangster and Western movies I watched would have understood, I thought. Plus, I wanted to do some jail time, so I could brag about it. Not only that, I knew I'd eat regularly and have clean clothes if sent away.

Finishing sixth grade in Boston normally meant moving on to junior high. I obviously didn't have the pleasure of attending William Howard Taft Junior High School with my friends. But they weren't the main reason I wanted to attend school there. For years I'd heard kids describe the mashed potatoes and gravy served along with other good food in the school cafeteria for only a quarter. I would have been overjoyed to eat one good meal a day.

Off I went to the Gertrude M. Godvin School, despite the long commute. To get there, I had to take a bus to Dudley Street Station and an El train to Eggleston Square. Once I left Eggleston Station, I had a two-mile walk up a steep hill. At that time, most El and subway stations were loaded with penny gum machines attached to the girders at eye level, so no one could steal them. While waiting for the El the first time, I delivered a hard kick to the bottoms of the machines. The sudden force caused pennies and gum to come sliding down to the tray where gum slid out if one paid for it. Gum and money for a few well-placed kicks became the best incentive for me to attend school.

When I arrived in Roxbury, I was surprised to find the disciplinary school situated in an old mansion. Inside, I could see it was a beautiful house at one time even though it had been scuffed up by unruly students. The staircases had finely carved handrails and wood paneling on the walls. The sixteen-foot tall windows held stained glass panels and wooden shutters that folded up into a recessed area called a pocket.

Godvin School had a lunchroom, but the food was barely edible. I never felt as safe there as I had in my neighborhood grammar school. And I didn't fit in. My sense of belonging plummeted. Half the students were African-American. That term was unknown at the time, and to call them "black" was an insult then. I'd never had dealings with colored people before, so when I found the schoolyard filled with colored boys, I was confused. Seven or eight of them sauntered over to check me out. It looked like I was going to get an education my first day.

"You got lunch money?" one asked, as the others circled around me.

"Hey, Joe." I looked over to see Donny Dawson walking up, one of the guys I knew from Brighton. At the sight of this big guy, the black kids dispersed. Soon after I started attending Dispy (our nickname for the school), Donny robbed a bank, got into a shootout with the cops, and fled to Hawaii, where he was captured. I never heard from him again.

A few days later, Jarvis, one of the black boys who had been planning to take my lunch money said, "I like boys like you."

Jarvis was about the same size as me and very effeminate. Unfortunately for him, he had girlish, bubble-like lips. In Hano, no one would be caught dead talking to a homosexual. They were considered sub-humans, to be ignored or punished, and no tough guys ever, ever became friends with one. So I said, "Fuck off."

"Don't get mad. I'll get my sister for you."

I didn't want any part of his sister, either. I figured she'd have bubble lips like him and be super ugly. I said, "Your sister is probably uglier than you."

Jarvis rushed me with his head down and arms swinging and proved to me that all "fags" weren't sissies. I hit the exposed top of his head and almost broke my hand. Then I knew the old saying, "Never hit a nigger in the head," one I'd heard for years, was true. (I mean no disrespect; this was the language we used then.)

Jarvis and I fought until the teachers broke it up. We never fought again. Like in Hano, once you fought back at Dispy when taunted, people tended to leave you alone.

The talk among the kids in the schoolyard was that the toughest kids in Boston attended Dispy, and that made me feel better about being there. The school was a warehouse for troublemakers, and I guess I fit the bill, with quite a few other fights. I remember liking to strut my stuff. In fact, I felt so tough that I tried to provoke a fight with a young male teacher who had been recently discharged from the Marines. He had schoolyard duty while we students were lining up, and told me to do something I didn't want to do.

"Meet me after school, and I'll kick your ass," I told him.

He looked me up and down and said, "I'm not allowed to fight with students."

I'm lucky that he didn't accept and kick my ass as he should have. If I was in his place, I would have met the punk kid I was and taught him a lesson.

My assignment to disciplinary school was designed to comply with the Massachusetts state law to keep kids in school until the age of sixteen. I attended Dispy from ages eleven to fourteen (1951 to 1954), and by the time I turned thirteen in January of 1953, I weighed one hundred and sixty pounds and stood close to six feet tall. I looked older than my years.

Not associating with girls or ordinary, well-behaved kids skewed my outlook on life. I neither competed in academic trials nor was challenged intellectually. I wasn't given any textbooks. No one at Dispy taught English, math, history, or any other academic subject. I never had any schoolwork at all. I simply watched the clock all day as I had through previous school years.

The teachers at Gertrude M. Godvin Disciplinary School were basically babysitters whose only goal was to get students to show up.

Supposedly, students were given vocational training. I was assigned to work in the school's print shop, located in the former coach house. The shop was far enough away from the main building to separate me from most teachers and kids. The printing press had type that needed to be set by hand. Even then, setting type by hand was antiquated. I spent hours picking letters out of a pile and placing them where they belonged on racks. I knew most everything I learned there would be a waste. If the authorities thought my brush with vocational training enticed me to attend school, they were sadly mistaken.

One day Joe LaPaglia, a kid with a face mottled by acne boils, mesmerized me with a story about a film he'd seen. I desperately wanted to see Marlon Brando in *The Wild One*, but I would get into hot water and then sent to reform school for truancy before I had the chance.

When I first began hooking school, I did it for the excitement. As time went by, my reasons changed. I never had clean clothes to wear to school, my sneakers usually had holes in them, and my skin was visible through the holes because I didn't own any socks. This was tough during winter when I had to trudge through snow and ice. I dreamed of having a pair of waterproof boots (a dream that didn't manifest until I was in my twenties). Also, I'd stay out until 1 or 2 a.m. selling newspapers and never had enough sleep by the time I had to get up for school. So I often found a place to sleep instead of going to school. Not having enough to eat caused me to feel worn out all the time. I never had much endurance as a kid because of my intermittent eating patterns.

And there were the fights I'd have at school because some kid would tease me about my shoes, clothes, or something else I lacked. I didn't respect any of my teachers except Mr. Scoffield, who carried a pointer stick in his pant leg. The first word or look he didn't like, he'd give me raps across the hand. Maybe I feared him more than respected him.

When I added all the negative factors up, it didn't seem worthwhile to attend Dispy. Hooking school was no longer fun.

Even in a place full of troublemakers, I was a wild card who didn't entirely fit in. But I had stopped caring about it.

Safe Cracking, Gay Bashing, Movies, and Booze

Jimmy Connolly may have been half-crazy, but he was knowledgeable about certain things. So in the summer of 1951, when he said, "Come on, I'll teach you how to crack a safe," I was more than willing to learn.

Cracking a safe was the apex of success for a young thief from Hano, and I couldn't wait to learn. In movies, the guys who knew how to open safes were always admired for their skills.

We broke a window on the backside of the clubhouse on Hano Street. Using a flashlight, we went to the second floor where Jimmy showed me a floor safe. "Turn that baby upside down, we're going through the bottom."

I tried, but needed Jimmy to help turn the heavy safe over. We pounded the bottom with a hammer and chisel that we found in the workshop on the premises. Then we chopped through several layers of cement and steel. After working feverishly for hours, we broke through the bottom of the safe. There were drawers inside we couldn't open because the door blocked them. The rest of the area inside was empty. It didn't matter, I was proud to have cracked my first safe. Now I was ready for the big time, I thought.

* * * * *

I often heard kids in Hano say that the only reason homosexuals exist is "so we'll have somebody to hunt and beat up on Saturday nights." Many of the gays (we called them "homos") cruised the Public Gardens and congregated in nearby restaurants. To us they weren't part of the human race, but strange entities with even stranger desires, who could be crucified just for existing.

When Jimmy Bryant and I turned twelve, we often listened to advice Jimmy Connelly gave us. Connelly was a few years older and had a queer brother. So when he said, "If you rob queers, they'll never call the cops," we figured Connelly knew what he was talking about.

And he made it sound easy: "They're sissies. All you have to do is scare them and they'll give you all their money. And they all have money."

Connelly said the Public Gardens across from Boston Commons was crawling with "cruising queers." He explained that cruising meant they were looking for sex.

We went to the Public Gardens to rob our first queer, and before we even got into the park, we were approached by a very tall, slender man.

"Hi guys, I'm Axel."

I stared at him, not sure what to do. Jimmy was quiet, too. Taller than both of us put together, Axel didn't look easily intimidated. I wondered if he'd really give us his money like Connelly said.

"You want to come to my apartment and have a drink?"

"Yeah, sure," Jimmy said.

We walked three abreast for about a block until we came to Axel's basement apartment. It was very luxurious, from my point of view. He noticed me looking at his reel-to-reel tape recorder. I was thinking how much I could sell it for.

"Do you want to hear what you sound like?" asked Axel.

"Sure I do," I answered.

Axel recorded Jimmy and I bantering insults back and forth.

"You're a dirty dago," Jimmy said.

"Shut up, Mick," I said.

"Guido the greaseball."

"Paddy-whacking left legger."

"Guinea, wop, greaser."

"Mackerel-snapper mickey."

"Hebe, hymie, kike, yid." Jimmy brought my mother's ethnicity into it when he ran out of Italian slurs.

This was the first time I'd ever heard my voice on a recording device and couldn't believe it sounded so different from how I heard myself.

Axel said, "Sit down, relax."

We sat on his couch, Jimmy on one end and me on the other. Axel sat between us and shut off the light. I didn't know what to do. Sitting on a couch with a homo two or three times bigger terrified me.

Jimmy wasn't scared. He grabbed Axel in a chokehold. Axel stood up with Jimmy's arms wrapped around his neck. Jimmy was trying to strangle him, but Axel peeled Jimmy's arms off. It was then that I knew Axel could easily overpower both of us. I wasn't sure what to do. If he could handle a tough guy like Jimmy, I imagined he'd easily kick my ass.

I don't know where I got the nerve, but I stood in front of this guy whose belly button stood even with my face, cocked my fist and said, "Give us your money or we're going to beat the shit out of you." I hoped the sissy would get scared and give up his money like Connolly said any gay guy would.

Axel laughed and set Jimmy down on the floor. I stood there with my fist cocked, ready to punch, but I knew it wouldn't hurt him. I looked at Jimmy for a signal to run. He looked confused, too. Axel took out his wallet, opened it and said, "Here, it's all I have."

It worked, I thought, *the sissy is giving us his money.* Other than a five-dollar bill, the wallet was empty. I grabbed the bill and Jimmy and I ran out the door. We kept on running until we were far away from Axel's apartment.

"We did it," Jimmy yelled. "We robbed a queer."

"We sure did," I said. I wasn't sure if our robbery was something to be proud of, but if Jimmy was happy, I guessed I was too. Looking back at this incident now, I imagine what Axel could have done to us and shudder. I'm thankful he treated us well.

Jimmy Connolly recruited me and my friends to go downtown with him to the Hayes & Bickford's restaurant where homosexual men hung out on Saturday nights. We went into the crowded restaurant and Jimmy threw sugar dispensers and salt and pepper shakers at the fags congregated there. They panicked and ran.

All the anti-gay activity among my peers was started by Jimmy

Connelly, who I later discovered was bisexual. I never thought then about why he led us on these forays against gays. I imagine by attacking them, he hoped to divert suspicion away from himself.

* * * * *

There were three theaters within walking distance of my family's apartment: the Capitol, the Allston, and the Egyptian. The Allston closed down soon after I moved to Hano. Between the other two, the Egyptian was my favorite. I loved the elaborate Egyptian-themed statuary and Art Deco décor throughout the theatre. (Constructed in 1929, the Eqyptian was demolished in 1959, sadly.)

I went to watch a movie every week. Kids from the neighborhood chipped in their pennies until we had enough for one admission. Whoever got elected to buy a ticket would go in and wait for the lights to go out and the movie to start. Then he'd open the fire escape doors to the twenty or so of us waiting to sneak in.

When the ticketholder threw the doors open, bright daylight illuminated the dark interior. A shout of "Close the doors!" went up from the audience as we ran in and to the darkest parts of the theatre. I always found an empty seat and slunk down low so the ushers who chased us wouldn't notice me. There were usually only two ushers, and we scattered every which way, so once we found seats they couldn't tell who had snuck in and who had been there legitimately. By now the audience would be chanting "Shut the doors! shut the doors!" so the ushers usually gave up after catching one or two kids and throwing them out.

The Egyptian was the "in" place to meet girls. After we'd entered the theater one way or another, we'd find some girls our age and sit next to them. When the time seemed right, we'd start kissing them and try to feel them up. The girls were there for the same reason, so it wasn't as if we were taking advantage of them.

Most families worried about their daughters running around with someone like me, and many managed to move from Hano regardless of the expense. When I reached the age of twelve, I was plenty interested in girls but had to go to other neighborhoods to find them. At that young age, I considered myself a grown man who could do whatever he pleased. I stayed away from home for long stretches of time, sleeping in parked cars, bus stations, or somebody's basement.

*****

All the kids I hung around with said they loved to drink, even at this early age. I hated the taste of alcohol, but I drank to fit in. Abstainers were called "chicken" or worse—"sissy boy." By my thirteenth birthday, I was drinking some kind of alcohol on almost a daily basis. I began to drink to reach oblivion, a place where I no longer had to think and feel.

Alcohol became a curse, and my life would have been better if I'd realized it wasn't my friend. But how could I, when it numbed my hurt and helped me forget all that was wrong? Once a habit is formed, it's hard to break. Everywhere I looked, injustice, hatred, poverty, and hunger ruled. I looked for good in everyone I met, but often discovered ill intentions. I thought I'd be glad to leave this world behind. Though there were many people I would have missed, I longed for a place where nothing seemed amiss.

On the other hand, maybe without the booze wiping my brain clean, I wouldn't have survived at all. But I began to suffer from blackouts. I was about thirteen years old the first time this happened.

"Let's go get Eddie Cronin's car," Jamesy Callahan said one summer night.

Cronin's uncle owned a liquor store in Union Square and was well-off for Hano. He had bought his nephew Eddie a '39 Ford Coupe.

Jimmy rang Eddie's doorbell and he came downstairs. I stood back to let Jamesy do the talking and heard Eddie saying, "No, you can't use my car."

Jamesy punched him in the stomach and then the face. "Give me the keys," he said, "and then go to your uncle's store and get me a fifth of whiskey."

"Here's the keys," Eddie replied, "but I can't get you any booze."

Jamesy hit Eddie repeatedly. I didn't like the idea, but if I would have objected, I would have gotten the beating instead.

"Okay, okay, I'll get it," Eddie said. He walked the two blocks to his uncle's store and snitched a bottle of whiskey for Jamesy and a gallon of wine for me.

The last thing I remembered was riding in the back seat, smelling the oil the car burned as we cruised around looking for girls. The next thing I remembered was opening my eyes in a damp, pitch-black place. I tried to figure out where the hell I was, fear welling up as I lay quietly with my head pounding like a wino's. I listened for a clue, but heard nothing. Finally, I cautiously stood up, nauseated from the drinking spree. I had to get out or my fear of the dark and unseen monsters lurking in it would get the best of me. I felt my way along a wall until I reached daylight coming through a basement window. Whose basement, I didn't know. Had I broken into someone's house? Had someone invited me in?

I found stairs, climbed to the first floor, and listened by the door. I didn't hear anyone, so slowly eased the door open. The house was empty. Later on that day, one of the younger kids in the neighborhood told me they found me passed out on the stairs outside, so they carried me down to the cellar so I wouldn't be arrested for drinking. I thought that gesture very kind.

After that, it seemed every time I got drunk, my memory would get wiped clean. I'd often awaken with blood on me, sometimes a lot, sometimes a little. I never knew if it was mine or someone else's. I couldn't remember if I'd been in a fight on the way home or if I'd had one of my spontaneous nosebleeds.

* * * * *

My best source for food continued to be Dorothy Muriel's Bakery, where I could still go practically any night for fresh-baked goodies. One night on my usual food raid, someone called the police. I saw two cops coming and ran. One chased me. I almost flew over a six- foot-high fence, but he grabbed my foot in his hands. I kicked with the other foot and he let go. I fell headfirst onto a block of cement. I split my right eyebrow open, and while peering over the fence as I got up, I noticed that the officer looked at me with concern.

Blinded by my blood, I got up and ran but had to stop to sit down. A woman heard my approach on her steps, peered outside, and saw me bleeding. She kindly opened her door and gave me a washrag to wipe away the blood. (Today I have a scar above my eye that reminds me of those hungry, thieving days.)

The injury didn't keep me from returning to Dorothy Muriel's to get something to eat a few nights later. Tommy Kelly and I decided to explore the bakery, and so we sneaked into the dark offices above the truck dock. I prowled through them more from curiosity than larcenous intent, when I discovered an open safe. I recognized the outline of a pint whiskey bottle. I snatched it and stuck it in my waistband while I continued to look around. We didn't find anything else of interest. I couldn't wait to get out of there to drink the whiskey.

At twelve or thirteen I wasn't yet a full-blown alcoholic, but I emulated the adults in Hano whose primary goal in life seemed to be to get drunk. You either worked or you thieved to get money. How you got the money didn't matter; only getting intoxicated mattered.

We left the bakery and went to Hano Park across the street. By the light filtering into the park from the surrounding streetlights, I showed the Four Roses Whiskey label on the bottle to Tommy Kelly. I unscrewed the cap, put the bottle to my lips and prepared to chug-a- lug as much as I could in one long swallow, the way a "real man" drank in Hano. Just as I tipped the bottle, Tommy yelled, "Wait, smell it first before you drink." I stopped to look at him, wondering why he'd make such a statement.

"The bottle wasn't sealed. Check it out before you drink it," he said again, taking the bottle from my hand. He put the opening under his nose and I watched his face wrinkle in disgust. I thought maybe he didn't like the whiskey smell until he said, "Fire extinguisher fluid. The kind of acid they put in fire extinguishers."

I took a sniff and sure enough, the bottle held some type of caustic chemical. I believe to this day that if I had swallowed it, I would have suffered a painful death. Why and how a kid like Tommy would have the presence of mind to stop me from chug-a-lugging from a whiskey bottle, I could never find an answer.

When I think of this incident, the old adage that "someone's looking out for you" always comes to mind. So does this quote from President Theodore Roosevelt: "A man who has never gone to school may steal from a freight car; but if he has a university education, he may steal the whole railroad."

Playing Jesus

Tommy Kelly and I were out hopping rides on slow-moving freight trains. All the loaded cars had wire seals on them. We jumped off one car and walked over to where twenty cars stood waiting for an engine to pick them up.

"See that metal seal on the door? If you break it, it's a federal offense," Tommy said."

"So what," I said and picked up a metal rod lying between the tracks. A broken seal would alert the railroad cops to the fact that someone had opened the door. I inserted the rod into the seal and twisted it until the metal strips snapped, then pulled the handle down and pushed the sliding door open.

I couldn't believe my eyes. Inside were hundreds—no, thousands of cases of Chef-Boyardee spaghetti and meat sauce.

"Let's take as much as we can carry and hide it behind the steel factory," I said.

Some days we hid out behind trees and bushes in an empty field behind the Harvey Steel Company, situated right beside the railroad cars.

"Okay," said Tommy, and he hefted a full case of cans onto his shoulder.

I did likewise and followed him into the trees and brush, where we stored the two cases. We went back nine more times until we'd cached twenty cases of spaghetti. I was happy to have the canned food, not only because I could eat for awhile, but because I knew the spaghetti was free of roaches. *If only we had a can opener at home,* I thought. My dad sometimes brought one home, but my mom would soon lose it among the piles of dirty dishes or junk scattered all over the house. She'd end up opening cans with a kitchen knife and that's what I had to use to open my spaghetti cans.

After eating most of the spaghetti, I returned to the freight yard in search of more food. I found lots of good stuff locked in the box-cars. I especially loved it when I found a caboose (the last car on a freight train where the crew ate and slept) because these were stocked with foodstuffs and drinks. Once I found a boxcar full of Army first aid kits. If I'd known about drugs, I could have made a bundle selling the morphine in them.

As I got older, I became more daring. Several of my friends and I broke into an enormous warehouse. It stretched along the tracks for a few city blocks and stood forty feet high; merchandise could be stacked all the way to the top. The warehouse held foodstuffs unloaded from boxcars every day.

Along the roof were windows used for ventilation that led into the interior. I went to the roof and climbed through a window. There were no alarms on the windows, so I thought the place hadn't been fitted with alarms. But when I opened a door to carry stuff out, I must have set off a silent alarm because police cars with flashing lights converged on the warehouse within minutes. Scared to death, I ran out the door and along the side of the building beside the tracks, and then turned toward the street. At the back of the building, I faced an eight-foot fence topped with barbed wire. I tried to climb over it and snagged my pants. While I was trying to untangle myself, two cops ran past me without looking up. If I'd jumped to the ground, I would have been caught. All my friends got away too.

A few days later, a bunch of my friends went back to the warehouse. This time they knew better than to open a door, so they hauled all their loot out the open window and onto the flat roof. And what great loot they snagged! Old Gold cigarettes and Chunky candy bars.

They gave me a share, and I had so many cigarettes and candy bars I didn't know what to do with them. Seemed like everybody in Hano was smoking and eating candy bars for a few days. One of the kids who broke in got arrested and ratted on everyone else. I lucked out by not being there the day he and his friends broke in. All the kids were sentenced to pay restitution, and I probably would have gone to reform school because I couldn't pay. Mrs. O'Donnell, the court clerk, would probably have gotten at me as well. Whenever I appeared in her court, she still liked to display her disapproval over Tony and me splattering her car with rotten fruit years earlier.

* * * * *

Easter 1952 came around, a big holiday in Hano, where 99% of the population was Catholic. My friends and I sat around drinking beer and wine on someone's front steps on Good Friday, when out of nowhere I got the idea to put on a passion play. I became a bit goofy when I drank wine and that day was no exception.

"Let's crucify Jesus," I said, and stood up, ready to give a speech.

"You're a Jew," Jimmy Bryant said, "so you get to be Christ. I'll be Pontius Pilate."

"Crucify him! Crucify him!" the other kids chanted.

Everybody drinking with me got into the act. I watched as Jimmy and two other kids tied a cross piece onto a railroad tie. "Here's your cross, and here's your crown," someone said and jammed a crown of thorns fashioned from a rosebush onto my head.

With my long curly hair, big nose, and blood running down my face where the thorns pierced my skin, I probably believably portrayed Jesus.

I placed the heavy cross on my shoulder and dragged it through the neighborhood. A large crowd of kids followed me. Some broke off branches from shrubs and trees to whip Jesus, getting carried away.

"You're no Son of God!" they shouted. "Kill the impostor!"

With their cries of "crucify him, crucify him," they played their parts better than I played mine.

The passion play was just a bit of entertainment for me. I never gave Jesus or his sacrifice to humanity a thought while we performed. So I was surprised the next day when nobody in the neighborhood would talk to me. I had no idea that people could be so easily offended. The priests from Saint Anthony's heard about my Jesus imitation, and this became one of the reasons they treated me with disdain. Quite some time passed before the incident was forgotten.

I gave the priests at St. Anthony's plenty more reasons to dislike me. One night I brought a pint of wine to a dance for teenagers at the school. I drank it in the bathroom and left the empty bottle there. One of the fathers found it.

He grabbed me by the collar. "You have a lot of nerve, DiBuduo. You come here and get drunk, then start a fight. I don't want you around here. Don't think about attending any more dances or anything else here."

The priest was angry because of a fight I'd had the previous week with a kid named Billy Collins. Billy had a nose that reminded me of a pig's snout. We danced around, punching one another for at least an hour as spectators jeered and cheered. He beat the shit out of me. My nose bled as it always did when I fought, and he kept asking if I wanted to quit. I did want to but couldn't with so many of my peers watching. Our mutual exhaustion finally ended the fight.

* * * * *

The black kids at Dispy had a vernacular that I thought was cool. All day at school, they called each other "motherfucker" and other colorful epithets while ranking each other. They'd say things like, "I saw your mother last night with a mattress on her back." The insulted kid would rank the other by retorting, "I saw your mother selling her ass, and she didn't even have a mattress."

One night when I was walking with Jamesy Callahan and Jimmy Bryant, thinking I was hep I said to Jamesy, "Hey, motherfucker!"

He stopped and looked at me. "What did you say?"

"I said, motherfucker."

"That's what I thought you said." He took a swing at me. A good boxer, Callahan broke my nose and blackened one eye.

I swung back. The fight went on for what seemed like hours in the blowing, swirling snow. The two of us danced like stick figures in the whitened street stained red by my dripping blood. I looked at the sky occasionally, appreciating the beauty of the silently falling snowflakes. It didn't matter to them whose head they landed on. Nor did they care if I fought or not. They witnessed my defeat. (To this day when I look to the sky and see snowflakes falling, I remember those that crowned my battered head that night.)

Jamesy Callahan and I finally backed away from one another, worn out by our sparring.

"You had enough?" he asked.

"Fuck you, motherfucker," I said. "I'll never quit."

"You're bleeding all over the place," said Jimmy Bryant. "Why don't you quit?"

"You know I can't," I said, dancing around, trying to avoid Jamesy's fists. "Everybody will call me chicken if I do."

"All right, I quit then," Jamesy said. "But if you ever call me motherfucker again, I'll kick your ass worse than this."

I wanted to tell him, "Thanks, motherfucker," but knew better.

* * * * *

When Jimmy Bryant and I were thirteen, we heard a rumor about a freight yard in Dorchester where freight cars were loaded with beer. We took an El train to Dorchester right away and started looking for beer-laden boxcars. A railroad security guard caught us peering into them. He grabbed us by our collars and held us until the police came. They took Jimmy and me to the station house and separated us for questioning. I vowed not to tell them anything. Let them figure out why we were there. All they could get us for was trespassing, I thought.

A big detective came into the interview room. He reached into his pocket and pulled out his sap—a black jack—and slammed it down on the table in front of me. "You little fucker," he said.

My face must have shown my fear, because the detective and the uniformed cop in the room laughed. Afraid or not, I was still stubborn: They could beat me to death but I wasn't ratting out my buddy Jimmy, no matter what they did to me.

When the two stopped laughing, the detective said, "You don't need to tell us anything. Your buddy already confessed that you came here to break into freight cars and steal beer."

"No fucking way," I said. "Jimmy would never tell you anything."

"Bring that other kid in here," the detective told the cop.

The cop soon returned with Jimmy Bryant.

"Tell your buddy what you told us," the detective said. Jimmy hung his head and mumbled something.

The detective slammed his lead-filled sap against the table again. "Speak up."

"All right, we came to steal beer," Jimmy said in a loud voice.

I couldn't believe it. Jimmy had ratted me out, something I thought he'd never do. At the time, I thought Jimmy was the toughest kid in Hano besides Jamesy. My idea of loyalty had been tested—my friend wasn't so tough after all. When put under enough pressure by authority figures, tough guys cracked like any other person.

Maybe I wasn't smart enough or maybe I was just too stubborn to change my ways. I never gave in, even when I should have.

* * * * *

By age thirteen, I'd accepted the premise prevalent in Hano that in order to live, you needed to get intoxicated at every opportunity. Alcohol was my number one desire and my only goal was to have enough cash to drink all day. I hated the taste but loved the oblivion it brought. By fourteen, I found a liquor store willing to sell me whatever I wanted. By buying booze for the other kids, I usually managed to finagle enough cash from them to buy my daily three quarts of Old India Ale for one dollar and five cents, and a pint of cheap wine for fifty cents. This combination fueled my goal of blacking out. I assumed that's why everyone drank: to wipe out thoughts of hunger and any other troubles. My mind was askew, but alcohol made me believe I was right and everyone else wrong.

The people I met while intoxicated and the places where I woke up after I blacked out are memories buried deep in the recesses of my mind; I don't want to recall the wrong I did to others and myself while under the curse of alcohol. But I do ask myself why I chose to drink myself into nothingness. Couldn't I have chosen a better path?

I discovered other ways to score alcohol, too. I'd go to the Paradise Café, a restaurant that also sold alcoholic beverages, located across the street from the Model Café in the Union Square area of Allston. I'd order a little food and pretend I had to use the bathroom downstairs where the cases of beer were stored. I'd put a few bottles under my coat and leave the restaurant.

Not satisfied with swiping a few bottles of beer, my brother broke into the Paradise Café and swiped several hundred dollars after it closed one night. Tony didn't tell me what he'd done, but I found the money where he'd hidden it inside a heating vent in his bedroom floor. I ended up spending more of that money than he did, but Tony was arrested and sentenced to work in the state police barracks as a cook. He received a salary plus room and board, maybe the best thing that ever happened to him. He'd come home some weekends wearing new clothes and have cash in his pocket. I thought he was living in luxury with all the food he could eat and a heated barracks to sleep in. I wished I could get into some trouble, so I'd get sent somewhere like that.

One week, at age thirteen, I ran away from home with Dickie Smith, a kid from the neighborhood.

Dickie said, "Let's take off."

I said, "Sure, where to?"

"I don't care. Anywhere. There has to be a better place than this."

Dickie was about my age, maybe a year or two older. We hitched a ride to the New York border when a guy picked us up in a convertible. Almost as soon as we got in the car, Bill Hailey's "Shake Rattle and Roll" came on the radio, the first rock and roll song we'd ever heard. A thrilling new musical world opened up for us.

Eventually, Dickie and I found our way to a restaurant in some small town. We sat at the counter drinking Cokes, next to two older women. By the looks they cast as us, I could almost read their minds. They were thinking about taking us home with them. I wouldn't have objected, but I was too shy to start a conversation and I think they were too scared to act on their thoughts.

After we slept on the side of the road a couple of nights, we decided that running away wasn't much fun after all. As we headed home, another guy picked us up. The way he talked, I figured he was one of those queers I disliked so much. He stopped to buy beer and handed us each a quart. "Drink up," he told us.

A cop riding behind us saw this guy passing beer to us and rescued us from what would surely have been an ugly scene, based on my attitude toward homosexuals then. Had the gay man tried to make advances, Dickie and I certainly would have tried to kick his ass.

Drinking and Fighting

Even though I attended school at Dispy, I still worked at night and engaged in all my usual activities. One night after playing pinball for a few hours and leaving the diner to head home, a guy bumped into me on the street as he left a three-story apartment building.

"S'cuse me," I said.

He turned and gave me a mean look. "Watch where the fuck you're going."

I surveyed the loudmouth. It was obvious he had been drinking. Nothing unusual, because lots of guys in Hano grew beer muscles and wanted to fight when they drank. I often had to fight some jerk like this because I couldn't refuse a fight if someone called me chicken. There wasn't a worse insult. This jerk was a bit smaller than me, so I didn't feel threatened.

He started mouthing off again. It seemed like every window in the apartment building opened automatically when he started yelling. I guessed this had happened before. Loudmouth here probably got drunk and started fights with passersby on a regular basis, and the tenants regarded it as entertainment. I looked up and saw spectators hanging their heads out of windows on all three floors.

"Kill that asshole, Pat!" they yelled. "Go on, Pat, show that punk!"

With people yelling for my blood, I got scared, but I didn't dare run from a fight.

Encouraged, my opponent aggressively came toward me in a boxing stance. I easily kicked him in the balls. I thought every street fighter knew to keep their legs closed to prevent that from happening. He doubled over. Surprised that my kick was so effective, I didn't follow through. In those days, a kick to the balls was my opening move in any fight, and when it worked, was the most devastating blow I possessed.

"Don't let him get away with that, Pat!" yelled one of the spectators from above. "Kill the fucker!" I wanted to run away but figured I'd be better off dead than called chicken.

Buoyed by the shouting, the drunk straightened up and came at me again with his hands raised in a defensive posture. I went into a boxing stance. I led with a left jab to the face, followed with a hard right to his chin, and knocked him down.

"Kill him! Get him, Pat!"

The guy looked at me from the ground. He was in no shape to kill anybody that night, but he kept coming at me, and I continued to beat the shit out of him. Once I had him beat for sure, I turned and left to the jeers of the spectators.

The next morning I went to Sam's store where I hung out with other kids from the neighborhood.

"Somebody beat the shit out of Pat Curran last night while he was drunk," I heard Jimmy Callahan telling Sam. "That guy better keep out of sight, because when Pat catches him, he's done for."

I almost wet my pants. Pat was one of the premiere fighters in

Boston, known all over the city for his toughness. If I hadn't beaten him, I wouldn't have believed anybody could. Scared to death he'd come looking for me, I went home and hid for three days.

I never saw him again. I figured he must have been embarrassed when he sobered up and realized a fourteen-year-old kid had kicked his butt in front of a bunch of witnesses.

* * * * *

Other than boxing, the only other sport I ever played in Hano was half-ball, a game that used a rubber ball cut in half and a stick for a bat. It only took two to play, a batter and a pitcher. One guy would pitch and once the batter hit the half ball, he would try to catch it as it rebounded off the building. We had to play next to the box factory so we could use its walls to judge how high we hit the half-ball. One story was a single and the fourth story was a home run, but if the guy pitching caught the ball falling from the building, it was an out. I never played any other competitive sports unless you consider street fighting a sport.

I assumed what went on in Hano happened everywhere else. I didn't know that people actually lived non-violent and loving lives. All I saw of "love" between married couples was arguments and fist-fights. I watched Jimmy Bryant's mother kick her husband's ass many times after he spent his entire pay in the tavern. My mother harassed my father, calling him offensive names in front of us kids, which I found that worse than a physical assault. Whenever I met

145

another guy, the first thought through my mind was, "Can I kick his ass?" because there seemed to always be an unwritten test to determine who was the toughest.

* * * * *

One day a little girl about four years old came into Sam's to buy some penny candy. Half her face was melted into a mask of wrinkled skin.

"What happened to her?" I asked Jimmy.

"Haven't you seen other kids like her? They all got scalded with boiling water by pulling over pots on the gas stove. That's what their parents always say, anyway. But I think one of their parents probably threw boiling water on them as punishment!"

I felt sorry for this poor little deformed kid who couldn't walk down the street without everyone staring. It was no wonder the girls thought I was cute when so many of my peers showed signs of abuse from living in a neighborhood filled with alcoholics.

I couldn't understand why so many parents didn't want their kids to play with me. I tried to act like cool guys in the movies. I wanted to be just like James Cagney in *Public Enemy #1*, and Marlon Brando in *The Wild One*. How was I to know then that movies glorifying the tough guys were make-believe? The films settings were a lot like Hano where everyone talked about the exploits of anyone who fought the cops. In my mind I was a hero. By the time I was fourteen, I would fight any cop or teacher, and never snitch on my friends. I thought that authority figures were enemies because they all treated me badly. That included all priests and nuns (except for Sister Conception, who was always nice to me, other than telling me that my father was going to burn in hell).

I saw myself as tough, and to me that meant I was a good guy. I fought constantly and it seemed I had a new black eye on a weekly basis. I didn't win many fights though. Most of the time I was scared and my arms would tremble and my knees get weak. No matter what, I fought back and never let myself become a "victim". After a while, I didn't have to fight unless I wanted to because other kids knew they couldn't push me around.

* * * * *

The situation at home was as bad as ever. We were still hungry, though occasionally our mother would have breakfast for us—a bottle of Pepsi and a donut. She'd never told us what a toothbrush was for; as a result, I had many cavities, and when I breathed through my mouth, cold air passed over the exposed nerves of my front teeth. I often lay awake in pain. Because I suffered so much, I found a dentist who extracted teeth for five dollars a tooth.

The dentist's office was located at Roxbury Crossing, a half-hour bus ride from Allston. I usually suffered quite a while before I could round up the five dollars each time I needed to rid myself of a painful tooth. By the time I turned fourteen, the five-dollar dentist had extracted all four of my upper front teeth. False teeth weren't even discussed. Whatever the cost, they were too expensive. Lots of Hano residents had rotten teeth and it wasn't unusual to see people with empty gaps in their mouth, so I didn't mind mine so much.

I told everyone they'd been knocked out in a fight.

I remember the dentist giving me nitrous oxide when I had one of the four teeth pulled. Though unconscious, I felt him hammering on my tooth to loosen it, then pain as he gripped the tooth with pliers and ripped it from my mouth. Next time I refused gas and got a shot of Novocain instead. When he started hammering on this rotten tooth, I heard the noise and felt the pressure, but the Novocain masked the pain.

* * * * *

Tony got a job at the box factory when he turned sixteen. He made more money than our father, and he wanted to combine Dad's wages with his own to keep the pantry stocked with food and pay the bills my folks were always behind on.

Mom went wild on the first payday Dad gave his money to Tony. She accosted him and Tony on their way home from the bank where Tony had deposited their wages.

"You gave him your paycheck? Well you can fuck him from now on. You're not fucking me anymore."

"But Mom," Tony said, "I'm only trying to see that we have enough to eat."

Mom reached into her dress, pulled out one of her large breasts, held it in both hands and aimed it at Tony. "You want to eat, suck on this. It was good enough when you were a baby, you little bastard."

Tony turned colors when she did that. I was shocked, but Tony was totally humiliated because people on the street saw and heard what she did.

I noticed more as I grew older how my poor father would come home to a slob of a wife who didn't appreciate a thing he did.

Her usual greeting when he walked through the door: "You dirty, one-eyed Italian bastard . . ." And she'd go on harassing him until she got whatever she wanted.

When she wanted sex, she'd get vicious with her verbal assaults. "You one-eyed Italian bastard. You're fucking your girlfriend, and that's why you can't get it up, isn't it?" She'd storm through the house swearing and throwing things. Dad would grab her by the arm and take her into the bedroom. After a short time, Mom would sheepishly reappear with a smile on her face. "Can I make you a piece of soup, honey?" she'd ask, a note of satisfaction in her voice.

Her nasty words still ring in my ears. My heart breaks when I think of my father, and I can only speculate why he stayed and took my mother's abuse. It might have been that he'd divorced once and never saw his other children. (Or did he?) Perhaps he truly loved my mother regardless of her insane ways. Or could it be that he was afraid to leave us kids alone with only our disturbed mother to care for us? I'll never know.

* * * * *

During the summer of my fourteenth year, I hiked several miles to Hammond Woods with other kids from Hano. Once there, Jimmy Connolly gathered some leaves and set them on fire. We played fire-fighters, using our jackets to try to beat the fire out. The swinging jackets sent flaming leaves flying every which way, and before we knew it, the fire had become a real forest fire. A troop of Boy Scouts came to help, and we soon beat the fire out with our jackets. Then Connolly spied a small hatchet one of the Scouts carried.

"Hey, can I see that?"

The Scout hesitantly handed it to him.

"Thanks," Connolly said as he put the hatchet's handle in his waistband. The Scouts were afraid or maybe too shocked to say anything. The rest of us Hano kids, seeing easy pickings, took their axes, hunting knives, and canteens. I can't remember feeling guilty, but I was thrilled to have a hunting knife and a canteen.

After that, the thought of running into a troop of Scouts and taking their expensive equipment motivated our trips into the woods.

Another time we were hiking in Hammond Woods, but we hadn't eaten all day. Me and Davy Bryant, my best friend's little brother, who was well over six feet tall, stole a few chickens from a hen house. Somebody fired a shotgun at us and we ran like hell. Davy and I each held onto one chicken as we ran. We cooked them with their feathers still on over an open campfire, the worst tasting and smelling chicken I ever ate.

On another excursion to Hammond Woods, we passed a car

with grocery bags on the seat. I popped open the door and grabbed two bottles of wine off the top of one bag. I drank most of one bottle, showing off that I could drink like a grownup. Intoxicated and thinking I was Joe Cool, I mooned passing cars and acted as stupid as any drunk ever had.

The Marines and Middlesex County Training School

At fourteen, I was big for my age and thought I could easily pass for seventeen, the minimum age to join the Marines. Because I fought all the time anyway, I thought the military would be a good place for me. So I went downtown to the recruiting station located on the Boston Commons. Impressed by the dress blues the recruiting sergeant wore, I could hardly wait to see myself in uniform.

I lied about my age on the paperwork the sergeant gave me. I passed the test he gave to see if I was mentally qualified. (I suspect knowing how to read was sufficient back then.) He sent me to the Statehouse to get my birth certificate. In those days, all one needed was a little ink eradicator to forge almost any document. When the worker at the state house gave me my birth certificate and I read "Giuseppe DiBuduo", I thought he'd made a mistake.

"That's not my name," I said. "Your father's Antonio, right?"

"Yeah."

"Mother's Miriam?"

"Yeah."

"That's you, Giuseppe," he said.

I didn't even know Giuseppe was Italian for Joseph. If I had called myself Giuseppe when I was younger, it would have added to my problems in my Irish neighborhood. But I loved the initials. I started using Oliver for a middle name because I had a crush on a girl named Jerrie Oliver. My name then became Giuseppe Oliver DiBuduo: G.O.D. Whenever anybody said, "Oh, God," I answered, "Yes?"

After I doctored my birth certificate with a little ink eradicator and India ink, I returned to the recruiting station expecting to get shipped to Paris Island for basic training. But to my dismay, a kid from Hano, Tommy McGary, stood in the recruiting office accompanied by Marty Hardiman, a minor politician who worked at the clubhouse in Hano. His first words to me were, "What are you doing here? You're not old enough to join the Marines."

Those words changed the course of my life. The recruiter studied my birth certificate carefully and saw my amateurish forgery.

"Sorry kid," he said. "Come back when you're old enough."

I think I would have made a good Marine, despite my young age, because they would have kicked my butt if I'd stepped out of line. A little discipline was just what I needed at the time, and I would have done almost anything to wear a set of dress blues.

* * * * *

Occasionally, the Boston municipal court would summon me for truancy. In 1954, I had a court date close to Christmas and my dad went with me to try to save my ass. Every time I went to court, I hoped to get sent somewhere that would provide food, clothing and a warm place to sleep, like my brother Tony had when he got sent away. So when the judge asked if I'd attend school faithfully from then on, I answered, "Why should I?"

"Middlesex County Training School for you," the judge replied.

Thinking how well off Tony was in the police barracks, I expected good things to result from my sentence. When I arrived at MCTS, I was pleased to see expansive lawns and clean-looking buildings. The campus spread out over many acres and had its own farmland with a barn that held maybe a dozen cows. There were chicken coops and horses as well. I thought this situation would greatly improve my life.

The guy who drove me from the court to the training school took me into a brick building with offices on the first floor and a dormitory on the second. He led me to a basement dayroom full of boys, took my handcuffs off, and handed a folder to a man named Mailey.

My stomach turned and I felt a chill pass over me when I met Mr. Mailey. The muscular, six-foot tall figure wearing Clark Kent glasses and a Tony Curtis curl hanging down the center of his forehead had a cynical look. His permanent squint and his tiny, cruel-looking mouth seemed to say, "Don't ever mess with me."

Like a "don't-give-a-damn-General-Patton," Mailey was formidable enough to scare any fourteen-year-old boy. "You obey the rules or else," he said, pulling himself ramrod straight and hitting my chest with his finger

I gave him a dirty look.

"Silent insolence doesn't go here. For that look you can spend the weekend on line."

"What's that?" I asked

"You'll find out soon enough."

I turned to walk away. He grabbed me by the shoulder.

"Listen to me, DiBuduo. You do what you're told or else I'll shave your head bald, like his."

He pointed to a baldheaded kid kneeling in a corner with his hands raised above his head.

That scared me. I wore my hair in a D.A. (duck's ass) that was the fashion for cool guys in 1954. I combed my hair from the front of my head to the back with a line down the center of the back. Terrified of losing my hair, I figured I'd better behave however he wanted me to.

"Why does he have his hands in the air like that? I asked.

"I learned how to apply discipline when I was a cadet at Annapolis," said Mailey. "So here's the rules—you tell me if you or anyone else violates any rule I've set down. If you tell on yourself when you break a rule, you'll receive a lesser punishment than if someone else reports the same infraction."

If that was how the military trained people, I was damn happy that I hadn't joined the Marines.

"Okay, but why does he have his hands over his head?" I repeated.

"He was already on line and he broke another rule. Now listen to what I have to say. I don't want to hear you crying that you didn't know what the rules were. I have all you boys line up every evening and come to my office to give me a daily report on any regulations you broke or any violations you observed anyone else making.

"It's the same at the other two cottages. The boys go into the master's office one at a time to report every night. The master interviews each boy, and if the boy doesn't have something to report, he'll get some demerits. You start out with a hundred points and deduct your demerits for the week. Fewer than eighty remaining and you'll spend the weekend on line."

I saw kids standing and facing the wall, looking down into Sunday prayer books and mumbling. They weren't praying; they were trying to memorize enough pages so they could get off line.

There were also a few boys on their knees in the corners of the room. Some read the missal and others, more severely punished, held their arms above their heads. It didn't look like something I'd be happy doing.

Mailey rambled on about his rules and regulations. "We take a roll call each night and you tell me how many demerits you're going to subtract that day for your bad behavior. If someone reports that you lied and should have taken some demerits, you'll be sorry and can count on spending a lot of time on line."

One thing I learned in Hano was to never rat on anybody. I wouldn't be reporting anything about my classmates during the nightly interviews. But I decided to report on myself when I had my first daily interview with "Master Mailey." I even made things up to pacify him. As a result, I had to take a lot of demerits and spent lots of weekends on line that I didn't deserve, but he never did shave my head.

I'd met many of the kids at Middlesex when we attended the

Gertrude M. Godvin School together. On my second day at Middlesex, I told a few "friends" of my plan to escape. Almost immediately afterward, Mailey summoned me. He repeated every word I'd uttered. I never dreamed that anyone could turn these tough kids into informants, but Mailey certainly had.

He put me on line that day instead of waiting for the weekend. It took a sadistically inclined mind to devise a punishment like that, I thought sourly. He insisted on being called Mr. before his surname, but I began to think of the word "asshole" first.

The kids on line either stood or kneeled facing a wall in the dayroom (unless assigned to work detail) while the other boys watched TV, did homework, played games, or just hung around. Usually we were on line four or five hours a day, but on weekends the days stretched into twelve to fourteen hours because there was no school or work detail. We could hear the other kids having fun, but if we dared turn around to look, we'd get an even worse punishment.

Mailey sat and watched us all day, probably getting his rocks off by seeing so many kids suffer. He sentenced kids to stand on line for a multitude of reasons, but the correction was consistent. While we faced the day room wall, Mailey made us memorize many pages from the Sunday missal. It was difficult to remember all the "thous" and "shalts" of the biblical language. If for some reason a kid didn't memorize his assignment on his feet, Mailey would force him to spend his days on his knees.

If any boy memorized his entire assignment, the rules stated he'd get off line. On my initial line assignment, I memorized entire

157

pages from the Sunday missal. A big mistake, because once Mailey knew I could memorize more than other kids, I could never get off line unless I memorized the entire assignment.

Later, I got sentenced to serve line time on my knees for what Mailey called "silent insolence" after he didn't like the way I looked at him. I never could hide my feelings and he could read the hatred in my face. After only fifteen minutes on my knees, it felt as though someone had hammered them. I spent entire days kneeling while trying to memorize the lessons and found it almost impossible to memorize anything while in such agonizing pain.

When kneeling and memorizing missals didn't get the desired results, Mailey made us raise our hands over our heads and keep them extended all day, pure torture. I'm sure if he'd known about waterboarding he would have tried that as well.

About one hundred boys slept and ate meals in each of three "cottages." The name made them sound small and cozy, but they were really two-story brick dormitories. Mailey was in charge of one, and the masters of the other two cottages reported to him.

Not long after I arrived at Middlesex, a new kid came to my cottage. He was about fourteen and I could see he didn't like it there, either. He fell to the floor and writhed in pain, pretending to have an appendicitis attack. Mailey carried him to a room next to the day-room and left him there. He pulled back a curtain covering a window between the two rooms and observed the boy through a one-way glass. From behind Mailey, I saw the boy stop acting sick when he thought no one was looking. Mailey rushed into the room with his shillelagh, beat the kid, then shaved him bald and put him on line with his hands held above his head. A shillelagh was a long, wide piece of wood with a handgrip and with holes drilled into the business end to overcome wind resistance.

There were other incidents at Middlesex that upset me: One night I was eating dinner in the cottage dining room where one table was for staff and eight tables for the boys. A kid at the table next to mine couldn't hold down the food and vomited it back onto his plate.

Mailey strode over with his face scrunched in anger. "You know the rules. Eat everything on your plate."

"But, I threw up on it," the boy said.

"The rule stands," Mailey growled. "You don't get anything else to eat until all that food is gone."

I felt sorry for the kid, but I couldn't do anything to help. At breakfast the next day, Mailey set the plate of pukey food back in front of the boy. It hurt me to see the desolate look on the boy's face when he realized Mailey was serious. I don't remember how many times the poor kid tried to eat, only to regurgitate what he forced down again and again. Somehow, the kid lived through Mailey's torment. Someone eventually took the plate away, and he got to eat regular food again.

To me, all the food at Middlesex tasted good. I can't remember a single thing that I couldn't stand to eat, and I looked forward to mealtimes. My childhood hunger helped make the food taste better, and when I was on line, sitting down at mealtimes was a welcome break. Sometimes, Mailey would make kids on line also eat their meals on their knees. The only break they had on weekends was bed-time. I was only surprised that he didn't make us kneel and pray all night.

Not long after the new kid faked appendicitis, my right arm swelled up and became as hard as a rock. I started to worry after a week had passed and I still couldn't move my arm. It hurt like heck and the pain went on for almost a month. I complained daily but Mailey ignored me. I worried it might be amputated if I didn't get help. On a Sunday while I sat in church, pus started pouring from a small opening in my forearm. It soaked through my shirt. After it drained, I could move my arm again.

"Look," I told Mailey, and showed him my pus-soaked shirt-sleeve. He gave me one of his intimidating looks. During my fourteen months at Middlesex, I never saw a doctor or dentist, even though my dad sent money whenever he could so I could go to the dentist because he knew I had cavities. The staff put his money orders into my file and held them until my release. By that time, though, I had a mouthful of cavities and my four front teeth were still missing.

As the days passed, I learned a lot about the staff at Middlesex by observing them at work. For example, a little kid named Smithy, maybe six or seven years old, lived in one of the other cottages. He often stood on line or got beaten for some infraction or another, but he was barely old enough to know right from wrong, let alone read that damn Sunday missal. Smithy's abuse went on from the time I arrived until my release. I hated the way all the staff abused him.

Boys also told me how Mailey's sister felt them up as she fitted them for clothing. As best I can remember, she was the only woman in the entire place, but she didn't behave any better than the men.

Mailey walked around carrying his shillelagh and beat anyone who defied him. I figured he could beat me in a fight, so never tried to fight him. But I did play-fight with his assistant one day, just like I used to do with guys in Hano. The assistant bloodied my nose, but I didn't think anything of it because my nose always bled when I fought or sparred.

Mailey came into the room and asked what happened when he saw blood dripping from my nose. I told him I had a spontaneous nosebleed. But I'm sure one of the other kids told him what happened, because Mailey fired the assistant. I don't think he was fired for bloodying my nose but rather for not telling Mailey the truth about our sparring.

Mailey often made me polish his two-door, black 1954 Mercury. Confused by this situation, I wasn't sure how to act. I was so tempted to do what he told me never ever to do—use steel wool to polish his car. But my better instincts stopped me. He liked that car better than any of the boys in his care and probably would have devised a barbaric punishment if I'd scratched his baby.

Mailey didn't have a woman in his life that I knew of, and he stayed on the grounds seven days a week. After a month or so at my cottage, I was transferred to another. My new master assigned me to work in the barn with a chubby Italian kid named Tomasso, two black kids whose names I can't remember, and the Clancy twins—identical blond, blue-eyed boys with very fair skin.

Trying to suck up, the two black kids told an outright lie. They said they witnessed Tomasso and I having homosexual relations. When Mr. "Asshole" Mailey heard this, he came rushing over and insisted I confess my guilt. I wasn't about to confess to something I hadn't done, especially committing a homosexual act.

"I want the truth, DiBuduo," Mailey said.

I knew the bastard wanted me not to confess so that he could continue to beat me. Even knowing that, I couldn't fake a confession. "I'm telling you the truth. I never did what they said."

"I'm going to beat you and Tomasso every night until you confess," Mailey said.

So after dinner every night for the next six months, Mailey would come over from the Reid cottage and say, "DiBuduo and Tomasso. Into the room." He'd pull out his shillelagh, and with a crooked smile on his face, say, "Drop 'em, Tomasso."

Tomasso always got his whacks first and always cried at the first whack. By the second one, he'd be pleading, "Tell him we did it, Joe, tell him, please."

I felt sorry for Tomasso, but I couldn't bring myself to confess. After about twenty whacks, my turn came. I never cried and with each whack I said, "I didn't do it."

After six months of daily beatings, Mailey decided to start beating the two black kids to see who was telling the truth. After one beating, they confessed they had lied.

After getting my ass kicked for six months, I got a simple "I'm sorry" from them. That was it. If he had wanted to be fair, Mailey should have beaten their butts for a few months. No such luck.

After they confessed, Mailey treated them well, probably happy they had given him an excuse to beat me for so long. It's no surprise that this incident also shaped my negative attitude toward homosexuality.

Master Sergeant and Barn Boy

I missed my family terribly after I arrived at Middlesex. The isolation and severe discipline made me regret every day that I'd smarted off to the district judge. One night at dinner, Mailey said, "Pray for one of you boys' father who had a heart attack."

Somehow, I knew it was my father. I found out later that he was near death, but asshole Mailey wouldn't even think about letting me visit. Fortunately, Dad pulled through and after I'd been at Middlesex for about three months, Dad paid someone to drive my family out to the school, located about fifty miles from Boston. When they arrived, asshole Mailey told them visitors weren't allowed because the flu was going around.

Dad had heart problems ever after. Later, when I was sixteen, he was hospitalized again. I visited him in the hospital several times, and he was always happy to see me. After he was released, I'd go see him in downtown Boston where he sold newspapers at night. I'd watch as he shuffled from restaurants to bars, or stood in the street selling papers, what I'd done as a kid. It seemed to me that the poor guy did nothing but work his entire life.

Maybe Mailey did feel a bit of remorse about beating me and keeping me from my family during my father's health crisis, because soon after the black kids had confessed, he gave me a work detail considered a privilege. The day after he offered me the job, two men in a pickup truck drove me to a big house situated next to a lake. When we got out, I noticed that one man was much older than the other, and that the younger one was built like a weight lifter.

"We're building a wall all around this house," the older man said. "We need to finish by the end of summer, so you need to work fast."

He pointed at a line scratched in the dirt, marking where they'd build a stone wall. It seemed impossible for two men and a boy to carry that many rocks in three months.

"What am I supposed to do?"

"Take this here wheelbarrow, fill it with rocks from the surrounding fields, and bring them back," the young man said.

As hard as I had to labor, I felt it was worth spending my days away from Mailey. At the end of three months, my arms bulged with muscles from lifting rocks and the wall was complete. To my dismay, though, I had to return to work in the barn.

Being a military man, Mailey made us march wherever we went. We also had to learn how to perform rifle drills to music and all sorts of other military stuff like learning the meaning of different ranks in the armed forces and who to salute or not to salute. We learned several types of salutes:—the hand salute, the rifle salute at order arms, a rifle salute at right shoulder, and the rifle salute at present arms. He even gave us ranks. My rank as a master sergeant made me the highest-ranking barn boy, so I had to get up at four in the morning to go milk the cows and march the others to and from the barn.

My job as the highest non-commissioned officer also meant I had to march the entire population of my cottage wherever we went. I suspected my promotion to master sergeant was Mailey's way of further tormenting me, although he probably thought of it as character building. He knew I didn't like ordering people around, but as master sergeant, I had to tell the other kids what to do and when to do it. I yelled marching commands whenever our group of boys went anywhere and had to learn all the different commands required for the fancy march formations that Mailey enjoyed watching. We had a drill field where we practiced, which I had to roll level every day in my spare time. I practiced until I could split my group of up to a hundred kids, space them out, and then have the separate groups march toward each other and pass through one another's ranks without colliding. I can still hear myself shouting the marching chant "left, left, left-right" to keep everyone in step. My voice became so strong and deep that when I spoke inside a room it seemed as though the walls vibrated from the timbre of my speech.

When I was first assigned to work in the barn, Mailey said, "DiBuduo, you and Tomasso are assigned the task of keeping the drill field in shape." He made sure we had no free time at all by adding this to our roster. It took quite an effort to muscle the heavy cement roller over the deep gravel to pack it evenly. As soon as we pushed it once across the field, Tomasso would tire out. I had to drag him along with the heavy cement roller, and his weight made it all the more difficult.

One day I was pitching hay in the barn for the cows and Tomasso walked in front of me. I stretched out and stuck one of the tines of the pitchfork completely through his left calf.

"Owww!" he screamed.

I smiled. I thought he had it coming because he was such an asshole. He went running to tell the barn master.

The barn master soon found me. "Did you stab Tomasso on purpose?" He gave me a look that let me know he thought I had.

"No, he walked in front of me as I threw the hay. It was an accident."

"We'll see what Mr. Mailey thinks of this." The barn master told me to report immediately to Mailey's office, then went off to call Mailey.

I figured I was in for another beating, but at least I deserved it this time.

When I arrived at his office, Mailey asked, "Did you do it on purpose?" He thumbed nonchalantly through a magazine, not even bothering to look up at me.

"No, it was an accident."

"Okay, be careful from now on," he said, still reading.

I could hardly believe he had let me walk out of his office without giving me a beating. He must have thought Tomasso deserved what he got, too.

In the barn, the Clancy boys milked the cows that had to stand with their heads trapped in stanchions allowing them to lie down or to stand. I felt sorry for the cows because that was all they did: stand, lie down, get milked, and eat. My job was to pour buckets of milk into larger containers and put them in the cooler. Then I had to clean the cement trench running behind the stanchions where the cows stood for milking. When they took a dump, the cow pies would fall into this trench. I pushed a shovel along until I came to the end of the trench, emptied into a manure room. The trench was about twenty feet higher than the room so it took awhile to fill it, but eventually the pile of manure rose to a height where no more would fit and it had to be cleaned out.

"Here you go, DiBuduo," Mailey said one day, handing me a pair of rubber boots.

"What're these for?" I took the boots and put them on.

"You can wear them when you go into the manure room to shovel it out." Mailey took me to a set of double doors under the barn and slid them open. A wave of steam came from the room as soon as the door opened, and the smell wasn't pleasant. The pile of manure rose all the way to the ceiling.

Mailey pointed to the truck he wanted me to load. "Fill it up and I'll have someone drive it to the fields where you can help spread it for fertilizer."

I started shoveling the endless pile of shit. As I worked, I sweated copiously because the pile generated heat. This was just one more chore added to my long list of chores. I hated every single one, but if I refused to do any of them, Mailey would shave my head.

Once we finished our early morning chores, we returned to our cottage and ate breakfast. After breakfast, I returned to the barn to feed the chickens. There were twenty hen houses jammed with laying hens, and I had to gather the eggs every day before I carried in bags of grain to feed them. The birds defecated everywhere and the henhouses smelled unbearably bad. I had to endure the stench of ammonia inside as I shoveled the chicken shit out of the henhouses once a month. As a bonus, I learned a lot about "fowl" behavior. Chickens are nasty—they'll eat anything they get their beak into. If any hen showed a sign of weakness, the other chickens would attack and kill her.

Thousands of young pullets roamed around in fenced areas on a large hillside where many more chicken coops stood. Because they ran around outside, they didn't smell as bad as the hen houses. I carried hundred-pound bags of grain to all the coops. When slaughter time came, we barn boys had to catch the chickens and tie their feet with a cord hanging from a crossbar. The guy in charge of us stuck a knife through their mouths and into their brain and then twisted it around with gusto. I watched as the chickens flapped their wings, bled, and died. I didn't have any choice but to participate. Even though I had to feed chickens and clean chicken shit all the time (or maybe because of it) I hated to see the birds being killed like that.

I grabbed each dead chicken by the feet, dunked it into hot water, and hung it up. Then I ripped the feathers off the carcass. The wet feathers gave off a terrible stench. The supervisor often told me I didn't do a good enough job of pulling feathers, but chickens constantly grow new feathers and these small pinfeathers were hard to grip and even harder to remove.

We had a team of horses that pulled a wagon used for heavier chores. I never drove them because I knew nothing about horses, but I was thrilled when I saw a mare birth a foal. I thought the baby beautiful but couldn't show any affection toward it. The school employees frowned upon showing affection toward any animal, stressing to us that farm animals were there to work or to be eaten. I sometimes wondered if they feared we boys would commit bestiality if we were allowed to befriend the animals.

During summer, we barn boys planted rows and rows of vegetables. I got on my hands and knees every spare minute to pull weeds from around the new plants. Then I'd have to load a dump truck with black dirt that I dug from a pile using a spade. I was the only boy assigned to the task, the only one given a spade for digging and loading. I figured Mailey made me use the spade to make it twice as hard for me to fill the truck, but I filled that truck every time within a few hours to show him I could manage without a shovel.

The farm overseer's name escapes me, but he was a neutral person—neither overtly mean nor exceptionally nice to us kids. But one day he gave us some soft, ripe cantaloupes to eat in the field. I remember how delicious they were and appreciated this singular act of kindness in all my days at Middlesex.

I learned to imagine I was elsewhere as I did my work. I closed my eyes while drinking water and pretended to be sipping Coca-Cola or some other beverage I longed for. The taste became whatever I imagined. Although locked away, my mind was free to roam. I traveled to different places, ate gourmet meals, met pretty women, and drove my dream car—a 1939 Ford coupe—all while incarcerated.

* * * * *

I knew nothing about sports, so of course Mailey named me captain of the soccer team, the football team, the baseball team and any other team sport we played. He probably hoped the other kids would get angry at my decisions and beat the heck out of me. That never happened because even though I didn't know the game strategies or the rules, I always gave it my best.

One day Mailey told me Bernard, my eleven-year-old brother, had arrived at Middlesex. He took me to see a kid I didn't know cutting grass with a push lawnmower. The kid's long skinny legs reminded me of a gazelle.

I looked at Mailey, puzzled.

"There's your brother," Mailey said. "You can go say hello."

After that, I hardly ever got to visit with Bernie during the time we were both there. His five years at Middlesex were quite different than mine. He was good at sports and got along well with those in charge. He received favors and incentives like getting candy, ice cream, and other treats because of his ability to play baseball well. (He was the only one of us five DiBuduo kids who became halfway successful in life, and I believe those years at Middlesex had much to do with that.)

My confinement at Middlesex lasted from December 1954 until January 1956. Sixteen was the legal age to quit school, so my release was scheduled on my birthday. (I told Bernie I'd come and break him out afterward, but never did.) During my last few days there, I nursed my resentments, telling myself that I'd never forgive or forget any wrong done to me there. I felt it was in my blood to hold a grudge. I dreamed of vengeance, returning every wrong to make things right. Everyone would pay for the treatment I received when I was young and helpless, I thought, when I was hungry every night and no one cared. I have regrets now because of this attitude, but I'm happy that I didn't do more to be sorry about.

My sixteenth birthday finally arrived on January 25, 1956. Mailey took me to the school office and gave me the money orders my dad had sent, plus a suit jacket and a pair of shoes made in the penitentiary to go with the pants and shirt I wore. The weather was cold, but Mailey didn't care that I didn't have a winter coat.

I heard about the major shakeup at Middlesex County Training School soon after my release. Mailey hired a new guy, and when this employee witnessed the kids' treatment, he reported the abuse to state authorities. I read what the new guy said in the newspaper: "Kids are treated inhumanely, they're beaten and abused. The place is run like a concentration camp." Mailey didn't get fired, but he began to give the kids some amenities. They installed snack and pop machines. But Bernie told me later that the beatings had continued as usual.

I recall my years at Middlesex County Training School as the most miserable time of my life. Standing on line was a terrible experience and not being able to trust other boys because they'd run and tattle about anything I said caused me to dislike most of them. I worked in the barn full-time and attended school four hours a day.

The so-called educational program was a joke, just like the disciplinary school's. We learned nothing. There was only one classroom
with grades 4 through 12, and I was in eighth grade. Whenever the
teacher would ask the class a question and no one could answer it,
he'd call on me and I usually had the right answer. It wasn't that I
was smart; it was just that the other kids were either dumb or totally
uneducated.

The worst aspect of Middlesex was the physical and psycholog-
ical abuse. When I researched historical records while writing this
memoir, I found that until about 1970, juveniles in Massachusetts
were not allowed what are now standard constitutional rights.
Many kids were sent to reform schools for "crimes" such as truancy
or "being a stubborn child." Though probably never invoked, an
old law remained on the books that allowed "stubborn children" to
be executed.

Though I didn't know any of this at the time, I certainly felt the
weight of it. I saw Mailey as a constant threat: It seemed he always
wanted to beat me or put me on line for something.

I don't hate many people I've come across in my life, but if anybody I've met deserves to burn in hell, I think it must be Mailey.

Footloose and Fancy Free

I wanted to whoop with joy when I went through the gate and left the Middlesex County Training School for Boys behind me. My family had moved to Dorchester while I was away. I didn't know anybody in that neighborhood, so I returned to Hano, where my friends were. Getting Bernard out of MCTS was the farthest thing from my mind. I had no way to get back to Chelmsford, nor did I have any idea what to do with Bernie if I did get him out.

I looked everywhere for a job, but with little education and farmyard skills, I couldn't find one. Most of my friends were still in school, so life settled into boredom quickly, with nothing to do all day.

I ran into Jimmy Bryant, who had quit school when he turned sixteen. The first thing he said was, "Let's get some dough so we can get drunk."

We started borrowing money (with no intention of ever paying it back) from anybody we ran into. "Lend me a quarter?" Jimmy would say, then stand face-to-face with his victim and look him in the eye.

"I don't have it," most kids said. Jimmy always replied with a scowl. "If I find out you're lying, you'll be sorry."

Because of Jimmy's badass reputation, anyone who had a quarter would give it to him. It didn't take long to collect the $1.55 we needed for three quarts of Old India ale, the cheapest drink around, or the 50-cent pints of port wine.

Jimmy really was a tough guy, and I wanted to be like him. We'd drink our booze and then go looking for a fight, almost always finding someone willing to engage in Hano's favorite recreational pastime. I recalled thinking while locked up that I'd lived a hell of an exciting life, and for a time, this made my dead-end ways seem worthwhile.

One night, we came across two guys waiting for a bus in Union Square. Jimmy walked up to them and said, "I need to borrow a quarter from each of you."

"Get lost," one said.

Jimmy swung at him, and as they fought I jumped the other guy. He fought better than me and was kicking my butt. Jimmy knocked out his guy and then knocked out the other one. That night we got our booze and sat on Kelly's back porch drinking with other friends who'd brought their own booze, too. Like addicts, we relived our fights dozens of times in the retelling.

"You should have seen Jimmy today." I took a swig from my pint of wine and continued. "He kicked two guys' asses."

"Yeah, but they were all right," Jimmy said. "They weren't sissies like so many guys who never fight back."

"That's right," I agreed, "Lots of guys give up their money because they're afraid to fight."

"Not in Hano, you don't," Kelly said.

"Not so much here, but in Roxbury, I saw white kids giving their lunch money to the black kids at school because they were scared."

School was a dreaded word. The thought of going to school to better ourselves never entered our minds. The only way to become a better man in our world was to drink more booze and kick more ass. Those who didn't were outcasts and called whatever derogatory names were stylish in 1956.

One night a cop who drove a three-wheeled motorcycle stopped to harass me as I sat on a bench in Brighton near the community showers.

"You don't belong around here. Get back to Hano or you're going to get your ass kicked."

It crossed my mind that I'd grown big enough to fight a cop and win.

"Take off your traffic stripes and I'll kick your ass," I said.

"You little punk, I'm going to beat you black and blue." The cop started to take off the white crisscrossed harness that Boston motorcycle cops wore. I hit him while his arms were still entangled in the straps. He fought back. We fell to the ground and rolled around in the grass. I ended up on top and he began yelling, "Help, police, help, police!"

I laughed until reinforcements arrived. The cops threw me into the back of the "paddy wagon," a term that evolved because these vehicles had a roof, enclosed sides, and an open back to toss the Irish drunks through.

"Tough guy, huh, DiBuduo?" one cop said and punched me in the face.

The other two cops holding my arms in the wagon punched me

with their free hands. I tried to kick and bite but wasn't successful. When we arrived at the garage of Precinct 14 in Brighton, cops pushed me from the back of the wagon. I ducked my head to clear the opening. I never saw the blow coming that hit me in the solar plexus or the one that knocked me unconscious. I awoke to the dull whack, whack, whack of billy clubs (sometimes called "paddy whackers") hitting my flesh.

When my senses returned, I found myself surrounded by a ring of cops with clubs in their hands.

"Come on, DiBuduo." Two cops stood me up, took me by the arms, and walked me to a set of cement stairs that led inside the police station. They backed me up against the steps while another one walked to the top step, about five feet higher than floor level.

"I'm going to teach you that hitting a cop is a losing proposition," he said, and then whacked me over the head with his club.

I think he cracked my skull because when I touched the side of my head I felt a piece of bone moving under the skin. (To this day, I still feel a bump on that side of my head.) I complained about my skull, so they had a doctor examine me in the holding cell where they detained me overnight. When I went to court, the cop didn't tell the judge that I'd fought him and I didn't tell the judge that they'd beaten me with clubs. The judge set me free.

I was satisfied: I'd fought with a cop.

The cops had kicked my ass and should have been satisfied but weren't.

From then on, we engaged in war.

Not long after the incident, I spotted a cop with a murderous look on his face approaching me while I stood on the corner of Brighton and Harvard avenues. I got ready to fight, but I didn't know he'd already called for backup. I wasn't prepared for the cops who snuck up behind me and aimed a blow to the back of my head. The fight was over before it had started. I quickly learned that I couldn't win a fight with cops because there were always too many of them. Still, I felt like a hero because I never backed down.

I had fantasies of getting my hands on a sub-machine gun and going to Precinct 14 when the cops lined up for roll call. I visualized myself mowing them down, row after row.

One day I was walking close to the Charles River when I came across a National Guard unit engaged in some sort of exercise. I went into their camp and picked up a sub-machine gun that a soldier had left on the seat of a Jeep. I pictured myself pulling the trigger and watching cops dropping one after another.

A soldier noticed me and ripped the weapon from my hands. A look of relief washed over his worried face. He probably saved a lot of lives that day—including mine.

* * * * *

Not long after my release from Middlesex, I purchased a 1948 Ford Coupe for $50. The master cylinder leaked, but not knowing much about cars, I didn't realize how dangerous this would be. In those days there wasn't any backup in the braking system. If the fluid got low, all four brakes stopped working.

I didn't know how to drive and didn't have a driver's license. I decided the only way to learn was to get some experience, so I drove. I learned to beep my horn when I came to an intersection because I couldn't stop. The brakes worked when I filled the master cylinder with fluid but would suddenly fail when the fluid leaked away. This often happened when I needed them most. With all the maneuvering I had to do to avoid smashing into other cars, I thought I'd become a pretty savvy driver.

One day I took a girl named Carol for a ride. To show off, I drove behind a factory on a hill that had a level spot in the middle.

"If I drive fast enough up the hill," I said, "my car will jump over the level spot."

Carol looked scared as I stepped on the gas.

The only hang-up was the busy cross street at the top of the hill. I put the pedal to the metal, jumped over the level spot, and slammed on the brakes. I pumped and pumped the brake pedal as fast as I could, but there was nothing. My car collided with several cars as it burst onto the busy street with traffic going in both directions. I got out. My car had smoke trailing up from the engine and wouldn't start.

Carol looked at me with questioning eyes.

"Run," I told her. I took off, leaving her to either get away or get caught. (She got away and wouldn't talk to me for a few years.)

When I reached a pay phone, I called my brother Tony. "Call the police and report my car stolen."

"Why?" he asked. "Just do it," I said.

I didn't hear anything about the crash until the police arrested me on suspicion of burglary a few weeks later. While I was in custody, an inspector from the Department of Motor Vehicles came to question me about the accident. My luck held again because one city cop told him, "Don't even worry about it. He's going away for a long time. He won't be driving any time soon."

Hearing the cop say "going away for a long time" worried me. I couldn't think of anything I'd done recently that deserved a long prison sentence. But he had me stand at one end of a room about fifty feet long, a space large enough for an entire shift of cops to line up in for their roll call. He made me put on a hooded coat that was several sizes too big for me, then brought his witness in and had him stand at the other end of the room.

"He's already confessed," the cop said to the witness. "All we need is for you to identify him, and he'll go where he belongs for a long time."

"That isn't the guy," the witness said. "Don't forget, I'm the one who grabbed the coat you've got that guy wearing. I got a real good look at the bastard, and it sure wasn't him."

The cop probably thought he could frame me. I could have kissed the witness for his honesty and independence. Most people would have believed I'd confessed or gotten confused and identified me. So the lousy cop did me a favor when he told the guy from the DMV not to worry. I guess the DMV inspector marked that case closed because I never heard from him again. Guess he figured I was going to prison so he didn't have to pursue the case. He should have, because a few weeks later I stole a 1949 Ford coupe one night while drunk.

My friend, Jacky Sandman, was with me as I sped along city streets. I'd just purchased an overcoat that we called "six-button Bennies" in the '50s—a heavy, dark blue, double-breasted, woolen job. I was fortunate to wear it on this night, because when I crashed the Ford, I was thrown and slid on my back long enough to wear a hole through the coat. Without that coat, my spine and the road would have made contact.

Jacky was thrown out the passenger side. Although he wasn't seriously injured, he was bleeding in a few places. I knew we had to get out of there before the cops came. I flagged down a car.

"What's going on?" the driver asked, pointing to the smashed-up car.

For the first time, I noticed that the car looked like a steamroller had run over it. "Can you take us to the hospital?" I asked. "My friend is hurt."

One look at Jacky and he agreed. But we didn't go all the way to the hospital, where the police would be looking for us.

I left Boston before the cops could question me about the smashed-up cars. I was still only sixteen.

I went to New York and rented a room in a Puerto Rican neighborhood. I soon caught the Puerto Rican landlord rifling through my belongings. I didn't do anything to him because this was my first day in the Big Apple, and I felt intimidated by the enormity of the city and the hordes of people. At 42nd Street near Broadway there were so many people walking so close together that if I tripped, I wouldn't have room to fall down.

I found a job soldering wires in stereos for a dollar and two-and-a-half cents an hour. The two-and-a-half cents went to the union to make sure the workers didn't form a real union. The wage wasn't enough to pay rent, so I moved to my Aunt Loretta's house in Mt. Vernon, New York. I had never met my mother's sister and knew only a little about her from the letters she wrote. It surprised me that Loretta was just a normal, middle-class woman who happened to love the color purple. Her carpets, drapes, bedspreads, and many other things in her home were purple. (My mother's other sister, Aunt Lillian, who had visited us in Boston, seemed to be mentally more like my mom, except that she kept herself well groomed and her house spotless.)

Aunt Loretta had a son, Nate, who was a few years older than me. We got along okay until I started wearing his underwear and socks. My uncle Frank sent us underwear a few times a year, so I was used to wearing it by then. In my mind, it was okay to wear Nate's underwear. Now I realize my ignorance. I stayed only a few weeks at My Aunt Lillian's because I wasn't truly welcome but rather tolerated because I was family. As soon as I found a place to fit in, I moved out of Loretta's house.

At work, I met Juan Sanchez, a swarthy guy maybe ten years older than me. He took me to his Puerto Rican neighborhood and I hung out there for the short time I stayed in New York. His brother owned buildings in the slum neighborhood, and I rented one from him. The rent was cheap, and it was my kind of neighborhood: gang fights, drinking, plenty of action.

Listening to the Puerto Ricans jabbering in Spanish all day, I learned to follow a simple conversation, but never spoke a word of it. Juan had a sister, older than me by about ten years. She liked me but Juan asked me to stay away from her. His brother liked me too because he was gay.

I missed Boston after a short time and figured I'd been gone long enough for the cops to forget about my exploits. It usually only took a few weeks for them to become distracted because so much happened in Hano. So I went home.

Back in Boston, I lived rent-free with my parents. When I got a job at the rug cleaning company, I used my pay to drink every day after work. Events started to catch up to me. A few weeks after I returned from New York, the police arrested me for public intoxication, and the court remanded me to the youth authority. Yes, I was definitely intoxicated, but people in Hano rarely got arrested for public drunkenness.

The youth authority in Roslindale—the Massachusetts Youth Service Board Reception and Detention Center—kept juveniles of all ages while they waited to go before a board that would decide their fate, release or incarceration. One of the worst punishments they could mete out was to send a boy to the Shirley Industrial School for Boys.

When I first arrived at the youth authority, an Italian kid named

Di Angelo, about sixteen years old, was molesting younger kids. When I heard about this, I grabbed him by the collar and told him, "I'll kill you if you keep making little kids suck your wiener."

Due to appear in front of the board, he stopped, and was soon on his way to Shirley Industrial School, where the youngest kids were fifteen. I hoped the inmates there would make Di Angelo suck their dicks.

I stayed in a state of suspense, wondering about my fate. Paul Carter, a kid I knew from Brighton, had hit a staff member over the head with a chair while trying to escape. However, when Carter went in front of the board, he was released. I figured I'd get released too, because I hadn't committed any crime other than drinking. Later I found out that Carter had a cousin on the board. The same board sent me to Shirley Industrial School for Boys for a year.

I'd spent over a year locked up for hooking school, and now I had to spend time for drinking. It didn't seem fair.

Maybe if I'm going to be serving time, I thought, I should become a real criminal but then realized I already was.

Joe DiBuduo

Shirley Industrial School for Boys

After I arrived at the Shirley Industrial School for Boys, I read the school history. The school had once been a Shaker village. I'd never heard of the Shaker religion before, and I learned that the Shakers sat in silent meditation, waiting to be "moved by the spirit." They trembled violently in response to this spiritual power, and would spin and dance. The more I heard about them, the crazier this religion sounded.

As someone who'd spent a lot of time away from girls, I was fascinated by the Shaker lifestyle. Shaker communities usually consisted of two "families" who each lived in a large house segregated by gender. Ann Lee, who brought the Shakers to America from England, experienced visions that revealed sexual activity as the main cause of sin. I guessed her followers believed what she said because there aren't any more Shakers.

The State of Massachusetts purchased the Shaker property to use as an industrial school for boys, what we now call a "reform school." The school existed in the town of Shirley from 1909 to 1972. Designed to shelter wayward boys from aged fifteen to seventeen, it provided a housemother and a housefather to teach them manners, and either academic classes or instruction in a trade. Good intentions—but as usual, I found that intention and reality are two different things.

The first night I arrived at Shirley, I was assigned to Cottage 4. I went to eat dinner in the dining room, and the houseparents seated me at a table located close to theirs. The houseparents (whose name I don't recall except that it sounded French) seemed like nice people and demanded obedience in a quiet and dignified way. They let the boys know that they expected to be obeyed without any threats.

Dinner was served: bowls filled with a dark substance that looked like molasses. I was reminded of my first dinner in a state institution when I'd been four years old.

"What is this?" I queried the kid next to me. I stuck my spoon in my bowl. When I tried to lift it out, the bowl stuck to the spoon and rose from the table. I twisted the spoon and turned the bowl upside down. By then, the contents had completely solidified, and I couldn't eat the stuff even if I'd wanted to. Things weren't looking good. I prayed that breakfast would be edible because I was hungry. At least eating everything wasn't a requirement at Shirley as it had been at Middlesex, thank God.

The next day, the houseparents on duty left for three days, and the Rujos started their three-day shift. That night when we sat at the dinner table, Mr. Rujo jumped up and shouted, "Quiet down!"

When the talking continued, Rujo threw a heavy silver napkin ring at a table where some boys had been talking too loudly for his taste. The ring hit a boy on his eyebrow and blood spurted from the gash.

"Next time I say shut up," Rujo said, "you'll shut up."

The talking started again. Rujo threw another napkin ring, and the boys hit the floor to get out of the line of fire.

"Get back in your seats!" Rujo roared.

Somebody laughed.

Rujo threw a dish in the direction of the laugh. Then he started throwing whatever he could get his hands on. They turned the tables on their sides to shield themselves from the projectiles. I began to wonder if Cottage 4 was for insane people.

Rujo was part American Indian and hated it when anyone called him "Chief." I, of course, called him Chief all the time, and it wasn't long before he named me "Anteater" because of my big nose.

When we boys were all seated in the dining room, I'd disguise my voice and yell out, "Hey, Chief!"

Rujo's anger flared and he'd start throwing things, usually the heavy napkin rings on the staff table. By the time the meal was over, he and his wife had both thrown anything they could get their hands on. The dining room usually ended up looking as if a riot had erupted, strewn with broken china and overturned tables and chairs.

Rujo did many other insane things. A kid named George had some sort of epilepsy and often spaced out, unaware of his surroundings.

"You, there," Rujo said to George at one meal.

George didn't respond. Rujo screamed at him and punched him in the face. "When I talk to you, you answer me! Understand?"

George stared ahead blankly. Rujo punched him again. "Did you hear what I said?"

George kept staring without making a sound. Rujo punched

him again, and again, and again. He should have become aware that George had a medical problem but continued to beat George the entire year I stayed at Shirley. I figured he was like Mr. Mailey at Middlesex, a monster who took pleasure in beating kids.

My first job at Shirley was picking weeds on the farm. I hated farmwork because it reminded me of Middlesex. My friend from Brighton, Donny Babbin, got to work in the auto shop, a choice job. I tried to get assigned there, but there wasn't an opening. I heard Shirley had a swimming pool but never saw one.

After farmwork, the regular houseparents assigned me to be staff waiter. That meant I served them the food that the wife cooked at meal times, and I was allowed to eat the same food as a privilege for my service. That worked out fine when the regular houseparents were there. But when the Rujos came on duty, I had to wait on them too. It wasn't easy to please the two psychos.

One day Rujo said, "Anteater, you're not to eat any of my food. Understand?"

"I'd rather eat institutional food than your grub anyway," I said. I got ready to run because I saw his face turning red. (I ran whenever Rujo wanted to beat me, which really frustrated him.)

"Listen, you jerk. You're not allowed to eat the state food, either." He said this with a smile, knowing that if I couldn't eat either the state food or the staff food, I'd go hungry.

But I wasn't going to let him get away with starving me. I went to the kitchen and reached under the refrigerator to grab a container full of rat poison. I dumped some into the food I had arranged for the Rujos.

Fortunately, a kid who helped me out in the kitchen saw me and his face darkened in a wary, disapproving look. "Don't do it," he said.

"I'm sick of him picking on us," I said, mixing the poison into the food so it wasn't noticeable.

"Yeah, but they're going to know it was you who poisoned them."

That stopped me in my tracks. The kid was saying he wasn't going to take any blame, meaning that he'd rat on me.

I then realized that my anger had taken control and shut out any common sense. Not only would the Rujos have died, it would have been obvious that I'd poisoned them. I dumped the poisoned food in the garbage and gave them something else for dinner.

During the time I was forbidden to have food, Mrs. Rujo stood and watched me whenever I worked in the kitchen to make sure I didn't eat. To feed myself while the Rujos were on duty, I snitched food from goody bags left by parents on a table in the recreation room. I managed to take enough food to survive the three days that the Rujos were in charge.

One of my other chores was to help Mrs. Rujo clean and make beds. She was the only female I had contact with, and I imagined her disrobing and lying on the bed naked. My raging teenage hormones must have caused these thoughts because I hated her with a passion. If she'd actually taken her clothes off, I'd probably have run screaming from the room.

189

* * * * *

Shirley had a central heating plant and a main building with a gym and classrooms, but we residents lived in the old Shaker houses. My Cottage 4 was next to Cottage 9, the only cottage with a fence around it to prevent the troublemakers and runaways from escaping. Two of the kids in Cottage 4 had killed their fathers. One seemed weird and told me how he and his mother had kept his father's body hidden in the attic for a few months. Others had committed robberies and other serious crimes. Yet I served the same sentence, punished for only public intoxication. Of course, I'd done many other things I'd gotten away with, but at the time, I didn't think my confinement was fair.

I often remembered how Mailey used to threaten to ship me off to Shirley when I was at Middlesex. Later, I wished he had carried out his threat because life at Shirley was a vacation compared to Middlesex. When I described Middlesex to the other kids at Shirley, they could hardly believe it.

At Shirley, a psychologist told me that I was an alcoholic (which I had no reason to doubt), and a dentist made me a partial plate to replace my four missing teeth. I had front teeth for the first time in years. The first day I wore them, I attempted to drink from a water fountain. The stream of water was so forceful that it knocked the false teeth loose and halfway down my throat. I almost choked to death getting them out. (This was only the beginning of the problems my new teeth would cause.)

The cottages at Shirley had rooms on the first floor for eating and socializing. The bathrooms and lockers were located in the basement, dormitories on the second floor, and a room on the third floor was reserved for a watchman who kept an eye on residents while we slept. My bed was close to the high windows always left open so that the dormitory wouldn't stink, and in the winter I'd wake up with snow covering my feet.

The dormitory toilet sat on a platform in plain view of everyone. The night watchman's job was to be sure the boys stayed in their beds. Whenever somebody had to use the toilet at night, everyone remained silent until that person perched on the platform, then the entire dormitory would start shouting. The kid would run to get back in bed, but when the watchman arrived, he'd beat the shit out of him, thinking him the instigator of all the noise. Only newbies used that toilet at night.

We were allowed four cigarettes a day, plus one before bed. One night I lit up while in bed—a definite violation of the rules.

The watchman saw me and yelled, "I see ya, you dirty bastard." He came running into the dorm ready to start beating me.

I yelled, "Wait, don't hit me! I'm sick, that's why I had to light up."

"Sick, what's da matter with ya?"

"I've got smokeramius," I said.

He scratched his head in confusion and said, "Okay, I'll give ya a break this time, but don't do it again."

* * * * *

Di Angelo, who I'd threatened to kill at the youth center for diddling with little kids, had been at Shirley awhile. He'd made plenty of friends by the time I arrived, so I was prepared for an ass-kicking from him and his cronies. To my surprise, he never said a word about my threat. Maybe he was embarrassed by what he had done.

But another kid harassed me by acting tough and trying to intimidate me. He belonged to a clique, so I knew he'd have plenty of backup if I started anything with him. I thought of a devious revenge, though. I took his giant-size tube of toothpaste from his locker, opened it from the bottom and stuffed my excrement into it. I closed it, cleaned it, and every time he brushed his teeth I felt avenged. Eventually, I heard, brown streaks started showing in his toothpaste. By that time, I'd made enough friends to back me up, so I told him what I'd done.

"I knew it tasted funny," was all he said.

* * * * *

I wanted to play football, but Hastings, the supervisor at Shirley, told me I couldn't because of my nosebleeds. He told me the same thing about boxing, but let me train anyway. There was a tall, lanky, black kid who beat everyone in the ring. I figured it wouldn't be embarrassing if he beat me, so I agreed to spar with him. I rushed in to pursue an inside fight where his long reach couldn't be an advantage. He wasn't that strong, and I got the best of him by forcing a close-in fight. After that, I thought I was hot shit because I'd done what no one else could.

One night the boxing team went to a men's club to put on an exhibition. The referee turned out to be Marty Hardeman, the same guy that opened his mouth when he shouldn't have and screwed me from joining the U.S. Marines. It didn't seem to bother him that I was in reform school when I could have been in the Marines.

"Are you on the card?" he asked me.

"No," I told him. "Hastings, the guy in charge of Shirley, won't let me fight."

When the announcer read the fight card, I was on it. My opponent was "Alley Oop." He acquired his name from a popular song about a caveman. He did look like one: fearsome, with long hairy arms like an ape.

The bell rang; we met in the middle of the ring wearing sixteen-ounce pillow gloves. Despite the name, the gloves hurt like heck when one connected with my face. I cautiously circled Alley Oop. I had never seen him fight, and it looked like one punch from his ape-like arms might put out my lights. He circled too, waiting for me to make the first move. I feinted with a left. He fell for the ruse and attempted to block a punch coming in on his right side. I unloaded a right roundhouse, catching him on the left side of his face and knocking him to the canvas.

I was sorry to knock him down so easily and I immediately tried to help him to his feet, but the ref waved me away. I knew how humiliated he must have been to get knocked down like that. I didn't want to hurt him psychologically, just physically.

Marty Hardeman came to my corner. "I thought you weren't supposed to fight."

I shrugged. I didn't know why they matched us up. Maybe no one else wanted to fight Alley Oop, so they put me in the ring with him.

A few days later, while playing basketball, a black kid named Wright attempted a jump shot. I jumped in front of him and blocked it. Coming down, he swung his elbow hard, hitting me in the eye. I knew he did it on purpose, but there were so many staffers watching us that if I retaliated, I'd get thrown into Cottage 9. Instead, I decided to ambush him at the end of the day when all the inmates lined up on a central field. My eye had blackened from the blow, and I was pissed. Hastings heard about our altercation and gave the kid an early release from Shirley, as though he wanted to make sure I didn't get even. I guess he either liked the kid or disliked me.

Shirley was known for its music program, and somehow I got recruited to sing in the choir for the Christmas pageant. Once the instructor heard me trying to sing, he told me to just move my lips. We dressed in the customary altar boy robes, and I looked like that famous picture of a choirboy dressed in robes and sporting a black eye. My father visited that day. Because he didn't have a car, he came on the train. When he attempted to return home, the trains had stopped running, and he was stranded overnight in the shitty little town of Shirley.

I sure made life harder for Dad than it should have been.

* * * * *

Jerome Miller, a former state Department of Youth Services commissioner, said the Industrial School for Boys was a horrific place . . . held together by threatening, intimidating, and beating. As head of DYS, he was responsible for closing down all of the state's reform schools in the early 1970s.

Miller said boys at the school were punished for running away by having their ring fingers bent back and broken. The conditions were so bad, he said, police hated to return runaways there because they'd hear them screaming. In the school's Cottage 9, where teenagers with disciplinary problems were held, the staff made them scrub floors with toothbrushes, he said, and the building's third floor held "the tombs," rooms without windows or toilets that runaways were thrown into naked as punishment.

—Julie Massis, *The Boston Globe,* July 19, 2009

Runaway

Some of my friends ran away from the Shirley Industrial School for Boys, so I decided to give it a shot. I'd never run away from Middlesex Training School because I feared getting my head shaved. The punishment for running away at Shirley was confinement to Cottage 9, where inmates were subjected to daily beatings and performing calisthenics for hours at a time. That didn't scare me. I'd always been impulsive, so when something crossed my mind I simply did it. There were no fences around the school, so one afternoon I took off running through the fields, sucking in lungsful of unconfined air.

This is great, I thought. *Free!*

But free to do what?

I had no plan and no idea how to get back to Boston. The farmers in the area were aware of the cash reward for returning runaways who were easy to spot in their state-supplied clothes. I started hitchhiking along a two-lane road anyway. A police car suddenly zipped toward me from the opposite lane. I attempted to scale an eight-foot high chain-link fence beside the road. When I reached the top and was about to jump to the ground on the other side, I heard a commanding voice say, "If you jump, I'll shoot."

I turned to see a uniformed cop not more than ten feet away with his pistol aimed at me. I slowly climbed back down the fence. He put me in his car and delivered me to supervisor Hastings.

"You know what happens to runaways," Hastings said to his assistant, smiling grimly. "Take him to cottage number nine."

* * * * *

Cottage 9 was the disciplinary cottage where all the runaways and troublemakers went. Its yard was fenced so we couldn't escape. I began to enjoy doing pushups, jumping jacks and the other disciplinary calisthenics. But some of the guards were mean and beat the boys. One of the kids told his brothers about such an incident on visiting day. The next day, the guard who'd beaten him came in with black eyes and bruises all over. We inmates were happy to see justice meted out.

One of the guards who worked at Cottage 9 took the time to speak with me about different things, and he told others I was basically a good kid and didn't belong at Shirley. After about a month, I was transferred from the disciplinary cottage and went back to work in the auto repair shop, where I'd been assigned to learn a trade. One day as I held a metal part to a grinder, something flew into my eye. I assumed it was a metal splinter. Because there were no preventative measures like using safety glasses, the school had to send me to a state hospital to have the splinter removed.

I never want to repeat my experience with hospital life. The food there was worse than the school's. I didn't see a doctor until weeks after I arrived, and I lost about thirty pounds in the six weeks I stayed there. No one seemed to know when I'd be treated or when

I'd be released.

The state hospital served as a warehouse for derelicts, and little in the way of medical treatment seemed to be dispensed to anyone. But this was a valuable learning experience for me. The hospital was full of alcoholics who had signed themselves in so they wouldn't freeze to death during the winter. I had no idea people would willingly come to a place like that. Tunnels connected all the buildings, and they filled with winos on their winter retreat.

After six weeks, orderlies took me into an operating room, where some doctors and surgical nurses surrounded me. One doctor used a cotton swab to remove a bit of grinding stone out of my eye. They seemed pissed at me and wanted to know why I said I had a piece of metal in my eye. I'd assumed a splinter had flown from the metal I'd been grinding, and so did the school employees. I told them I guessed I was lucky. One of the doctors told me the piece of stone had stayed on the surface of my eye, unlike a metal splinter, which will lodge deeper into the eyeball with blinking and eye movement. Of course, no one mentioned any of the problems I could have had by the time they bothered to take the piece of stone out. The next day I was on my way back to Shirley.

There wasn't any academic program at the industrial school because a boy sentenced there had to be at least fifteen (working age at that time), and so we all had jobs in vocational training programs. When Donny Babbin finally volunteered to take a job working outdoors, I got his job in the auto shop, a garage big enough to hold four cars. I hoped to learn how to earn a living as mechanic or body man, but all I ever did was polish cars and watch kids sniff gas.

I worked with Phil Sheehan in the auto shop. When I first met him, he wore greasy clothing, and had a wide grin on his face when he asked, "Wanna get high?"

"On what?"

"Gasoline."

"How do you do that?" I asked.

"Watch."

He put his mouth over the stem of the gas tank of the vehicle he stood beside. He sucked in as hard as he could, stood straight up, and then fell backwards to the cement floor. I didn't want any part of getting high like that.

* * * * *

While I was away at Shirley, Dad had purchased a house on 17 Tucker Street in Dorchester, a white neighborhood where black families were moving in, causing real estate values to drop. As usual, Mom had a steak for me to eat on my release date, and Dad was at work.

By then life was looking up for my family. Dad had retired from the Marine Hospital after thirty years. He'd started collecting Social Security and a government pension—both while still earning a salary from his new job after he'd graduated from trade school, where he learned to tend steam boilers. So my younger siblings' lives had improved in my absence, and to this day, they don't recall the hunger that haunted Tony and me during our childhood. Because my father had more money, he would often bring food home. (I'm sure he was the one who made sure my younger brother and sister had enough to eat.) By then, Tony was working and I'd been absent for years, so my parents had two fewer mouths to feed. But one thing that never changed was my mother's behavior—she continued to nag my father until he died.

After a good meal at home, the next thing I did was make the two-hour bus ride to Hano to get drunk with my friends. The buses stopped running around 1 a.m. I'd often get stuck in an MTA station on the way home, and end up sleeping on a bench until the buses started running again. Lots of stuff happened on the buses, like fights and problems with homosexuals trying to molest me while I was drunk. Traveling through black neighborhoods alone late at night was the cause of many confrontations. Drinking and fighting were all I knew how to do, maybe all I wanted to do at the time. Every week my nose got bent in a different direction and I sported a new black eye. I still wasn't a very good fighter, but I didn't let that stop me.

Middlesex County Training School finally released my brother Bernard in 1957 when he was fifteen and I was seventeen. We chipped in together and bought a 1938 Plymouth sedan. I drove it for only a few days before I rammed it into the rear of a city bus and damaged the bus engine badly enough that the bus had to be towed away. The Plymouth survived with only a small dent. The bus driver didn't call the cops. Of course, I didn't haven't any insurance. Bernie drove it with a learner's permit to Cape Cod, hitting 109 miles per hour at one point, but the engine blew a rod, so we had to junk it. I was without a car again.

One night, drunk as usual, I missed the last bus going to Dudley Station, where I'd transfer to a trackless trolley that went to Codman Square in Dorchester. I usually walked the last few miles to my house, and often saw a guy closing up a bar along the way. It seemed as though he tempted me purposely by turning his back to me while locking the door. He had his cash box tucked under one arm so he could use both hands to lock the door, and I could see a pistol in a holster peeking from under his jacket. Every time I saw him, I felt tempted to grab his pistol and rob him, but I never did.

This time when I missed the last bus, I stole a car. I reached under the dashboard, pulled the ignition wires loose, wound two together to make a circuit and then touched the starter wire to them to fire up the motor. When the engine started, I pulled that wire away.

I don't remember much about that night except that I passed out in the car. I must have awakened at some point and taken the bus home. The Brookline police found the car later that day with my partial dental plate on the floor. The Brookline PD turned my teeth over to the Boston PD in Brighton, because I'd stolen the car from Brighton. The cops in Brighton put two and two together as they knew me well enough to know my four front teeth were missing.

The police came to my house and arrested me on a Friday night.

"Why is it you always arrest me on a Friday?" I asked the cop as he snapped handcuffs on my wrists.

"We want to be sure you're available Monday morning to appear in court."

"No, you want me to spend an entire weekend locked up in a tiny cell with nothing to read or do. No heat, no blankets, and no sheets."

"Better than sleeping in an alley," the cop said.

Each cell had an iron cot and a stinking toilet. Every now and then, a smartass cop would come around and harass the prisoners.

After having nothing to eat for three days but two bologna sandwiches, I appeared on auto theft charges in the Brighton District Court, where my nemesis Mrs. O'Donnell still ruled with an iron hand.

"Nice to see you again, DiBuduo," she said. "We've got you this time."

O'Donnell still remembered us kids pelting her car with rotten fruit by the disgusted looks she cast at me. She smiled with satisfaction as a cop testified.

"Your Honor, the defendant's teeth were found lying on the floor of a stolen car."

The cop held my false teeth up for everyone to see.

"Mark them as an exhibit," the judge said. "What other evidence do you have?"

Mrs. O'Donnell started to speak, but my lawyer—my father's friend Zoloti—spoke first.

"Where were the teeth found?"

"In a stolen car," the cop said. He looked at me with a satisfied gleam in his eyes.

Zoloti nonchalantly rummaged through his briefcase. "Where was this alleged stolen car recovered?"

"Brookline Center," the cop said.

Zoloti's face lit up. "Then what are we doing in a court that has no jurisdiction in Brookline?"

"He's right," the judge said. "Case dismissed."

"Just a minute, Your Honor," Zoloti said. "The police are holding my client's property and I'd like it returned now that the charges are no longer valid."

The judge motioned at the policeman. "Give the defendant his teeth."

The cop handed me my false teeth. I was thankful to have them back and thankful for Zoloti's representation. Without his help, I would have been sentenced to prison.

The Friday after my court date, I celebrated my victory. Celebrating always meant drinking. After a party, I went into Donovan's Drugstore in Allston.

"Hey, good looking," I said to a girl who sat at the soda fountain.

She narrowed her eyes and frowned at me. "Go away. I don't want to be bothered."

"But how can you turn down an opportunity to go out with a suave, sophisticated, good-looking man like me?"

She threw a glass of water in my face. Instinctively, I punched her in the mouth and chipped her tooth. The police came and arrested me. I spent another weekend with my bologna sandwiches.

Monday morning came and a Station 14 cop paraded me into the courtroom. Mrs. O'Donnell looked as if she had me nailed.

"What have you done now?" the judge asked me.

"Assault and battery," Mrs. O'Donnell said and pointed at the girl. "He punched this poor girl and chipped one of her teeth."

Zoloti defended me again. "My client is the victim here. That woman assaulted him and he acted in self-defense."

When the judge heard the girl had thrown water on me before I'd reacted, he said, "If you agree to pay to repair her tooth, I'll dismiss the charges."

I agreed. Mrs. O'Donnell glared at me with tears of frustration in her eyes because I'd escaped her clutches one more time.

Adult Detention

I turned seventeen a few months before I left the Shirley Industrial School—old enough to go to adult detention if I got caught doing something illegal. Unfortunately, that fact didn't change my behavior. One night I was with Jimmy Bryant and a group of guys walking over the Market Street Bridge, which spanned the Boston & Albany Railroad tracks that ran through Hano. Other than the traffic traveling over it, the bridge was secluded when we met another group of guys. We tried to start an altercation and threw a few punches, but they were timid and didn't want to fight because they were "sissies".

"Give me your fucking sweater," Jimmy Bryant told one of them.

Jimmy walked away wearing his new sweater. We thought nothing of this. If we needed something, we took it. This time the victim called the cops.

Jimmy and I found ourselves in the Charles Street jail, charged with robbery. The seriousness of the charge didn't sink in until I heard the cell doors clang shut. Other than the local lockup, this was the first adult facility I'd been in, a real prison with steel bars everywhere. Most of inmates were serious criminals, grown-up murderers and robbers locked down twenty- three hours a day. The place scared me, but I couldn't show it. All we'd done to get there was what we'd done all our lives: take things we needed.

Fortunately, I wasn't held in custody long. My dad came up with bail money for me. Jimmy sat in the Charles Street Jail until our trial, which was months later. I ended up with a one-year suspended sentence for each of three criminal charges.

*****

I often traveled to different areas of Boston to visit the friends I'd made at Shirley. Some of them lived in Hano, my old stomping ground. Many times during the trip home to Dorchester (a two-hour ride on three or four different buses), I'd be intoxicated and pass out.

About three months after receiving my suspended sentence, I went to Roxbury to visit Vince Ceccone, whom I'd met at Shirley. He was a barber there, and he'd cut my hair when I came to visit. On my last visit, we'd had too many drinks before he began to cut my hair. He attempted to make what we called a box-cut, a straight line low on the back of the neck. He wasn't satisfied the line was straight enough, so he raised it a bit and cut it again. He wasn't happy that time either, so he trimmed it again, and again, and again. The line was above my ears by the time he gave up trying to make it straight. I never let him cut my hair after that.

Vince belonged to the National Guard. I attended a meeting with him and enlisted, but I only went to one more meeting because I had a court date for breaking and entering. To get home in Dorchester, I often walked along the railroad tracks. One night, I broke into a coal company's office in a railroad yard close to my house. I was so drunk that the cop caught me standing there trying to figure out how I'd bounced my flashlight beam off the high front window (theirs) when my light was aimed at the floor. He arrested me.

I had a jury trial not long after. I testified that the door was open when I entered. In his summation, the prosecutor asked, "Can you believe his story . . . can you?"

A juror jumped up and said, "No, no, I can't believe him!" He looked around sheepishly because of his emotional outburst.

I knew then it was all over. After the guilty verdict, the judge asked my lawyer what he could do with me. If I'd had half a brain, I could have told him I was in the National Guard and would volunteer for active duty. But like an idiot, I kept my mouth shut. I was timid about speaking up unless I got angry, and then I sometimes blurted out things I'd feel sorry for later.

I meekly waited for the sentence. The courtroom went silent as the judge proceeded to read off four different charges (because I had violated my probation while taking the sweater with Jimmy): Three counts of robbery plus the one breaking-and-entering charge equaled four different sentences. I'd serve all four at the same time because the judge said each charge would run concurrently.

"I sentence you to one year and a day to be served in the Deer Island House of Correction," said the judge. Any sentence over a year was considered a felony, so by adding one day, I was now a convicted felon.

I don't remember how my father reacted because I was too self-absorbed. I recall my mother saying that I made it hard for my little brother Andy to keep friends because of the newspaper report about my arrest for the "great sweater robbery". Even so, going to Deer Island seemed like an adventure. By this time, I'd spent so much time in reform school that I thought it no big deal to do another year in jail.

Deer Island is located in Winthrop, Massachusetts, the town my mother lived in before she married my father. The prison is literally on an island, connected to the mainland by a road. Convicted criminals were sentenced to serve time there for misdemeanors as well as felonies. (I believe that the longest sentence allowed at the time was two and a half years.) There weren't many career criminals at Deer Island and most guys were there for non-violent crimes like non-support, shoplifting, or auto theft—things I didn't think serious at all.

The tone of my stay at Deer Island was set on my first night after one of the inmates had received a "Dear John" letter from his girlfriend. He was found hanging from a noose in the morning. I wondered how often that happened.

I have to admit I was taken aback when I walked into the "New Prison," a deceptive name because the prison had been used to hold Civil War prisoners. The long brick building had four stories with a cellblock in the center of each. Each cellblock consisted of about fifty cells side-by-side on each row, about one hundred to each floor, making the prison population around four hundred men. A locking mechanism consisting of one lever controlled the locks on entire rows of cells.

After all the state facilities I had been in, I shouldn't have been surprised by the conditions. Birds flew in and out of glassless windows and cats sprang around trying to catch the birds. The beds had springs wired to the frame and probably dated to the Civil War, too. The middle of the bed springs touched the floor. Sleeping in them felt like dangling in a hammock. The only thing that kept me sane was books. I would trade anything for a book, and when lucky enough to acquire one, I'd read as slowly as possible to savor the words.

We were released from our cells around 7 a.m. for work detail and weren't locked up again until after dinner. We weren't watched closely because it would be hard to escape from the island. Even so, living inside a cell barely big enough for the bed and "shit bucket" (as we called them) sucked. Every cell had a radio, though, and once we were locked in for the night after dinner, it seemed that all four hundred radios were tuned to a different station and playing at full volume to drown out the others.

There was no plumbing, no toilets, no sinks, and no showers. A trustee made rounds once each night to fill the prisoner's tin cups with drinking water. Our toilet facilities consisted of a covered wooden bucket that we poured some disinfected water into after we emptied it each day. At least it didn't stink inside the cellblock; the ocean breeze blew through the broken windows, carrying the odors away.

We had to empty the shit buckets into a large open trough when we were released from our cells for our morning work detail. That's when the fun began. A strong ocean breeze almost always blew through the cell block, and I soon learned to duck when emptying the shit bucket. This gave me an idea about how to antagonize someone if I didn't like them. I'd get in front of them in line, and when my turn came to empty my bucket, I'd throw the contents high into the wind and duck down. The wind would blow the contents back over my head and soak the guy behind me.

Once a week, inmates went to the shower room in the laundry building. I witnessed a few fights in there whenever an inmate made sexual advances on another. I never had a problem like that. I guess my stance made it obvious that I wouldn't let anybody get away with trying, or maybe I was just too ugly for those weirdos.

While I served time on Deer Island, my friend Joe Gillis made his girlfriend write to me every week. He did this because most guys I knew didn't write letters. It was a woman's job to do that. (I was supposed to be Joe's best man when he got married, but I was still locked up when that happened.) In one of my return letters I wrote, "The food is great here, ha-ha." Shortly after I'd mailed the letter, the prison director, known as "Lampshade Kelly," called me to his office. The inmates gave Kelly this moniker because it was rumored that he stood in his window to observe what went on outside and supposedly wore a lampshade on his head as a disguise.

When I walked into his office, he was sitting behind his desk with my letter in his hand. "What's this supposed to mean?" he asked. "Are you implying there's something wrong with the food here?"

I burst out laughing. Of course, the food was worse than what most people on the outside throw in the garbage.

He sent me to the hole for ten days of solitary confinement. The hole was a cell in a dark, walled-off section of the cell block, furnished with just a shit bucket and a blanket to sleep on.

The law stated that prisoners only had to be fed once a day, and that's what they did. Once a day, a guard delivered a tray of garbage. This was another instance where my imagination served me well in jail. As I ate the crummy food, I saw and tasted fried chicken or Joe & Nemo hamburgers. My mind travelled to faraway places during the long hours in the bare, dark cell.

One day the guard ordered me to hand the tray to him.

"You want it,"I told him, "come and get it."

That got me another ten days in the hole. I chalked that experience up to another thing my movie heroes had accomplished: spent time in the hole without whimpering or complaining.

Once I completed my sentence in solitary, I went to work on the island's pig farm. There I encountered a guy from Maine so big and muscular that he probably could have picked me up with one hand. He wasn't too bright, though, and didn't know when to quit joking or fooling around. This annoyed the hell out of me.

When a man is locked up, he can't let anybody harass him. If he does, the harassment catches on and others start doing it. I saw something similar happen with chickens when I was at Middlesex: One chicken would get injured, and the others would peck it to death. I didn't think prisoners were much different than chickens, so I had to stop this guy before others joined him, because I figured he could easily beat me in a fight.

Around the pigpens lay many things that could be used as weapons, but no one seemed to care. One day after the big guy had harassed me, I found him lying on the grass near the sea wall. Sick of his mouth, I found a piece of iron pipe about two and a half feet long. I gripped the pipe tight as I walked near him, calling him by name. When he lifted his head, I swung the pipe up and over my shoulder, and hit him directly on top of the head with all my might. The sound of pipe smashing into bone overwhelmed the sound of the ocean breeze. Upon impact, the pipe vibrated and broke free of my grip. Time stopped as we watched the pipe, transfixed as it spun thirty feet into the air, reflecting sunlight off the ends. Still spinning end over end in what seemed like slow motion, it descended and bounced off a rock with a clang, rolling off the seawall and into the ocean.

After it disappeared, this guy looked at me and said, "Huh?"

Surprised that he showed no effect whatsoever from being smashed in the head, I held out my hands as a sign of peace. "Hold on," I said. "I was only kidding,"

Uncertain how to react, he didn't do or say anything. But I knew it wasn't over between us. I figured he would wait to get even.

The next day we walked in a double column from the mess hall, located on a hill in a newer building that also housed prisoners about a half-mile away. The big dumb guy was directly in front of me as we walked past a half-demolished building. I picked up a half of a "Kelly brick" (what we called a red brick) that weighed a few pounds. I drew my right arm back and swung as hard as I could, landing a blow on his right temple.

"Huh," he said as he spun around.

"I was only kidding," I quickly said again. "We're friends."

And we were friends from that time on because I knew the only way to get him out of circulation would probably be to kill him. I didn't want any part of killing someone, and I didn't think he wanted me hitting him on the head again.

Friends and Foes

My prison adventure quickly became routine, and I couldn't wait to get out. I kept a calendar in my cell and marked off each day of my sentence with an X. I tried to educate myself as best I could in that environment so I could find some employment after my release. A clergyman helped me enroll in a correspondence course. Like an idiot, I chose Radio and Television Repair—a bad choice when there's no equipment to work with. I've always regretted not taking some type of art course, because all I did in my free time was try to draw pictures.

Before my conviction, I often looked for work but never found a decent job. I used to dream about being a plumber or electrician, and couldn't imagine myself holding a better job than these. Another friend of mine at Deer Island worked in the prison laundry and he recommended me for a job as the gardener after I told him about my experience working on the farm at Middlesex County Training School. The position consisted of maintaining the shrubbery and flowers growing around the laundry building.

The gardening job moved me up in the prison's pecking order. I was transferred to what used to be the women's prison—luxurious compared with the New Prison, because the cells had toilets and sinks with running water and intact windows. It was almost a pleasure to return to a quiet bird-, cat- and rat-free cell every night.

214

The Women's Prison was almost silent compared the New Prison's cacophony. Unfortunately, it now held only men.

Occasionally I'd see Judy, a girl I knew from Winthrop, riding on the back of a motorcycle headed to a military radar station on the end of the island. Prisoners weren't allowed to go there except when Red, one of the guards, took us to the mounds behind the firing range to dig out spent bullets. He'd melt them down to mold weights for scuba diving belts.

A week after I became the gardener, construction began outside the laundry. The ground and plants were torn up. There was nothing for me to take care of, so I sat in the sun part of the day, enjoying doing whatever I wanted. A guy named Castrucci and I got some plastic buckets, filled them with cement, and stuck an iron bar in the center of each bucket, one at a time. When the cement dried, we had a heavy weight to lift. We made several different barbells of different weights, built a bench, and were all set to start lifting weights. We had a bar in the laundry for chin-ups, and I filled empty potato sacks with sand to use as a heavy punching bag. Castrucci later became a hardcore body builder.

Other than playing cards, this was about the only recreation we had, so I worked out every day. I got to where I could do twenty-five chin-ups and fifteen behind the neck. I did these several times a day and worked out on the punching bag. Two guys who worked in the laundry—Sully, who was close to my age, and an ex-fighter named Johnny Rossi, who was in his fifties—taught me to throw combination punches. This instruction helped hone my fighting skills. I figured I wouldn't be on the losing end as often after my release.

Sully was a good-looking guy with a broken nose that added to his rugged good looks. He had an Irish father and an Italian mother and seemed to have inherited the best of both ethnicities. Always ready to either laugh or fight was the Irish part, and the loyalty to friends, principles and his desire for fairness seemed to be the Italian part. Sully had a pleasing but crooked smile and one never knew if he was glad or about to take someone's head off. He was also tough and knew lots of tricks. Regardless of this, he was one of those people with whom it was always a pleasure to associate.

Sully's cell was next to mine on the second tier of four tiers. Lights out came early, but I could see to draw because of the bare bulb lighting the walkway for the guards. One night I thought I'd done a fine job of a self-portrait. I stuck my arm through the bars and passed the drawing over to Sully's hand.

"Does that look like me?" I asked.

He laughed so long and hard that it made me laugh, too. It seemed we laughed for hours over that stupid drawing. That's the way it was in jail—you had to see the humor in every situation. If it wasn't for humor, I would have become bitter.

* * * * *

When my release time approached, I was offered a job working in the garage at Deer Island. A guard would drive me and another prisoner, Henry, into the city every day to pick up day-old food from the city hospital to help feed the prisoners. Henry had half his nose cut off and I never could get used to looking at him. I tried to be polite because he seemed like a nice man, but I'd flinch from the sight of his exposed nostrils.

Sunday was a day of rest, and rather than make us stay in our cells all day, the prison showed movies on Sunday afternoons. The guy who brought the movies would drop his car off at the garage to be cleaned and detailed. I'd do that, and he'd leave two Bensedrex inhalers in the glove box for pay. In those days, one of the main ingredients of the inhalers was Benzedrine, soaked into a strip of cotton inside the inhaler.

To make the inhalers last, I cut the cotton from each one into six pieces and swallowed one piece at a time. By eating the cotton I'd get an effect we called "speeding." My mouth would get dry, my eyes stay open for days at a time, and I'd talk incessantly.

As I lay in my cell at night after eating Benzedrine, I'd look past the bars and through a window at a flashing red maritime or aircraft warning light on an antenna located on a military base on another part of the island. Every time the light went out, I'd see some kind of picture, and when it came back on seconds later, the picture would disappear. It was like watching movies all night.

An older black guy we called "Big Al" used to hang around with Tommy Priday and a few other guys I knew from the outside, whenever we were allowed to participate in sports or other outdoor events. Joining us was "Bomber," a young white guy serving six months, called that because he'd made a false bomb report aboard a U.S. Navy ship

217

so his friends on shore leave wouldn't have to return right away.

One day we were watching a ball game on the field when I had to pee. I pulled open the door of a porta-potty and there was Bomber bent over with big Al's dick up his ass. I closed the door, shaken. I always swore never to have anything to do with a homosexual while I was locked up. I believed a man could grow to like other men rather than women if they screwed one often enough.

Big black Al was from the South End of Boston. Priday and I ran into him one day after we were all released and he was flush with money. He gave Priday some (I don't know how much) but I wouldn't take his money. All I could picture was what Al was doing in the outhouse and didn't want anything to do with him.

When my release day at Deer Island arrived (around 1958 or 1959), I had been eating Benzedrine inhalers for several months. These were available in any drugstore, and knew I could have an unlimited supply on the outside. The first things I did was move my sparse belongings into my parent's apartment, ate the steak my mom cooked for me, and then went to the nearest drug store, where I discovered the inhalers cost only a buck apiece. At Deer Island, these things were so hard to come by that I'd had to ration my supply to make them last. Outside, I lost control. With no limit I began to use all I wanted. I soon swallowed so much cotton that I got constipated. I didn't think about what this drug was doing to me until one night I overdosed.

I went home after eating more cotton from an inhaler and soon my hands folded up into claws and my body tightened up all over.

My breath came in spurts and I couldn't get enough air into my lungs because I'd inhale, then forget how to exhale. I remember thinking that I didn't care if I died, but while waiting for death to arrive I then started thinking about all the things I'd never experience if I did: revenge on those who had it coming, all the beautiful girls I had yet to meet, and the excitement of doing new things. Whenever life didn't seem worth living, I always remembered the reasons I didn't want to die.

My dad took me to the hospital in a cab, terrified to see me sucking in air and nearly passing out before I exhaled. A doctor understood the problem at first glance. He gave me a brown paper bag and told me to blow it up and then inhale. As long as I could watch the bag expand and contract, I was all right, but as soon as I'd pull the bag from my mouth, I'd start sucking in air again.

We returned home, and I breathed into the bag until I went to sleep. But the next morning I awoke to a crowd standing around my bed—women, men and children, all staring at me. Who the fuck let them in my room? I was nude under the blankets and had to go to the bathroom.

"Everybody get the fuck out!" I yelled.

No one moved.

"Maaaaaa," I said, "come and tell these people to get the hell out of here."

I heard her bulk come trudging down the hall. Everyone scattered, ran and hid. One person hid behind my bedroom door, two in the pantry, and two girls crawled under the kitchen table. I didn't see where the others hid after they ran away.

"What are you talking about?" she asked. "What people?"

"They're hiding." I slipped on some jeans and walked to the bedroom door.

"You must have been dreaming," Mom said.

"No, I wasn't dreaming. Look, there's someone's hiding behind the door."

I yanked it away from the wall expecting to expose the person, but there wasn't anyone there. "I saw one of them hide here."

"Were you dreaming or are you drunk?"

"Right there," I pointed. "There are two guys hiding in the pantry."

Mom opened the pantry door. No one was there.

"Okay," I said, "I saw two girls crawl under the kitchen table."

I walked over and tipped it up. No one was there.

My mom turned around and walked away, shaking her head.

I was still sure I saw people, whether they were now there or not. I dressed, and as soon as I left the house, I heard someone calling, "Joe, Joe," every few minutes. I'd look around and see no one. I didn't know what to do but have a few drinks to drown my hallucinations.

That night I went with friends to Ringers Park to drink beer. I soon saw a girl sitting on a rock a few feet from us.

"Who's that sitting over there?" I asked Jimmy Bryant, who was sharing beers with me.

"Sitting where?" he asked. "I don't see anybody."

"Right there." I walked toward her, but she disappeared in a flash.

No one else could see her. These apparitions only lasted a day but showed me what drug addiction and insanity were like. The incident scared me but unfortunately didn't change my behavior much. I stopped using inhalers and stayed away from hard drugs like heroin, because I eventually lost friends in New York to smack. But I'd try almost anything else.

* * * * *

I got a job at Albany Carpet, a rug cleaning company located across from the asphalt park in Hano. The large plant had machines that pulled big, expensive Oriental carpets through on a conveyor belt, spraying them with soapy water. After the washing, the rugs went through a blow dryer. Workers then rolled up the rugs in paper, and some were stored for the summer on wooden lanes of the bowling alley where I'd once worked as a pin boy. No one bowled during the summer before air conditioning was common, and the lanes were a perfect place to store the rugs. Apparently, many people took their carpets up during summer and lived with bare floors to keep their houses cooler.

As a helper at Albany Carpet, I earned minimum wage, seventy cents an hour. My buddy Jimmy Bryant worked there, too. My job was to help a driver deliver clean rugs, lay them out in client's homes or place them in storage, and to pick up dirty rugs and bring them back to the plant for cleaning. By the end of the day, we had a truck full of soiled rugs to unload.

One time when delivering carpeting to a doctor's office, I looked through the many bottles of pills lying around and snitched several with labels warning that they couldn't be distributed without a prescription, I figured these must be mind-altering drugs.

I swallowed the entire contents of one bottle. My rationale for drinking and taking whatever drugs were available was to help me forget my miserable life. The pills I swallowed that day helped me forget, all right. My first aware moment after taking the pills surfaced when I found myself sitting on the steps where I used to live in my old neighborhood in Hano, at 33 Blaine Street in Allston. I checked a calendar when I went home and found that a week had passed.

Once I hit the streets again, I began to exact my revenge on those who had enjoyed kicking my ass while I was weak and undernourished. It felt good to be the one to administer a beating instead of being the one getting beaten. I'd developed a muscular frame from lifting weights and had gained a pretty good punch with my right. I could grab a guy by the collar or throat with my left hand, pin him against the wall with my arm straight out, then work him over with my right fist. I beat up a few dozen guys, and that was enough to satisfy me.

One night I was in Union Square where Jamesy Callahan hung out with his buddies. He had beaten me for hours in a snowstorm a few years before, and everyone still considered him the toughest guy in our age group. He approached me, followed by several of his friends.

"Hear you've been kicking ass," Jimmy said.

His slurred speech told me he had been drinking. I didn't answer, because I didn't think I'd ever be able to beat him in a fight, especially with so many of his friends backing him.

"Come on, Joe," Jamesy said, swinging a roundhouse right at my head. "Let's see if you can take me."

I ducked and came up with a right uppercut to his jaw, knocking him to the ground. It was too easy. Alcohol must have slowed him.

He got up and came at me again with his gang rooting him on. "Get him, Jimmy!"

I knocked him on his ass again.

"He's really going to kill you now!" his followers shouted.

I continued to knock him down every time he came at me. The crowd didn't like seeing their idol lose. They were getting ready to kick my ass when George McDonald said, "You better get out of here before they all jump you."

It was like the time I fought Pat Curran. I could have kicked Jamesy's ass that night, but when he sobered up, I'd have to face him and his brothers, so I took George's advice.

I went to see Jamesy where he worked in the box factory a few days later. He had bruises from the fight, but he wasn't upset. Fighting between friends was often forgotten when the sun rose— though sometimes a fight could start an ongoing feud. One never knew what to expect in Hano.

A few nights later, I went to Brighton Center, a few miles from Allston. The kids there were middle class, and I liked to go to war with middle class people for looking down on me. Earlier that night, I'd fought with three guys around my age. I can't say that I won, but they couldn't subdue me. Later, I was standing behind an old railroad car used as a diner when those same three guys and a bunch of their friends showed up. One started fighting me. If I beat him, his friends would jump me. I wrestled him to the ground. He was on top and appeared to be winning the fight, but I kept jamming a small razor knife into his crotch and slicing. With his adrenaline flowing, he didn't feel me cutting him, and when the police came and broke up the fight, no one noticed my opponent's injuries. Later he had to go to the hospital to get his wounds treated. I rarely used a weapon, but in this instance, as there were so many adversaries, I felt I had to take any advantage.

A few months later, I was standing in front of the donut shop that had opened where the Paradise Café used to be when a car suddenly stopped. The door flew open and a guy I didn't recognize jumped out, ran up to me, and kicked me in the balls as hard as he could. I doubled over in pain.

"That makes us even," he said, and I realized he was the guy I had cut.

I accepted what he said and figured we were truly even.

Tough Guy

Because of attending the Gertrude Godvin Disciplinary School, Middlesex County Training School, Shirley Industrial School, and spending a year at Deer Island, my tough guy reputation became widely known. I knew kids from almost every neighborhood in Boston. Of course, most were criminals, drug addicts or alcoholics. On weekends, I'd go downtown to drink, and if I stood on the sidewalk, it seemed like hundreds would stop to say hello. I felt like a politician greeting so many people. Of course, knowing people doesn't make them friends, but then it didn't much matter to me if they were real friends or not. I could always find something exciting to do with one group or another.

John Mendez, a kid I'd met in Shirley, became my best friend for a few months. He was so black his skin seemed to absorb light. Bigger than me, his size and menacing, cold stare intimidated most people and stopped them from crossing him.

We'd drink together and he'd often spend the night at my house. In the morning, I'd supply him with clean clothing. At this point in my life, I was making enough money by committing various crimes to afford clothes and have them cleaned. One of the ways I also acquired new clothes was to take a few dirty items to a dry cleaners. When they were ready to be picked up, I'd bring Tommy Priday, an exceptionally handsome kid, to flirt with the girl behind the counter while I ran the automated rack, pretending to look for my dry cleaning but instead grabbing anything else that might fit. For the price of getting a few things cleaned, I usually scored another outfit or two.

One night John and I were hanging out downtown. A group of black kids formed a circle around me, and began hassling me like the black kids used to do when they wanted to take my lunch money at Dispy. John stood behind the circle. Once you're surrounded, you don't have much of a chance if you stand still. I learned to always charge the guy directly in front of me before another could jump on my back.

I wasn't worried about my safety and figured the two of us could kick all their asses. But to my utter surprise, John sided with them. I barged through the circle and escaped.

John's actions opened my eyes: Not many people would defend me against "their own kind," not even my so-called friends.

* * * * *

The Palace, a downtown bar, advertised that it had the longest bar in the world. One night, intoxicated as usual, I bought a drink for everyone at the bar. I have no idea how much it cost or where I got the money. Having money and not knowing where it came from wasn't unusual. I sometimes had friends ask me things like, "Did you get that safe open?"

"What safe?" I'd ask.

"The one you told me you were working on the other night."

I wouldn't know what they were talking about because alcohol washed my memories away.

I put my dad through a lot during the summer I was nineteen. One night, drunk as usual, I fell asleep while smoking and the bed caught fire. My dad couldn't wake me. In the morning, I awoke to a soaked mattress burned black up to an inch away from my body. I know he saved my life by throwing buckets of water onto the burning bed.

Other times I'd wake with bloodstains on my clothing, sometimes mine, sometimes somebody else's. I knew the blood was from fights, but I couldn't remember where I'd fought or with whom.

Once, while searching our pantry for something to eat, I noticed a pillowcase on the top shelf. I took it down and looked inside. It was filled with money—lots of money. I never counted it, but every day I would take a handful, tuck pillowcase far back on the top shelf where no one ever looked, and go happily on my way to another day of drinking and drugs, if any were available. That money lasted the entire summer of 1959.

* * * * *

"When you get out, come and visit me," Sully had said.

So I went to visit him in Boston's South End. He took me to the Universal Café and introduced me to his brother, a bartender there. I felt right at home in the Universal, among the thieves, crooks, whores and other unsavory types who hung out there.

One day, drunk as usual, I went there looking for Sully with my friend Jonesy, who was brilliant but a little insane and feared no one.

"Hey baby, how much?" he asked a hooker sitting at the bar in a loud voice, grabbing her ass.

A tall, well-built black guy stepped in front of Jonesy. "Keep it down. Just be cool, man."

Jonesy was the same height as me, over six feet, but had a slender build. I stepped between him and the black guy. "Okay, we'll be quiet," I said, "Now go sit down."

"You telling me what to do?"

The guy's attitude pissed me off. I pushed him up against the bar. "Yeah, so what?"

He reached into his pocket—I didn't know for what—so I slugged him with a right to the belly. I felt my fist sink into it as air whooshed from his mouth. I followed through with a left to the stomach, a right to his jaw, a left to the other side of his jaw, then a right to the head. I was connecting with a lot of punches when Sully's brother hit me over the head with a club he kept behind the bar.

"Hey, don't you know who I am?" I shouted in a daze from the blow.

"Yeah, but he's our bouncer."

That did it for me; this was one battle I wasn't going to win. I went outside. It was then I discovered that I'd been stabbed twice. Both times the blade had struck bone. The wounds weren't deep, but they hurt like hell. I was too dense to learn a lesson from that fight.

Days later, I got into an argument with a few guys in a downtown Boston bar, and we ended up outside. I stood with my back to an alley and three of them faced me.

"C'mon tough guys." I gestured for them to come at me. This wouldn't be the first time I fought more than one guy at a time. When I did, they were usually confused and didn't know who was going to do what. I knew exactly what I had to do, and as a result often did better in a fight with multiple opponents than I did one-on-one. While I confidently dared them to come and get me, something hit me behind the knees and I fell to the ground.

Two of their friends had gone around the building and came up the alley behind me. I not only got my ass kicked, but one of those jerks stabbed me in the leg. That and getting stabbed a few days before gave me a fear of knives. From then on, whenever someone pulled a knife I'd break out in a cold sweat—but would only fight harder because I was scared to death of getting stabbed again.

* * * * *

I met this kid Louie in Boston's South End in the summer of '59. He had a scar under his left eye where someone had slashed him, giving him a cruel appearance. While hanging around the South End, he introduced me to a pretty blonde about twenty-two. He told me she used to turn tricks for him, but had left him for a lesbian she now gave her money to. I met her three-hundred-pound black girlfriend and was somewhat intimidated by her fierce looks. A few months later, the lesbian was sent to jail. The blonde hinted that she wanted me to be her pimp. I said no. It wasn't because I had scruples of any kind. I think it was because I saw how pimps mistreated their girls and knew I could never treat any woman that way.

The South End was loaded with prostitutes. People came from all over to cruise the streets looking for hookers. Business was so good that hookers from New York City would come to Boston for the weekend. One night I was hanging out on the street when a car pulled up with two guys who looked a little older than me. "Hey man, where can we find some hookers?"

Thinking I was cool, I said, "I'll take you to a whorehouse where they have the best- looking girls in town. They'll do anything you want for a cheapo price, too."

"Jump in," the driver said.

On the way, I told them, "This place has the best pussy around, but you better only bring enough money to pay for what you want, or they'll take it one way or the other."

"How much do we need?" asked the guy in the passenger seat.

"Fifty bucks each will take you around the world," I said.

We drove to Tremont Street where I knew there was a whorehouse. I showed them where to park. They were overly eager and hurried to get out of the car.

"Go ahead," I said, "but don't blame me if they take all your money."

They couldn't wait to get to the whorehouse, so I said, "Leave your money with me. I'll sit right here and wait for you."

Their small brains must have been doing the thinking, because they both handed me their wallets and money, then went inside to see the girls, with only fifty dollars each to pay them. As soon as they went through the door, I took off running.

The next day there was a write-up in the *Mid-Town Journal*, a local newspaper referred to in the '50s and '60s as the "South End scandal sheet." The article mentioned how a city slicker had taken two rubes for their money. I was proud that my crime had made the newspaper. I was beginning to live up to my childhood dream of becoming famous like all my movie heroes. Hell, maybe I'd even stand alongside real criminals like Machine Gun Kelly, Pretty Boy Floyd, or even John Dillinger.

* * * * *

Sully had to leave town in a hurry. He went to New York City and told me to look for him around Eighth Avenue and 42nd Street, if I ever got there. It wasn't long before I too had to leave town in a hurry, because the cops were looking for me about some crime I'd committed. (I can't remember which one because there were so many.) I went to New York and looked for Sully, but couldn't find him. With no money, I didn't know what to do. By then, I was a full-grown man weighing over one-hundred-seventy, so I was big enough to take care of myself if hassled.

I walked around Times Square without a dime in my pocket, enticed by the aromas of different foods coming from restaurants and bars. I pictured myself as one of those cartoon characters who smell something good and float through the air with their arms outstretched toward the source of the aroma. Some windows displayed large wheels of roast beef sliced for sandwiches. From pizza parlor windows, cooks tossed dough into circles (a rarity today). The fresh-baked pizzas had the most enticing scent of all.

As I walked down 42nd Street, a guy asked me for a quarter.

"Sorry, I don't have any money," I said, "but if I did, I'd certainly give you a quarter."

He reached into his pocket, pulled out handfuls of quarters and held them out to me.

"Here, take what you need," he said.

Shocked, I took enough for a sandwich. This guy was making a fortune by begging quarters. I felt too proud to panhandle, but it would have been better than what I ended up doing.

For a few days, I continued to walk around hungry. I snuck into twenty-four-hour movie theatres to sleep. Then I decided to do what I had always done when I needed something: take it from someone who had it.

Hunchback of Eighth Avenue

In New York City, the older walk-up apartment buildings usually had a set of stairs leading to the front door. After sleeping in theaters and going hungry for a few nights, I saw a guy putting his key into his front door lock. The thought of robbing him made my adrenaline flow. My arms and legs got weak, my knees shook, but my hungry stomach ruled. I bounded up the stairs, grabbed him by the collar with my left hand and made a threatening fist with my right.

"Give me your money."

He looked at me, confused.

"Your money or I'm going to beat the shit out of you."

He reached into his pocket and took out a roll of bills. I snatched it and ran. I didn't go far, just to the nearest pizza parlor on 42nd Street, and ate enough to satisfy my growling stomach.

That crime started my career as "The Hunchback of Eighth Avenue," (a name given to me by the guys I hung around with), because their conception of a mugger was a thug jumping on a victim's back, something I never did. I always faced my victims. Any time I needed money, I'd go to the uptown side of 42nd Street on Eighth Avenue, in mid-Manhattan near Times Square and the eastern edge of Hell's Kitchen. (Mayor Giuliani "cleaned up" the area in the 1980s, but the former redlight district that I prowled had been known since the 1920s for hustling and crime.)

My mugging method was simple: I'd grab the first guy who looked like he might have money and take it from him. I never looked for anyone weak, used weapons, or ever thought about robbing a woman. If a man had money and I was able to take it from him, he was fair game, I rationalized. The strong survive.

I felt invulnerable in the Times Square area. There were so many people, I figured the cops would never catch me. Every day I saw cops chasing some guy or another through the crowded streets, but never witnessed them catching one. Some of them truly ignored anything that happened.

Me and Tiny Dumbrowski, another guy from Boston hiding out in New York, walked up Eighth Avenue just past 42nd Street where two men held signs proclaiming the world was about to end and shouted Bible verses to a crowd of onlookers.

One of them tried to hand a brochure to Tiny.

"Stick it up your ass," Tiny said, loud enough for the crowd to hear.

But the preachers didn't turn the other cheek. One of them said, "You're going to hell, you unbeliever."

"No, you're going to hell," Tiny said, and punched him.

The other preacher jumped on Tiny's back. I grabbed him, and we grappled and fell to the ground, wrestling. Tiny and the first preacher rolled around on the ground, wrestling too. The crowd cheered, but I didn't know if it was for us or for the preachers. Some cops stood nearby, and we rolled right into their legs, but they didn't even turn around. They kept staring at the buildings across the street, pretending they didn't see us. The fight ended without bloodshed, and Tiny and I continued on our way, amazed by the policemen's behavior. (Fighting with a street preacher was something I'd never done before and have never done since.)

One night, Tiny and I planned on breaking into a grocery store. I stole an old 1940s Plymouth to haul our loot. As Tiny and I drove to the store, a cop car started tailing us. I stepped on the gas. The old Plymouth didn't have much power and no way could it outrun the police car. The side streets around Eighth Avenue in Manhattan were too narrow for the cops to navigate ahead to cut me off. I put the pedal to the metal, the engine straining to make its puny horses run faster. I couldn't allow them to catch me, because it meant going to jail if they did.

The officers chased us in close pursuit for several more blocks. When I lost control going around a corner, the Plymouth jumped the sidewalk and smashed into a building.

I leapt out the driver's door and Tiny exited the passenger side. I paused to look at the old Plymouth crumpled up against the building. I turned around to run, but two cops stood with their legs apart not more than five feet away, pointing their weapons at us. Tiny and I looked at each other and instinctively knew what the other would do. We sprinted off at the same instant, Tiny one way, and me the other.

One cop chased me, and the other went after Tiny. No one yelled, "Stop or I'll shoot," like cops do in the movies. They started shooting as soon as we ran. My anger rose when I realized they were trying to kill us.

Stoned on speed, my thoughts took weird, delusional twists during the chase, like how I couldn't haul any merchandise from the store because the cops made me crash my car. I ran with my hands clasped around the back of my head, thinking this would deflect the bullets.

Pop, pop, pop, pop, pop, pop! The gunshots rang in my ears and bullets zipped past my head, spattering bits of brick into my face as they slammed into the buildings nearby.

Six shots. I remembered from eluding Boston police that they carried six shooters, so they had to stop and reload. I figured this New York City cop carried the same weapon.

I turned to face him. "What're you gonna do without bullets, motherfucker?"

He aimed his gun at me and shot three more rounds that whizzed past my head and exploded into the brick wall, showering me with more fragments.

I turned around and ran like hell, zigzagging through the streets until I lost the cop. When I turned a corner, a black and white police cruiser rolled slowly down the street.

My heart jumped into my throat. Nowhere to hide, I flattened myself up against a wall in the shadows. The car came closer. I pushed myself flatter against the wall, wishing I could merge with it so they wouldn't see me. The squad car stopped directly in front me. What could I do? I couldn't outrun their car and the cop on foot might show up any minute. Like a deer caught in the headlights, I remained frozen to the spot. To my amazement, the squad car kept rolling past and down the street.

I felt like one of my celluloid movie heroes as I dashed into an apartment building. The doorman asked me where I was going.

"I'm being chased by a bunch of guys who want to rob me. Could you please get me a cab? Quick!"

"Sure, kid," he said.

He whistled for a cab, and I took it to Times Square. Almost immediately, I spotted Tiny sitting in a restaurant. To be honest, I hadn't even thought of him until then. Self- preservation, I guess. But I felt relieved he'd gotten away, too.

After that, when we needed some quick cash, Tiny and I targeted one of the numerous fleabag hotels around Times Square. We'd tell the desk clerk we needed a room, but all we had was a hundred dollar bill. Did they have change? Desk clerks almost always glanced toward their cash drawers as they considered this.

"Stand back and you won't get hurt," I'd say. Then I'd jump over the counter and rifle the cash drawer. No one ever tried to stop me, and if they had, I'd probably have robbed them too.

We got substantially more cash doing this than from mugging guys on the street. Robbery didn't bother my conscience at all. I needed to survive, and this was the only way I knew how. A job was out of the question because I could never last long enough to wait for a paycheck, and I knew nothing about day labor. My career as a hotel robber enabled me to eat and rent a room when I didn't feel like sleeping in a twenty-four hour movie house. I never had enough cash to rent an apartment or establish a stable life.

* * * * *

One day while looking for another way to get my hands on some money, I strolled past the theatres on Broadway. There were always hordes of tourists there, milling around the theatres and staring up at the skyscrapers. A sure way to tell a stranger from a New Yorker was if they looked up instead of down. I spotted a guy pushing his way through the crowd and my jaw dropped. I stopped dead in the middle of the busy sidewalk to hug Sully, my buddy from the South End. "I can't believe you're here, Sully."

"Great to see you," he said. "You hungry?"

"Starving," I said. "I haven't scored for a couple of days."

We went to the automat on 42nd Street, and Sully handed me a roll of bills. "Here, get anything you want."

I got some change, went over to the wall of little doors and deposited the required amount to stock up on pie and coffee.

"Thanks for the money," I said, "Where'd you get so much?"

"Man, this town is full of queers. They're always hitting on me. I go along with one and pretend I'm interested. Once I get inside a hotel room, I ask him to take a shower. The guy usually gets so excited he jumps right in the shower. As soon as he does, I go through his pants, take his wallet, money, watch, and any other valuables lying around. It's so easy. Want to try it?"

I figured Sully to be bisexual, but I didn't know for sure and didn't want to know.

"No," I told him. "I've got a way to get money when I need it. I just go over to Eighth Avenue after dark when it's deserted, and grab the first guy I see who looks like he has money."

"How do you do that?"

"I grab him by the collar and tell him to give me his money or I'll beat the shit out of him."

"What if he doesn't give it up?"

"Then I forcefully take it."

* * * * *

Sully had recently married a beautiful redhead, Patsy, but thought she might be a lesbian. He mentioned that she had a recent discharge from the Marines, and he suspected it was because of homosexual activity. One night soon after we'd discovered each other in Manhattan, we went out drinking, but he wanted to get back to where he and his wife were staying with a lady friend.

"I'm going to surprise her," he said, "and if she's wet down there, I'll know she's been fooling around."

He went home, barged in, and gave her the finger test.

"She passed," he told me the next day.

I don't know if he just stuck his hand in her pants or feigned amorous intentions to accomplish his goal, but he was satisfied.

Beansy, another fugitive from Boston, stole some U.S. savings bonds from Patsy's friend. He tried to cash them at a bank the next day. They told him they'd check the value of the bonds and to come back the next day. I never would have gone back, but Beansy did, and the bank cashed the bonds. He shared the money with Sully and me.

I ended up getting an apartment with Sully and Patsy. Sully came up with enough cash for the deposit and first month's rent after he'd ripped off a queer. Sometimes I'd stay at home while Sully went out to do his thing. Patsy often walked around wearing nothing but one of his button-up shirts. She'd sit on the couch next to me and wrap her arms around her knees. If I'd looked, I would have seen her exposed. The heat from her body spread to me, and I could smell her. She wanted me to make a move. But Sully had told me how disappointed he was in his brother because he'd fooled around with his first wife.

Though I robbed people for a living, I never messed around with a friend's wife. This time my "small brain" didn't take over, but it tried like hell. I resisted Patsy and soon met Dianne, a pretty girl around my age. Dianne moved in with me and that solved the temptation problem. Patsy gave up trying to seduce me and we all lived together in peace for several months.

Cruising for a Bruising

I used to hang out at a bar on Eighth Avenue about half a block up from 42nd Street. My usual dinner, along with a dozen or so beers, was a bowl of chili for fifty cents with all the oyster crackers I could eat. One night, while eating my chili and watching a boxing match on TV, I felt a hand on my shoulder. I turned and looked at a black guy smaller than me.

"What the fuck are you looking at?" he said.

"You little shit," I said, "You want trouble? I'll give you more than you can handle."

He assumed a fighting stance. "I'll take all you can give me."

I didn't want to fight there because I'd probably get barred from the place, so I said, "Let's take this outside."

"Let's go."

I led the way and turned to face him. He ran at me with his head down, and I did what I always did when some asshole left himself unprotected. I aimed my foot at his balls and kicked as hard as I could. I heard a squishing sound as the tip of my shoe sunk into his groin. He bent over to grab his balls, and I smashed my knee into his face while I pushed his head down with two hands.

After the devastating blow that normally would have knocked any opponent unconscious, he was still able to grab me by my legs and yank them out from under me. I rolled away from him and scurried to my feet to be ready for when he came at me.

A crowd started to gather, so I wanted to hurry and get the fight over with. This guy charged me time after time. I kept kicking him in the balls and smashing his face against my knee. He somehow kept going. He continued to yank on my legs after I kicked him and knock me to the ground. I knew he must be on some type of drug where he couldn't feel pain, and if he ever got me down where I couldn't get up, it would be all over for me. Short of killing this guy, I wasn't going to win this fight.

I'd gotten a bit smarter as I grew older, so I turned and ran. I felt like a coward for running in front of a large crowd of onlookers, but it seemed like the smart thing to do. It must be okay to quit if the circumstances called for it, I told myself.

The next day my buddies said the guy came back looking for me later that night, packing heat. Good thing I wasn't around to get shot.

Not long after that, a white guy named Bob was hanging around the same bar. We once shared a hotel room, and Bob lay on the bed, sleeping with his eyes wide open. He thought he was tough, but the one time he went out to mug somebody, his victim turned the tables and took all Bob's money. Everybody laughed at that story.

I never liked Bob, but he knew the guys I hung around with, so I tolerated him. He'd worked at a company that paid its employees in cash delivered by messenger. So Bob recruited a few guys from the bar, and they caught the messenger on an elevator and relieved him of his cash.

When Bob was flush with dough, he became obnoxious. One night we were in a restaurant on lower Eighth Avenue when he insulted the waitress.

I'd had enough of his aggravation. "Having money doesn't agree with you, Bob. All it does is make you a bigger asshole."

"You best watch your mouth or I'll shut it for you."

"Ha, ha. You and what army?"

He came running at me with a knife in his hand. My fear of knives caused me to turn and run. *Maybe running away from a fight has gotten to be a habit,* I thought.

Bob chased me down the street until I ran into a row of garbage cans. (In New York City there are few alleys, so businesses put their garbage along the sidewalks and curb for pickup.) Trapped, I turned around to face Bob, armed only with a heavy cardboard box from the top of a garbage can, the only thing I could see that might work as a weapon.

He charged me. I attempted to hit him with the box, but when I swung, the cardboard ripped and I ended up waving a piece in his face. His knife hand forcibly hit my left side. I thought I was done for.

The blade tore a hole in my heavy winter coat but didn't penetrate my flesh.

I grabbed his knife hand. Rage overcame me when I saw he held a butter knife: He'd made me look and feel like a coward. I beat him viciously.

Bob lay crumpled on the sidewalk, unconscious when the police arrived. Witnesses reported how he'd chased me with a knife, so the cops let me go.

* * * * *

I returned to Boston with Dianne and a few of my friends. We stayed at my parents' apartment for a short time. (They'd lost their house in Dorchester because of my mom's wild spending.) My dad quickly got tired of having extra people in the apartment and told me to move out.

Beansy, another criminal I'd met in New York, rented a furnished apartment with Dianne and me in the Back Bay area of Boston. We sat around on the last day of the month, wondering where we'd get the money to pay our rent the next day. Getting a job wasn't a consideration, because I'd have to find one first, and then have enough money for food, bus fare, cigarettes, and other needs and wants until my first payday, which was always two to three weeks out.

"Don't worry, opportunity will knock," Beansy said.

The words had hardly left his mouth when a knock sounded at the door.

When Beansy opened the door, a tall, middle-aged black man stood there. "Hi, I'm your upstairs neighbor."

I knew he wanted something from us and we sure wanted rent money from him.

"Come on in," Beansy said, sizing the guy up.

"I'm Jared," he said, not taking his eyes off Dianne. "I'm on the way to the liquor store and wondered if you wanted anything."

"Sure, you can bring me a quart of vodka," she said.

He moved beside her and whispered something in her ear; she smiled and whispered something to him. He stood up, took a wad of bills from his pocket, then peeled off ten twenty-dollar bills and handed them to her. He turned and said goodbye as he went out the door.

"What was that all about?" I said.

"He invited me up to his place for the weekend to get high on anything I wanted. I told him if I didn't have $200, I'd have to move today. So we've got our rent money."

I don't think she ever intended to keep that promise. But who knows? There were a few bucks left over after we paid the rent, so I went to the Shamrock Inn—a seedy bar I usually drank in—to have a few beers.

I was ready to fight every time I went into an Irish bar. After tipping a few back, Irishmen—the ones I knew anyway—grew beer muscles and wanted to prove how tough they were. But the Back Bay area wasn't what it used to be. This bar had quite a few derelicts nursing a glass of wine or beer so they could sit in a warm room rather than stand out in the cold.

I noticed a guy around thirty as he walked up to the bar.

"Give everybody a drink on me," he said, pulling a fat wad of bills from a pocket.

I took one look at that roll and figured I'd make it mine. I bought him a drink and introduced myself. Then I invited him out back to smoke some dope. He happily agreed. Out in the alley I said, "Give me your money."

He turned to run, but I grabbed him around the neck, reached into his pocket, and took out his roll of bills. He struggled to get free and squirmed out of his coat. I was left holding it as he ran down the alley, yelling for help.

I later found a paper in a pocket of his coat showing that the poor bastard had just been released from some type of institution. My stomach turned when I saw that lousy piece of paper and I sorely regretted what I'd done.

Some things I can't forgive myself for, and this is one of them. If I could go back in time and redo my life, I know I would change that moment.

* * * * *

John McDonald, called Mac by his friends, lived in Washington D.C. and sold used cars for a living. I knew him from Brighton, Massachusetts. He was only around twenty but looked forty because of chronic alcoholism.

Jonesy and I went to the car lot where Mac worked. A small building with a desk, three chairs, and a couch served as an office. I heard Mac talking to his cousin on the phone about a Volkswagen. His cousin insisted he didn't want one with a sunroof, and Mac agreed. "No sunroof, absolutely no sunroof," he said again. "Come on over, I have the exact car you're looking for."

An hour later, his cousin walked through the door, and Mac took him outside to see the Volkswagen. I followed close behind and when Mac walked up to a VW with a ragged sunroof. I was more shocked than his cousin.

"I told you I didn't want a sunroof." The cousin turned to leave.

"This is the best deal you'll ever get," Mac said. "Having a sunroof adds to the resale value. Get in—see the AM/FM radio? Comes with the car free of charge, the tires and brakes are brand new and so is the tranny."

Mac rambled on and on and browbeat his cousin into buying that car, sunroof and all.

After the sale, Mac bought a few cases of Schlitz and a fifth of Four Roses, and we sat around the office drinking all day. Mac passed out, sprawled on the floor asleep when his boss walked in. Jonesy asked the boss if he wanted to buy a car. He turned around and left. The next day Mac told us he got fired from that job.

Mac had lots of friends in the car business and access to many different cars. We'd often drive from D.C. to Baltimore in the early morning, around 4 or 5 a.m. when traffic was light and a heavy fog hung over the Beltway. Mac would straddle the divider line, barely visible through the fog. He'd go as fast as the car would allow. If another vehicle had been coming in the opposite direction, it would have been all over for us. I accompanied him several times on his death-defying drive; though scared to death, I found it exciting.

After spending a night at Mac's apartment, with a fridge full of booze but no food, Jonesy and I were famished. We only had twelve cents between us, but we saw a sign advertising a hamburger—a "twelve-cent special"—on the front of a sparsely furnished diner. We ordered one at the front counter and then sat at one of the few tables, waiting with our mouths watering. When the burger emerged from the kitchen, we couldn't believe the tiny bun and smear of beef that looked like a dab of peanut butter. We laughed so long and hard that we never did eat it.

A few days later, one of Mac's friends had a fender bender in his Corvette. Repairing the car's fiberglass body was an expensive proposition. The owner wanted the car stolen so he could collect the insurance. I agreed to do it for $300. I used some money he gave me to buy gas, and then Mac and I drove the Corvette to Boston. I got Jonesy a train ticket, because the car only sat two.

I figured on using the car profitably before I destroyed it.

Armed Robbery and the City of Angels

I'd labored at one job or another from the time I was six years old until I was sentenced to Middlesex County Training School at fourteen. But it became harder and harder to find work as a young adult, especially with my series of arrests. When I applied for local jobs, someone always seemed to warn the prospective employer about my exploits.

My friend Bobby Hill, whose father worked as a bricklayer, told me to go to his father's company and say that he'd sent me.

On the way, some cops stopped me. "Where are you headed?" one asked.

"Looking for a job," I said, and like a dummy, I told them where.

They called ahead and warned the owner that he'd be asking for trouble if he hired me.

If I'd had a definite opportunity at that time, I think I would have done my best to acquire enough money to last the two to three weeks before my first payday and gone back to work full time. Instead, I went to see my friend Dippy DiPalmo in Brighton, and picked up my Colt .32 revolver from him. He'd been holding it for me while I did time at Deer Island. I owned the gun because someone had given it to me instead of the money he owed me. I'd never fired the old revolver and had no idea if it worked. The cylinder was loose and would fall open on its own, exposing the shells.

I showed the .32 to Mac and said, "Now that we've got a gun, we can use that Corvette for a getaway car before we dump it."

"Good idea," Jonesy said. "I'm tired of being broke. Liquor stores do a booming business on New Year's Eve. Let's hit a few."

Mac and I squeezed Jonesy into the middle of the Corvette, and the three of us went on a 1960 New Year's Eve robbery spree. We agreed to take turns robbing stores, and I volunteered to go first, as we only had one gun.

We pulled up to a liquor store on Commonwealth Avenue that I'd never been inside. I went in by myself without wearing a mask or any disguise. There were several people in the store. "Hands up," I shouted, waving the .32 for all to see.

Half a dozen men stopped what they were doing and stared at me. I wasn't sure what to do next. In the movies, they always locked the customers in the walk-in cooler. Such a cooler stood right behind the counter.

"Everybody into the cooler. Now!" I shouted.

They hesitated and looked at me. I pointed my revolver toward the ceiling. When I raised the barrel up, the cylinder popped loose. I almost wet my pants when I heard the rounds clatter to the floor.

The six men I held at gunpoint looked at the bullets on the floor and then looked at me. I looked down at the bullets, then raised my eyes to meet six angry stares. Their faces told me they didn't think I had any bullets left. I glanced down again at the bullets lying on the floor and tried to think what to do next.

All six took a step toward me.

I leveled the .32 and shouted, "I've got one left, one more step and I'll shoot."

They stood still.

I didn't know if I had one left or not, but neither did they. I emptied the cash register, ran out the door, and jumped into the Corvette's open door. Mac stomped on the gas and we spun rubber, fleeing the crime scene.

I handed the .32 to Jonesy.

He opened the cylinder to find it empty.

That was my first and last armed robbery. I knew I would have shot someone if they had tried to apprehend me. That is, if the gun would've had bullets. I never wanted to hurt anyone, but realizing that I could and would made me vow to be more careful in the future, so that I wouldn't harm anyone not deserving of it.

Mac took his turn at the next liquor store we found. He made off with plenty of money and booze. Then Jonesy's turn came around. I drove up to a brightly lit liquor store near Charles Street jail. Mac handed him the .32 and a nylon stocking to wear as a mask. Before he went in, Jonesy checked to see if the .32 was loaded. I got out when he did and walked up to one of the windows of the store. Three customers had lined up to pay for their liquor, a last-minute New Year's Eve rush before the store closed in a few minutes.

Jonesy pulled the nylon stocking over his face and went in. I watched through the window, listening to Jonesy's voice boom through the window glass.

"On the floor, motherfuckers!" Jonesy yelled as he rushed toward the line of patrons.

Stunned, they just turned and looked at him.

"Motherfucker, I said on the floor." He slapped one buyer in the face with the .32.

The other customers dropped to the floor. The clerk stood with his arms on the counter.

"You deaf, motherfucker?" Jonesy headed for the clerk who then dropped to the floor.

Jonesy emptied the register and then walked around and took everyone's wallet, watch, jewelry, and any loose change in their pockets. A chime went off and I watched as a new customer walked through the door. Jonesy ran to him, grabbed him by the collar and threw him further into the store. The new customer started to protest and got the gun barrel whipped across his face.

Jonesy repeated this performance as more last-minute customers waltzed through the door. He seemed to be in some sort of trance, getting carried away on a power trip. I heard another chime and saw the store filling up. I figured I better get him out of there before he seriously hurt someone.

Jonesy grabbed me by the collar as I went through the entrance.

I said, "It's me, asshole," before he could hit me with the gun.

He looked as if he could have gone on all night pistol-whipping whoever came through the door.

"We better go now!" I yelled. My words brought him out of his trance.

We ran out the door. Jonesy paused outside and put all his loot into the nylon stocking he'd worn until it overflowed with money and jewelry. He handed me the .32. Mac gunned the Corvette engine to remind us to get the hell out of there.

There was more money in my pocket than I'd ever had at one time. Though the adrenaline-stimulating action revved me up, my gut also churned with anxiety. I guessed this half-terrified, half-exhilarated feeling was why so many guys turned to crime. Not just for the money, but for the thrill.

Jonesy, Mac, and I divided the money evenly and went our separate ways for the evening.

Mac had joined us on the robbery spree to pay his lawyer for a drunk driving offense in Washington D.C., so he took the Corvette to do some business and spent the night at a fleabag hotel.

On New Year's night, Mac drove to Hano where Jonesy and I were drinking beers in the Blueplate Café on Harvard Avenue. He walked in looking despondent. "Buy me a drink," he said. "Someone robbed me while I was sleeping at the hotel."

I figured that was a bad omen, almost as crazy as Jonesy standing around pistol-whipping people during his robbery.

"Did they get everything?" I asked. "How're you going to pay your lawyer now?"

If he was dumb enough to get robbed, I wasn't about to give him my money. "Let's dump the car before we get caught with it," I insisted.

Mac drove the Corvette to the Charles River, frozen solid in

January, while Priday and Jonesy followed us in Priday's car. Mac parked the Corvette by the river's edge. I put a brick on the gas pedal, dropped it in gear, and jumped out. We watched as it coasted onto the ice and rolled halfway across the river. We never considered that if it didn't break the ice, it might continue rolling across the river and onto the opposite bank. If that happened, we'd find ourselves in deep shit because our prints were all over it.

But my plan worked: A loud crack echoed in the frosty air as the car broke through the ice and began to nose down into the river. A loud hiss and a cloud of steam rose as the hot engine hit the icy water. Finally, the car stood straight up and slowly went under just like sinking ships in movies.

* * * * *

The next day I went out to party with my newfound wealth. While sitting in a strange bar by myself in Somerville, a Boston suburb, the local toughs started harassing me. I offered to go outside and fight them one at a time. I don't know where I ever got the stupid idea of fighting a bunch of guys one at a time. The idea must have come from a movie I'd seen at some point in my life. (I based many of my questionable actions on Hollywood film propaganda.)

The group of around a dozen or so guys followed me out the barroom door. I reached into my jacket pocket, put my hand on the .32 and listened to the jerks as they chattered about having fun kicking my ass. I pulled out the gun, pointed it at them, cocked the hammer and said, "Who's first?"

One of them yelled, "He's got a gun!"

They all took off running, and I went back into the bar to finish my beer.

The owner walked over to me. "If you ever pull a gun on me, you better use it or I'll kill you."

"Okay, I'll be sure to do just that," I said.

I finished my beer and took the subway home.

That .32 is going to get me in trouble, I thought. So I stored it in a locker in the Boylston Street subway station. In the '50s, before people started planting bombs in them, train stations, bus stations, and subway stations all had coin-operated lockers where packages could be stored for twenty-four hours for twenty-five cents.

When I went to retrieve the .32, I found I'd lost the key. I panicked. Both the key and the gun had my fingerprints all over them. If someone found the .32 in the locker, the police might check to see if it had been used in any crimes. I had to retrieve it, at any cost. I called the operator at the locker company and they sent a guy out to open it.

The guy from the locker company had a ring of keys and reached out to open the locker.

"What's in here that's so important, anyway?"

"Just my .32 and some ammo," I said.

Wrong answer. He quickly relocked it and strode away.

Cursing myself for my stupidity, I went and got a tire iron to force the locker open. I jammed the tire iron into the locker door jamb and yanked on it with all my might, but all I did was bend the door. The lock held firm. By then I was sure the guy had called the cops, so I left without my .32.

The next night—January 3, 1961—Priday, Jonesy and I went cruising in a cab. Whenever the three of us gathered in one place, it always meant something was going to hit the fan. Sure enough, Jonesy harassed the cab driver, who then used his radio to call for help. It seemed like only a minute had passed before police cars surrounded us.

Taken in handcuffs to Boston Police Headquarters (a seven-story building), we boarded an elevator and took it up to where a fingerprint unit took up the entire floor. There was a lot of equipment in that room that I hadn't seen before.

In order to take my fingerprints, one cop unlocked my cuffs, grabbed me by the arm and escorted me to a table where another cop sat.

"Give me your right hand," said the seated cop.

I held it out, and he grabbed it and rolled it in an inkpad.

"Press down," he said, as he placed my thumb in a box on a fingerprint card. "Put your fingers together." He rolled them one at a time on the inkpad, put them back together and pointed to a larger box on the fingerprint card. "Press down here."

While watching him roll my fingers, something bashed me in the head.

"What the fuck?" I said and spun around.

A short cop, about 5' 5", had smashed a board onto my head.

The look of surprise on my face made the fingerprint cop laugh. The blow made my adrenaline flow. I didn't find the stunt funny at all.

After we got fingerprinted, the short cop handcuffed me again and forced us to sit on a bench—me in the middle, Jonesy to my left, and Priday on my right. Soon he and another cop escorted us toward the elevator that would take us to the lockup.

The cop who'd smashed me in the head with the board leaned toward me. "Did that hurt when I hit you?"

"Fuck no."

He punched me in the face three times.

"Did that hurt?"

Handcuffed, I couldn't raise my hands to block his punches, but I wouldn't give him the satisfaction of knowing he hurt me, so I said, "My mother hits harder than that."

He punched me in the face several more times.

My anger took over. With adrenaline-fueled strength, I wrapped my arms around the cop and swung Jonesy and Priday around him. Trapped in the elevator between the three of us, the cop couldn't move. I bit his ear and kneed the tough guy in the balls. "Does that hurt, motherfucker?"

The other cop set off the alarm, and I heard a multitude of footsteps and then the *whack-whack* on flesh sound that I'd experienced when cops had beaten me years before in the paddy wagon. But now I felt nothing: Jonesy, Priday, and the abusive cop all took the blows administered by "Boston's finest," and I never felt a thing at the bottom of the pile.

"Now you're in trouble," a detective in a suit told me after they'd taken us all to lock- up. "You've assaulted a police officer."

"Are you kidding me?" I said. "He punched me over and over while I was handcuffed. I got pissed off because he was such a coward."

"It doesn't matter why you did it. The officer went to the hospital for treatment."

"If he's injured," I said, "you guys hurt him while you were trying to get me."

The next day in court, the guy from the locker company pointed at me during a cross-examination. To my surprise, no one mentioned the .32. Rather than charge me with attempting to break into the locker, I was charged with assaulting a police officer. The City of Boston prosecutor could nail me with that charge but seemed worried I might sue because I had two witnesses to the policeman's assault on me.

The judge called my name and read the charges.

"Your honor," I said. "I was handcuffed between two other prisoners, and he punched me repeatedly." I pointed to the wiseass cop, who showed no signs of being injured. "He should be the one charged with assault, not me."

Then Jonesy testified and told the judge what had happened.

Then the cop described his hospital treatment due to the blows that were actually inflicted by the other cops. I didn't get a chance to testify because the judge suddenly banged his gavel and said, "Thirty days in Deer Island for assault."

By giving me only thirty days instead of a year or two, I knew the judge believed me, but he had to find me guilty. If he didn't, I'd have grounds for a lawsuit.

In the future, every time arresting officers saw "assault and battery of a police officer" on my record, it wasn't good for me.

Deer Island Redux and the City of Angels

Back at Deer Island with only thirty days to serve, the prison staff assigned me to the New Prison, and I had to once again endure the stench of unwashed bodies and unemptied shit buckets.

I was sent to work at the pig farm that supplied the jail with meat. There, I hung around playing cards for a few weeks in the stinking piggery until the "screw" (what we called a guard) told me to shovel pig shit.

I refused.

He had me thrown in the hole for ten days. Like before, there was no running water in isolation, just a blanket on the floor and a shit bucket that went unemptied for ten days. Hungry all the time because they only fed me once a day, I sat and dreamed about food. In my imagination, I dined at gourmet restaurants, vividly imagining the flavors of food and drink.

I couldn't brush my teeth, so I took out my partial plate and wrapped it in toilet paper. To pass the time, I'd roll toilet paper up in balls to toss into the shit bucket as though to play basketball. One day I picked up the toilet paper my teeth were wrapped in and whooshed it into the shit bucket. I'd never see those teeth again.

When I got out of the hole, I only had a few days left before my release. I went to get a haircut, and the inept barber just about shaved me bald.

I left jail with no teeth and no hair.

* * * * *

To my disbelief, I met a couple of good-looking girls soon after my release. I was spending the night at their house when the police came looking for me at my parents' place. I figured the cops had my fingerprints from the .32 and wanted me for the armed robberies, so I decided to leave town before they caught up with me.

My brother Tony had just purchased a 1953 Ford, and he agreed to take the trip to Washington, D.C. On the second night there, a bunch of guys with drawn guns came through our hotel windows and door, shouting "FBI! FBI!"

We didn't dare resist.

No one explained the reason for our arrest—the agents just separated us and locked us in cells, and I'm not sure if we ended up at a federal facility or a District of Columbia Metropolitan Police lockup.

An enormous cockroach crawled under the bars into my cell and stood staring at me, waving his antennae back and forth. I swear he must have sent some kind of signal to his brethren, because more and more roaches lined up beside him. My childhood fear returned and I felt certain they were considering me as a meal. The leader moved forward and the rest of the roaches did likewise. Then the leader moved forward and the rest followed again. It looked almost as if the insects were formulating plans, waiting for reinforcements before they attacked. I seriously didn't think I could kill them all before they overwhelmed me. It appeared that my worst nightmare of roaches crawling all over me was about to come true.

Suddenly I heard jingling keys as an officer in uniform came to open my cell door. I was never so happy to see a cop before or since. He took me to a perp lineup—the real thing, just like in the movies. A bunch of guys of various heights stood against a wall with bright lights shining on them. The cop told me to stand against the wall with the others. As I walked over to the place he pointed at, I saw the owner of the Corvette.

After I stood against the wall, the Feds kept pointing at me and asking him, "Isn't he the guy you had take your car?"

"No," he replied every time. "The guy I gave it to had curly hair and wasn't missing any teeth."

I thanked my lucky stars for losing my partial plate and hair.

Since the Corvette's owner was brought in for questioning, I figured someone must have written down the license plate number at one of the robbery scenes.

I stood against that wall for a long time. I guess they were hoping someone might identify me as the perp for some other crime.

Eventually an agent pulled me aside. "Your friend Jones is going to prison for the armed robberies, but we're letting you go. I'm warning you, if you go back to Boston, you're going to the penitentiary. If I were you, I'd head for California where no one knows you and start a new life."

I liked the idea of starting over. Maybe I could find a job and a better life without my lousy reputation. I also figured California was a place where they'd understand the things I'd learned from my celluloid heroes.

Tony and I were released a few hours after we were picked up. I told him what the agent had said. But Tony wanted to head for Chicago, and since I had to run or go to jail, I was more than happy to head there because it was on the way to California.

The year was 1961. I was twenty-one when I cancelled the remainder of my stay at the "graybar hotel" and fled west. I don't know what happened to Mac and never heard from him again.

* * * * *

Leaving D.C., Tony blew a tire at 105 mph. He lost control, and the '54 Ford rolled into a heap. I was scared, yet my adrenaline flowed as the car rolled over and over. Neither of us got hurt, but the car was totaled.

Tony sold the Ford to a junkyard for $15. A Greyhound bus carried us through four more states. The last stop was Chicago, Illinois, where we bought a green 1948 Buick Roadmaster for fifty bucks. We took it to a back alley mechanic who straightened the spark plug wires out so it ran smoothly.

Tony didn't like Chicago and agreed to head on to California with me. On the way, old Nat King Cole sang on the radio: "Get your kicks on Route 66...." We headed west along with the crooner, driving on four slicks ready to blow. The Buick coupe coughed, smoked, and was hard to brake.

The city signs seemed to whisper, "A new day begins," as we sped by. Our first stop was St. Louis, Missouri. Then the Buick roared on to Oklahoma City, Amarillo, Texas, and Gallup, New Mexico. I didn't stop unless I had to, even though our tires were bald and I couldn't let them get too hot. But when an eighteen-wheeler got close to our tail as we roared down a narrow mountain road at a high velocity, I feared that the Buick, Tony and I would end up planted in a garden of memorial crosses that grew at every curve.

I barely had a chance to read the roadside signs: *Slow down, Joe! ... sakes alive...* (I missed signs three, four and five) *... Burma Shave.*

Burma Shave signs were everywhere back then. The small, rectangular boards on posts appeared along the road in sets of five or six, with each sign appearing about a hundred feet past the other. The next one read, *Don't lose your head ... to gain a minute ... you need your head ... your brains are in it ... Burma Shave.* Another read, *Speed was high ... weather was not ... tires were thin ... X marks the spot ... Burma Shave.*

We made it to the bottom of the mountain and almost as soon as we hit the straight road, our two back tires blew out. We looked at each other. I know we both thought how lucky we were that they hadn't blown out on one of the steep curves.

The Buick limped on through Flagstaff, Arizona and then San Bernardino, California. As we approached the coast, we were thrilled by the sight of the City of Angels rising from a cloud of sunburned smog.

* * * * *

Our first day in L.A. wasn't the heaven I expected. Tears filled my eyes and ran from the smog. An older woman tried to pick me up, but I refused her attention. Tony had to take a leak, so we went into an alley that stunk from all the garbage piled up at the backside of a row of restaurants. For the first time ever in my, life, I witnessed people eating from garbage cans. Way before dumpsters became common, restaurants still used metal garbage cans with round covers. A half-dozen bums each held a garbage can cover in one hand like a tray while they fished through garbage with the other. They gave Tony and I dirty looks, like we better not disturb their dinner.

I watched as these men sorted through the overflowing cans. Once they found something edible, they'd lay it on their garbage can cover. To see that people actually picked through trash to survive scared me. Would I end up like these guys? I made a vow I never would. Hell, I'd rather be in jail than eat garbage.

And I thought we'd had it bad back in Boston!

I nudged Tony. "How's life going to be here in paradise? Think we'll have to come down here to eat?"

Tony puked into a garbage can after watching a bum taking a bite out of a rancid, maggot-infested piece of meat.

"Let's go to Hollywood where things are better!" I said.

Tony wiped his mouth and nodded his head. "Yeah, sure, it has to be better than this."

We headed to Hollywood and Vine to see movie stars and celebrities. I'd come all this way to start a new life and vowed to do my best to remain honest, stay out of jail, work for a living, and even be a good citizen.

I added "Never, ever eat out of a garbage can" to my list.

Tony's Ideas

We arrived in Tinseltown. Ironically, I wasn't trying to emulate any of my old celluloid heroes any more. After Tony and I rented a room, we looked for work, but all we found was a job for a jewelry store, selling on credit stupid-looking clock radios shaped like sailing ships.

The owner instructed us how to make sales. "Go to the colored neighborhoods and tell them they can have this beautiful piece for only $29.99. They'll start to close the door, and that's when you say, 'A dollar down and a dollar a week and it's yours to keep.' Then put the thing in their hand and take their dollar."

Tony's face lit up. "You're saying all I have to do is get a buck and you're going to pay me a ten-dollar commission?"

"Well, you do have to get them to fill out a credit application and have it approved before they get the merchandise."

I knew it sounded too easy, but we went knocking on doors in black neighborhoods anyway, looking for credit-worthy customers so the store could load them up with high-priced junk. It didn't work out so well for us because no matter how many signed contracts we scored, we only got paid after credit approval, and that turned out to be rare.

Then Tony came up with one of his brilliant ideas. "We're in Hollywood and all the women here use lots of cosmetics. Maybe that's what we should be selling."

He showed me a magazine named *Specialty Salesman* that featured ads with a line of cosmetics called Cover Girl. "Let's go talk to the company," he said.

So off we went to the Cover Girl headquarters on Hollywood Boulevard. As Tony was a persuasive talker, he got the receptionist to tell the president of the company that two potential sales reps wanted to speak to him.

To my amazement, the girl told us to go on back to his office. We went through the door and a well-dressed man jumped up and shook hands with Tony and me.

"I'm planning to start a multi-level sales organization," Tony said, "and I'd like to use it to represent Cover Girl cosmetics." He rattled on about how he would recruit and train women to be sales people. "All I need to get started is an office where I can have my potential employees come for an interview. Once I find a place, I'm ready to go."

"Tell you what," the president said, "I like your ideas, so why don't you use my office for recruiting?" He waved his hand as though displaying the available space.

My eyes followed his hand and took in the wood-paneled walls and pieces of expensive artwork, the plush carpeting, leather chairs and couches, marble coffee table, and fully stocked bar. My mouth hung open in astonishment. Tony agreed to use the office and said he'd be in touch.

The next day I said, "I can't wait to start hiring girls. Imagine all the good-looking ones that will apply for a job and see us sitting behind a luxurious desk. We're bound to get lots of dates."

Tony looked angry. "Forget it. We're not doing it."

"Why not? The guy agreed to everything you said."

"For starters, we need money to put an ad in the paper, and then I need to print brochures and other sales paraphernalia. Plus, our rent is due in a few days and we don't have much money. We need to find a job that pays by the hour first."

This wasn't the first time success stared Tony in the face and he'd found reasons not to succeed. Sometimes he'd even get everything ready to go and then come up with an excuse why he couldn't do it. For example, when I was about sixteen, he had our house in Dorchester filled with vending machines that dispense a little toy in a plastic ball. This was a brand new fad then. Tony was set to go when some official told him that he technically needed a license to distribute the machines, but "to not worry about it," the guy added. That was enough for Tony to quit. Never mind that a business license for such an endeavor probably didn't cost much.

Another example: Before Manpower spread across the country, Tony got a franchise for Boston, but he never opened an office.

So instead of basking in the glow of some cover girl smiles, we looked for work at the California Employment Development Department in Hollywood. They sent us to Long Beach, where there was a job on the boardwalk. The job consisted of sitting in a cage while people threw balls at a target on the cage. If they hit it, the bench gave way and dunked you into the water. Neither one us wanted the job.

Tony's next idea was to go to work in the agriculture industry. There was a law then that farmers had to hire Americans over Mexicans. So we went to work picking lettuce, the only two gringos there. Tony sat on his ass, knowing he couldn't get fired. I worked alongside the Mexicans and equaled their amount of labor. We carried knives that we used to cut the lettuce from its roots and then we'd put the heads of lettuce into a crate we carried with us. As soon as it was full, we'd carry the crate to the truck, then get an empty one. By lunchtime, Tony was tired of sitting on his ass and wanted to quit. I can't say I was sorry. My feet were sore from scrambling over the rocky soil where the lettuce grew. I gained a lot of respect for Mexican farmworkers because I saw how hard they worked for almost nothing.

The "Oriental" guy in charge (what we called Asians back then) was happy to pay Tony and me so that we'd leave. "No American will work as hard as Mexicans for such low pay," he said, counting out our wages.

Tony's next idea was to go to Riverside and pick oranges. On the orange farm we visited, they had a bunkhouse where the laborers slept. We spent one night there, ate breakfast the next morning, and then Tony decided he didn't want to pick oranges. So we headed for San Diego and, with the last of Tony's savings, rented an apartment from a chiropractor named Elmer Winter.

We were out of money after paying Elmer a week's rent. Same old, same old for me: no money and no food. But I found about twenty jars of sauerkraut under the sink. Tony and I hated the taste but learned to appreciate it since there was nothing else to eat. (To this day, I eat it every chance I get, and it always reminds me of San Diego.)

It wasn't long before Tony wanted to go home. He couldn't find any work in San Diego, but had a job waiting for him in Boston. I couldn't go with him because the cops would be waiting for me, so I stayed in California.

I went to the California Employment Development Department office in San Diego and took an aptitude test for the carpenters union. It consisted of visual things, like fitting pieces into holes and piecing together blocks of wood like a jigsaw puzzle. I finished at the top of the list, but got no job offers.

I met a guy there around my age who'd also taken the test and passed it. We got along well. He had a brand-new pickup truck and we drove to Tijuana in it.

Still young enough to feel immortal, I didn't hesitate to hang around in several bars and get drunk, even when the patrons cast me lots of dirty looks. I don't remember what I did to rile up so many Mexicans, but the next thing I knew, I was standing in the bed of the pickup throwing rocks at a crowd chasing us as my friend drove away. We zoomed across the border and they couldn't follow. I thanked my lucky stars the next day for that border crossing. After the truck owner dropped me off, I never saw him again.

A few weeks later when I couldn't pay the rent, Elmer had me move into his house so he could rent the apartment to a paying tenant. Elmer and Tony had taught me to play chess, and I had a knack for it. I started doing housekeeping tasks in exchange for my room and board. Elmer was so cheap that he'd drive to Tijuana to buy anything he needed because most everything was less expensive there. Gas was so cheap back then it didn't even figure into the equation.

One day Elmer asked, "Ever been to México?"

"No," I lied.

"Now's your chance. Get in the car."

I got into the old Ford that he'd purchased at an auction. I wouldn't have known it was an old Highway Patrol cruiser if he hadn't told me, because he had painted it solid black.

The Mexican border was only about twenty miles away. Once we crossed it, I could hardly believe my eyes: cardboard shacks, unpaved roads, and obvious poverty I'd never known existed. I realized that as bad as I thought I'd had it growing up in Boston, these poor bastards had it worse.

Elmer drove downtown to the shops. Crowds of kids surrounded us to beg for money as we walked down the street. I didn't have any to give, or I would have. Elmer had plenty but gave nothing.

I followed him to a butcher shop where meat hung unrefrigerated on hooks, flies and other insects buzzing over the bloody slabs. Elmer picked out a couple of chunks and the butcher wrapped them in brown paper.

Next, we went to a tobacco store. I smoked at the time, and Elmer offered to buy me a carton of brown Mexican cigarettes. They were five cents a pack. An entire carton cost the equivalent of one pack in the States.

Elmer was clearly in heaven. "Even the women are cheaper," he told me.

He said he could speak Spanish, but he often created misunderstandings because he wasn't fluent. On our shopping trip in Tijuana, he made a date in his stumbling Spanish, and the whore thought he meant for her to bring a friend when she came to his house. I didn't know about his blunder until the woman drove up from México and brought a friend with her. Elmer told me to take a ride so he could be alone with his "girlfriend."

I drove to the beach and had sex with the friend. It turned out that she wanted to be paid for it. I had no idea. I thought she liked me. I was twenty-one and had spent most of my years locked up since age fourteen—plus I'd gone to the all-boys disciplinary school before that. I didn't have much experience with women. I figured a hooker would have asked for money before we had sex, a situation I understood from hanging around in Boston's South End where hookers were plentiful.

I had to ask Elmer for money to pay her when I got back.

He turned red. "Did you have sex with her?"

"Uh, yeah, I did."

He angrily pulled some bills from his wallet and paid her. I could see he didn't want to, but he probably figured that if he didn't, his "girlfriend" wouldn't come back.

Elmer was going through a divorce and wanted to talk about his problems all the time. Later that day, he talked to me about his estranged wife. "If she'd get sick," he said, "she'd want me to call a doctor. My first wife was frugal and never called a doctor when she was sick. She died in my arms and never asked me to call one."

I kept my mouth shut. After listening to this talk, I knew money was foremost in Elmer's brain. No wonder he was pissed off when he'd had to pay the hooker for me. I didn't understand how much money could mean to anyone—but how would I know, since I rarely had any?

"She was a good wife," Elmer said again. "She never wanted to call a doctor."

The deluded man didn't stop to think that his frugality probably cost his first wife her life. He continued to rant about his current wife. "Just because she's sick, she'll go to see a doctor. I can't afford her extravagant ways. Not only does she run up doctor bills, she wants to eat gourmet food, too."

I figured "gourmet" meant meat from a sanitary place.

Frugality had become a disease with Elmer. He had more money than he could ever spend. At the time, the City of San Diego was building a freeway and he was acquiring vacant houses for free. All he had to do was move them onto land he already owned. One day we went to the bank and he came out with a handful of $1,000 bills (still in circulation back in 1961). I knew he wasn't lying about having money.

Elmer used to take me to coroner's auctions where the county sold the belongings of people who had died without heirs. Elmer bid on boxes of personal belongings and filled his basement with them. Sometimes we'd find beautiful diamond, ruby, and emerald rings as we looked through the boxes before storing them. True to my vow to remain honest, I put aside any thoughts about how much cash I could get for the treasures we found. I never stole a single thing from Elmer.

Elmer's sister brought his daughter Eva out from Minnesota for a visit. His sister told me that Eva had come to live with her because she was afraid Elmer would let her starve to death. Eva was a pretty blonde about my age, and we got along well.

A few weeks later, I came home and Elmer's Doberman pinscher Sam ran up to greet me.

"Get back there." Elmer kicked Sam and pointed the dog to the fenced-in area he stayed in.

"Why'd you do that?"

"I want him to be a watchdog, not friends with any bum who comes around here."

Sam and I had been buddies since he was a pup. Elmer had just made it abundantly clear that he didn't want me around his daughter. My heart went out to Sam. Now he'd be in for a beating every time he ran up to me.

I can't blame Elmer for wanting a suitor for his daughter who at least had a job. Even so, I wished I could find a way to stay in San Diego so I could pursue a relationship with her and watch out for Sam. This turned out to be another time when I didn't fit the societal norm, and running was again my solution.

On the Road Again

I didn't have much money, but I took a Greyhound bus to San Francisco, hoping to find work. I went to the painters union and found they needed someone to do swing stage work.

A pro painter looked me over. "Do you know how to tie the knot that keeps a stage from falling?"

"Yes," I lied.

He held out a length of rope. "Show me."

I didn't have any idea how to show him, and he picked up on this right away.

"Sorry," he said. "I can't send you on the job if you don't know what you're doing. Someone may get killed, and it would probably be you."

The way things were going, I didn't much care one way or another.

After my botched interview, I wandered around, stopping in restaurants and hotels to ask if they were hiring. No luck. I eventually found a job selling newspaper subscriptions on the phone, and worked for two days. I didn't sell a single newspaper, let alone a subscription. No sales, no pay. I had no money for a room or food, and no idea where to go or what to do. I vowed to kill myself rather than turn to crime and go to jail again.

I walked past a bar and a guy came running out. "Hey kid, buy you a beer?"

I stopped and looked at him. I knew San Francisco was loaded with queers, but this guy looked straight. "Sure, I could use a beer about now," I said and followed him inside.

He paid for a beer. I sat down beside him and looked around. A row of men nursed their drinks along the bar. I didn't think this unusual because Boston had taverns that didn't allow women inside.

The beer tasted great. My mouth started to water when I glanced at a man eating a hamburger across from us.

"My name's Jim," my benefactor said. "You look hungry. Want a hamburger?"

Uh-oh, I thought. *This guy wants something.* While I waited to find out what, I figured I'd eat the hamburger. "Sure," I told him, "I'd really appreciate it."

Jim ordered a burger and fries for me, then put his hand on my thigh. I knocked it off. "I don't like to be touched."

"Don't be rude," he said. "I'm just being friendly." He reached out to put his hand on my leg again. I stood up, swallowed the remainder of the beer, and said, "I ain't no fucking queer."

Then I walked out, wishing I hadn't said anything until I'd eaten the hamburger.

* * * * *

Without job prospects, I decided to hitchhike back East. When I reached the far side of San Francisco Bay, the temperature seemed to

277

rise about thirty degrees. It felt like a hundred degrees in the sun, so hot I could hardly breathe.

One hard knock led to another. I found myself on the road for over a week and hadn't even crossed the Continental Divide. It took me days to get another ride every time someone dropped me off, probably because I looked scary from not showering or changing clothes. On one day that seemed to stretch out forever, a double rainbow appeared, reminding me of the distant, unattainable legendary pot of gold at each end. But those rainbows were so far away I could never find the ends even if the legend had been true.

On one cold night along the deserted highway where I'd tried to thumb a ride for over a day, I heard a car coming but saw no lights. Within a minute, I heard brakes squeal and a car so old I thought it could be a Model-T stopped right in front of me. I don't know how the driver could see me on that moonless night.

"Want a ride?" he shouted over the engine noise.

"Sure do!" I opened the door, threw in my bag, and climbed inside the antique car. I was a bit nervous about riding in a vehicle with no light, but anything had to be better than spending a freezing night out under the stars.

I studied the driver's face by starlight, gauging if he were some kind of nut. "Why don't you turn on your lights?"

"Blew a fuse and don't have a spare," he said.

I dropped my gaze. "If you wrap tinfoil around the blown fuse, it'll make a circuit and still work." I knew that from stealing cars.

"Tried that, but it didn't work. Wish it would have, because I've got a hundred miles to go, and not being able to see, I'll never make it in time to go to work."

He went on to tell me how he worked for a crew that installed asphalt driveways. They had to start work by sunup, as the heat from the hot tar was too much to take by noon.

I noticed a flashlight on the floor. "Do you want me to try aiming the flashlight on the road to help you see?"

"Nah, it's not bright enough...but wait a minute. If you'd ride on my fender and hold it out in front, I could see to increase my speed and make it to work on time."

He stopped the car and I got out. With my feet on the old jalopy's running board, and my body curled over the fender, I aimed the flashlight beam so he could see the road ahead. After three hours, the sun rose and I was practically frozen, but he made it to work on time, and I had another hundred miles under my belt.

Afterward, I stood for hours beside the highway—dirty, thirsty, hungry and broke. Suddenly an old station wagon appeared and clattered to a stop. I ran up to the open passenger window.

"Name's Harlo," the driver said. "I'm headed to Yellowstone to work as a cook. You're welcome to come along. You can probably get hired on, too."

I figured fate would intervene, and it looked like it had shown up. The only thing I knew about Yellowstone was that Yogi Bear lived there, but heading somewhere beat waiting for a ride to nowhere.

As we sped along a deserted mountain road, I noticed Harlo

grinding his teeth.

"You doing speed?"

"Prescription medicine." He showed me a bottle. I didn't bother to read the label. "Here take a couple of these," he said. "They'll wake you up."

I swallowed two little white pills he gave me. I was worried if I did fall asleep, Harlo might turn out to be some sort of maniac and I'd wake up with my hands tied—or not wake up at all.

He gave me a few more pills after a few hours passed. I swallowed them, still wide- awake.

Harlo had three different prescription bottles in his hand, and he shook one of them. "Almost empty. I need to get these refilled or I'm going to get awfully sick."

"Stop at the next town and get them filled," I said.

As we pulled into a little town, Harlo glanced around. He pulled up in front of a Catholic church. "I can't go any further if I don't have my medicine. I don't have any money and don't know what to do."

I knew what that implied. He wanted me to go in and ask the priest to get his prescriptions filled. I didn't want to beg, but didn't see that I had a choice. I took Harlo's empty bottles, went to the rectory, and rang the bell.

A priest answered.

"Look," I said, "I hate to ask you this, but the guy driving the car—" I pointed to the old station wagon, "Harlo's taking me to Yellowstone National Park where there are jobs waiting for us. He doesn't have money for his medicine, and I'm broke." I handed the empty bottles to the priest. "If you can get these filled, I'll repay you when I get paid."

The priest looked at the bottles. "Take these to the drug store on the next street and tell the druggist to call me."

"Thank you, Father," I said, truly grateful not only for his generosity, but also because he didn't make me pray for his kindness. One of my lasting regrets is that I never repaid him. I quickly forgot what town and what state we were in, as well as the name of the church. If only I could remember, I'd retrace my route and return the money now.

After Harlo had an adequate supply of amphetamines, it seemed as if we drove and drove for weeks, though it was likely only another day or two. This perception of life moving in slow motion was unusual for me, because time usually goes by in a blur on speed.

When we reached Yellowstone, the security guards at the entrance waved us through when Harlo told them we were looking for jobs. We were both hired, and I was assigned to cook for the employees. It was to be a great place to hang out. Most of the employees were college kids on their summer vacations. I could hardly believe the way they all walked around singing to one another instead of talking in the kitchen. I felt as though I lived in some kind of musical comedy.

Women outnumbered men by a big margin at Yellowstone, so I was more than happy to be there. I took a girl to a mountain lake and got a severe sunburn on my legs. This surprised me because the weather wasn't hot. But the rays were stronger up in the mountains. I experienced many other firsts at Yellowstone. I went trout fishing there for the one and only time in my life. (I loved standing in the river but hated killing the flying insects we used for bait.) I visited Old Faithful Geyser and Glacier National Park as well, searching all over for Yogi Bear, the cartoon character popular at the time. I saw plenty of bears, but never came across Yogi.

The Northwest was wild and pristine, and I loved living there, even more so because no one knew anything about me. I felt like I'd come home.

Harlo wanted to leave before the summer ended. Like a dummy, I left with him, probably because I felt a sense of loyalty to him for bringing me there.

*****

When we hit the road again, we didn't take any speed, and other than almost hallucinating from lack of sleep, we made it to Wisconsin in good shape.

We went to the state employment office. It listed a job at Tecumseh Lodge at Eagle River, near Rhinelander, Wisconsin, a boys' camp where the stove had blown up and injured the cook. The camp needed a new cook and an assistant cook, so we drove to Rhinelander for interviews. The facilities impressed me— the camp had canoes, a speedboat for water skiing, horses, and many buildings for recreation and accommodation, including the mess hall where I hired on as assistant cook.

Faye Dorfman and her late husband William had owned and operated the Tecumseh Lodge for many years, and when I was there, her son-in-law, Ira Lustig, assisted her. Well over six feet tall, redheaded Ira weighed in at two hundred and fifty pounds and ran the business end of the camp as athletic director. He was maybe five years older than me, and was married to Faye's daughter, Ila, who taught horseback riding and waterskiing to campers. Ira and Ila had a son named Billy. I playfully chased Billy around the camp just to hear him laugh.

Faye dropped in for coffee every morning at the kitchen where I worked. An intelligent woman and an artist, she treated me as an equal, probably the first time in my life that any middle-class woman had done so. I secretly fell in love with her, though she was in her fifties and not trim or athletic.

The counselors were around my age, so I got along fine with them. The campers were teenage boys of various ages. Despite my problems with never getting enough food as a kid, I never realized teenage boys could consume such huge amounts of it until I had to cook for them. I teased the kids whenever they wanted extra food, and they appreciated my sense of humor.

"Who has the prettiest legs in Wisconsin?" I'd ask them. "You'd better treat me right or your 'Egyptian eyeballs'"—a fried egg in the center of a piece of toast—"will be burnt!"

Bea, the camp nurse, liked me and told Faye that she could see from my good manners that I'd had a good upbringing. If only she knew about my checkered past! I also got along well with another assistant cook, a black lady in her forties. Actually, I got along well with everybody at Tecumseh Lodge. In the Northwoods, there were no drugs or alcohol to tempt me, and I began to think I could forget my past and start a new life.

Because I got along with the family (Faye, Ira, and Faye's daughter, Ila), some of the counselors bent over backwards to flatter me. One guy even let me use his car anytime I wanted. So I went into Eagle River and drank with the local yokels on my time off. But the counselors' actions also showed me how kiss-asses operated. Their motivation was to use me to get what they wanted from Faye. I despised their efforts and never tried to help them in any way.

One night, after all the boys and counselors had gathered in the recreation hall, Ira heard me make the kids say I had the prettiest legs in Wisconsin. He suggested we have a contest to see who had the prettiest legs. I guess he thought he'd win because he was the head honcho and instructed the kids in athletics. But one kid was a real loudmouth. He kept yelling, "Joe does, Joe does!" for so long that he wore out the kids who were voting for Ira. When I told people years later that I'd won a vote by a loud majority for having the prettiest legs in Wisconsin, they gave me funny looks.

The scene of Lon Chaney turning into a wolf in the film *Wolf Man* had haunted me ever since my mom had taken me to see it when I was five years old. My fear that the creature really existed stayed with me. I figured I could overcome any fear, and waited for the full moon to go for a hike alone in the woods near Tecumseh

Lodge. Things went well until scurrying noises erupted all around me under the canopy of tall pines. Clouds blew across the moon, and the woods filled with strange shadows. Suddenly, the Wolf Man stood in front of me. Knowing I'd created him with my imagination, I refused to panic. I kept walking, but as the noises around me became louder, my vision of this half-man, half-beast became clearer. When I saw its hands sprout claws, hairs pop from its face, and fangs grow from its animal-like snout, I ran all the way back to camp. Low-hanging branches left welts and scratches on my bare arms and legs, and I must have looked like I'd been attacked by something. I never told anyone of my fear, and I even tried to walk alone in the night woods several more times. Each attempt ended up with me running for my life from my imaginary Wolf Man!

* * * * *

When camping season was over, Harlo took off without me. We hadn't been getting along because I no longer got high with him. Faye looked concerned when I told her I didn't have a way to get home. "That wasn't very nice of Harlo to leave you stranded here."

"Doesn't matter," I said. "I was hitchhiking when I met him. Guess I can continue hitching from here."

"My nephew Al is coming up to his Jack O' Lantern Lodge for a vacation. Why don't you work for him for a few weeks to put some money in your pocket?"

"Sure," I said. I really didn't have much of a choice, as I probably would have starved to death before I got a ride out of the Northwoods.

I went to the Jack O' Lantern Lodge, also near Eagle River, the next day, but Al hadn't arrived yet. He and Saul, his vice president, had a business meeting to attend before they could go on vacation.

I met Saul's wife and his daughter, a pretty, well-proportioned girl close to my age. I took her out that night and we went drinking at a local bar. A bunch of guys came in and acted like guys always do when a good-looking girl enters their territory.

"Hey baby," one guy said.

"Mind your manners," I said.

"Be quiet, or you might get hurt," another guy said.

My beer muscles took over. After a few beers, I wouldn't take bullshit from anyone. "I can see where this is going. You assholes want to fight? I'll fight all of you, one at a time."

Must have been those stupid movie actors again, inspiring me to do things that looked cool in the movies but never turned out well in real life.

The boys took me up on the offer. I walked out of the bar, leaving Saul's daughter alone—a nice Jewish girl from Chicago who'd probably never seen a fistfight before. What she would have witnessed was a total embarrassment for me. The toughest guy fought me first. He kicked my ass and wore me out. Being stupid and stubborn, I wouldn't quit before I fought every one. There wasn't much fight left in me after the first, but I still stood after seven fights, defeated but not bowed.

Saul's daughter never went out with me again.

From the Northwoods to the Cook County Jail

Faye's nephew Allen Dorfman, and Al's insurance company VP
Saul, came in to Tecumseh Lodge late on the night of my ill-fated
serial fistfight, probably around Labor Day weekend. I was up at
around 5 a.m. because Saul's wife put reveille on the loudspeakers
and woke everyone up. Al came charging down the stairs, spotted
me, and viciously chewed me out.

I stood there, rolled my eyes at the guilty party, and let him
rant. I wasn't about to tell him who really did it. But she must have
told him later, because Al couldn't do enough to be nice to me after
that.

I figured that most people Al yelled at pointed their finger and
blamed someone else. He must have gained some respect for me
when I stood there and let him browbeat me.

Al told me how the Jack O'Lantern Lodge used to be owned by
Al Capone, and that there were tunnels built under it so the patrons
could escape if the place got raided. I had no idea at the time that his
stepfather, Chicago-based gangster Paul "Red" Dorfman, had been a
lieutenant for Capone, or anything about how Al had bought the
lodge in 1950, or anything about how he used the lodge to wine and
dine high-ranking members of the Teamsters Union. I also discovered years later that after former Teamsters Union leader Jimmy
Hoffa disappeared, the FBI had searched for his body, among many

other places, in the Northwoods around the Jack O'Lantern Lodge.

Anyway, Al said there was lots of gambling equipment from the Capone days in the basement that would be worth a fortune in Chicago. I offered to drive it there, but he said, "No, it's too dangerous—you'll probably get caught by the Highway Patrol."

Al's wife and two sons came with him to the camp. The boys were maybe eight and ten years old and nice kids that Al treated kindly. I liked his sons. Al seemed to like me a lot, but I don't think his wife cared for me.

Al told me he'd once been a physical education teacher and how if the rewards were equal, he'd choose teaching over the insurance business. "How did you get into a position where you don't have any money, anyway?" he asked, checking out my Jewish-Italian face.

I didn't know what to say. Being broke and hungry seemed like a natural state for me.

"Come to work for me in Chicago," he said.

Afterward, two business agents from the Teamsters Union vacationing with Al also told me to come and see them in Chicago. I mentioned that Al had already offered me a job.

"Go with Al," they said.

After considering it, I heeded the business agents' advice. I went to stay at Al's house in Deerfield, Illinois, a suburb of Chicago, where I met a woman who did his laundry and ironing. She had a retarded son around my age, and she'd bring him with her when she came for pickups and deliveries. I treated the young man as I would any other person and I never paid attention to his disabilities. One day at her house, I was goofing around with him and I saw the happiness in her eyes when she looked at us. I knew she was happy because of the way I treated her son, and I was happy to be doing something good for a change.

Al had built his mansion around a large tree in the middle of his living room. There was a formal dining room, many bedrooms, and a servant's quarters, where I slept. Two black girls who worked as housekeepers stayed there too. One liked me, but I wasn't interested.

I spent most of my time in Al's swimming pool. One day I looked in Al's closet and couldn't believe that one man could own so many suits. There had to be at least fifty jackets and matching trousers neatly hung on hangers, with a pair of shoes under each one.

One day Al conducted a business meeting, and I overheard him talking. "You want trouble? I'll give you trouble." The guy he spoke to practically cried while insisting he didn't want any trouble. (I liked that line and used it several times in my life. One time I was on Rush Street in Chicago and a waitress short-changed me. The management tried to ignore my complaint until I used Al's line. The manager quickly returned my money.)

I'd drive Al to the train station for his morning commute to his office in Chicago. I assumed I was there as a bodyguard in the event something happened. Al told me on one of our morning jaunts that he was going to get me into his country club and find me a Jewish wife. The Jewish wife part scared me to death. My mother was Jewish, and I sure as hell didn't want a wife like her.

Being twenty-one and not smart enough to take advantage of the offer, I told Al, "I've been in the Northwoods all summer, and now I'm stuck out here in Deerfield. I've got to get back to the city lights."

So Al gave me a job at his insurance company in Chicago. Mike Breen, his office manager said, "Give me a sample of your handwriting, Joe. It needs to be legible if I'm going to make you a claims examiner."

I gave him an illegible handwriting sample, so he put me in the mailroom. I guessed that was an insult, but it didn't bother me. I was happy to be working in an office with so many good-looking women, and Faye worked there as a receptionist.

Al was such a nice guy that I was a bit shocked when I finally learned his family was considered one of the top gangster families in Chicago. Red Dorfman had been a lieutenant for Al Capone, and Red had helped Hoffa get to the helm of the Teamsters Union. Hoffa returned the favor by putting Al in charge of the Central States Pension Fund.

Red Dorfman ran the Waste Handler's Union, and was married to Faye's sister, Rose. Apparently. Faye's husband William Dorfman was no relation to Red Dorfman; she told me it was coincidental that she and her sister shared the same married name.

One day I was teasing Red's other son, Jay, whom I thought had some sort of mental problem. He had a hammer and wanted to kill a squirrel that the mailroom guys had been feeding as a pet. Unbeknownst to me at the time, Red stood at the bottom of the stairs listening to me. Guess I was lucky Red didn't get angry with me, or who knows what would have happened.

Allen Dorfman worked as co-counsel for Hoffa's legal defense team in the "Test Fleet" prosecution brought against Hoffa by the Justice Department, then headed by Robert F. Kennedy. After the trial resulted in a hung jury in December 1962, Al Dorfman, along with other Hoffa allies, was investigated for jury tampering. I heard that Al had been mentioned in President John F. Kennedy's book, *Profiles in Courage.*

Now, years later, I read that the FBI thinks Jack Ruby received payoff money from Al Dorfman for killing Lee Harvey Oswald. It turns out that Red Dorfman took over a union that Jack Ruby had run, and moved to Texas. What a twist of fate if all this is true.

After being in the boonies so long, I thirsted for some excitement. A few days after I left Al's house, he had another guy drive him to the train station, and a couple of thugs shot out the front tire of his car in a kidnap attempt. The driver took off on the flat tire. I often thought if I had been driving, I may have stopped. If I had, the next shot would've been to my head. Maybe somebody up there was still looking out for me.

* * * * *

I stayed at the YMCA until my brother Tony came to Chicago. We got an apartment together at 1117 N. Dearborn Street. A guy and his girlfriend who studied acting at the Art Institute befriended us. They lived across the hall. I met their friends and enjoyed their company, and they enjoyed mine because I had a lot of stories to tell. When I was drinking, I guess I told them well. I almost fit in.

Once I started drinking again, I also started taking speed again. One night when I was at Clark and Division, a major commercial area, I watched the hypnotic swaying of a purse that a black woman carried. The impulsivity that ruled my life took over, and I snatched the purse from her. To this day, I'm ashamed of doing that. It went against my perceived code of honor to pick on anyone weaker than me, and my victim was a woman. I would have been able to control my impulse if I hadn't been stoned on alcohol and drugs.

I ran down Dearborn Street with the police in hot pursuit. I committed that crime, but not from need or even greed. I let my dark side take over for an instant. When I realized what I had done, I immediately threw the purse away, but it was too late. As I ran by pedestrians, I saw fear on their faces, and the fear caused me to stop running and give up. I've never understood how or why I could care enough to stop, but I did.

Al bailed me out the next day and sent his lawyer and office manager Mike Breen to court with me.

"Just tell them you work for Allen Dorfman," Mike said. "The judge will dismiss the case."

But the day I had to appear, Al's picture was plastered on the front page of every paper in Chicago. He had been indicted for fraud. Now that he had problems of his own, I couldn't use his name. Eventually, Al was sentenced to the Marion Federal Prison Camp.

The prosecutor in my case won a grand jury indictment and raised my bail to some astronomical figure. After my hearing, I was taken into custody to await trial, and placed on tier E-3 in the Cook County Jail. A tier consisted of about sixty cells, thirty on each side of the aisle. Each tier had a dayroom with tables and benches, a TV, and a shower. E-3 housed the hardcore felons. F-3 housed the homosexuals and perverts. (I hope I'm not getting the letters mixed up).

The prisoners were allowed to use the dayroom during the day, but after I'd been there a few weeks, the cellblock became so crowded that guys had to sleep on the dayroom tables and floor. The shower was in view of the dayroom and anybody could watch anybody shower. I couldn't help but notice that the story about black men being better endowed than white men seemed to be true.

As far as I can remember, those of us who weren't yet convicted of any crime had to wear our own clothes. I didn't have anyone to bring me fresh clothing, so I must have stunk from wearing the same outfit day after day.

Sitting in jail for another idiotic crime made me feel like a real loser. I had an opportunity to live a normal life and I blew it. I wondered if I'd become institutionalized and therefore uncomfortable if not locked up. I knew guys like that. They couldn't make it on the street, but they thrived in jail or prison. Twenty-one now, I'd been in and out for seven years, so I fit right in.

I met a guy named Mulligan who helped publish the weekly jail paper. I told him I held a black belt in karate, and a few other impressive lies. I figured those who could read wouldn't mess with me after seeing the article.

I was surprised to hear that Brown, the guy who ran our tier, was a convicted murderer. Brown was an apt name, because of his skin color. I can't recall if he was under a death sentence; if so, I thought murderers were always kept in isolation. But this was how the local authorities operated Cook County Jail. They used what they called the "barn boss system." They put a guy in charge that had nothing to lose by keeping the other prisoners in line. What would they do if Brown killed someone—execute him twice?

Unwittingly, I almost got mixed up in a power struggle between the killer who ran the tier and another killer who wanted his job. The other guy used the old "send the little guy over to start a fight, and then the big guy takes over the fight" strategy, the same strategy they used in Dispy back when I was a kid.

Once I pushed the little guy away when he cut in front of me in the chow line. Then the big guy—the killer—tried to intimidate me. I held an empty metal food tray and put my left foot forward so I could pivot, gripped the tray as tight as I could, and figured out the trajectory so that the edge of the tray would hit him in his Adam's apple. If he made a move, I'd have swung the tray backhanded and sliced into his throat. When he saw I wasn't backing down, he walked away. No one bothered me after that.

My assigned cellmate was black, as were about 80% of the prisoners in the Cook County system. Another black guy told me he had a one-man cell next to the one I shared and that he wanted to trade cells. I gladly accepted, but then I had to listen to him and my former cellmate having sex all night.

The women's tier was directly above ours, and we could communicate with them by yelling into the airshaft located in every cell. Notes, cigarettes, and candy bars were passed down to our tier by the women attaching items to a length of string and throwing the string out the window just a few feet from the bars in our cellblock. The guy in a cell could then reel it in by throwing something that would snag the string. Then he would attach whatever he wanted to send back, and the woman above would reel in her string. With all that going on, it was hard to sleep some nights. Every night, one guy would repeatedly scream into his airshaft, "Jewish pussy stinks! They don't believe in douching!"

The four-term law in Illinois stated that prisoners must be released if not brought to trial after four months. Al had paid a lawyer for me, but the lawyer was incompetent. Over four months went by and the lawyer told the judge I should be released. If the defendant asked for a continuance, it voided the law. The judge told my lawyer that I had asked for a continuance, so I had to stay in jail until I went to trial. I'd never asked for a continuance, and the lawyer didn't even argue or correct the judge's statement.

While sitting in jail, I saw lots of guys come and go. Many on my tier went to court and came back with sentences of thirty, forty, fifty years or more in the state prison—serious time. Your life was over with a sentence like that. Up to this time, when I went to jail, I always knew plenty of guys inside and it was fun to talk about old times. But here in Chicago, I didn't know anyone, and the sentences handed out to inmates were so long, it scared me.

I wanted a jury trial, but more than six more months would pass before I even went to trial. When I was offered five years' probation and six more months in jail, I grabbed it, pleading guilty.

When I got out of Cook County Jail in the spring of 1962, I'd be twenty-two.

Electric Chair

Because I was from Boston, the guy who owned the jail commissary probably figured I wouldn't know other inmates, so he chose me to work for him. On the first day of work, I went to the basement where the jail kept commissary supplies. Along the way, guards who didn't have anything better to do searched me twice.

"I'm going to show you the ropes," said the trustee in charge of the cart. "Watch close."

The cart stood about six feet high and three feet deep. It held shelves and compartments for razors, deodorant, candy, cigarettes, hot chocolate, instant coffee and other items. I watched as he tore the wrappers off the packages and threw them into a large canvas bag hanging on the side. When the cart was about half full, he started loading cigarettes on it. He snuck a carton into the garbage bag every so often and covered it with trash. We counted everything else on the cart before we went out the door. No one knew about the hidden cigarettes, which we left on a cellblock tier to sell after work. I was a thief at heart, so I thought it great to rip off merchandise to make my life a bit better. I didn't stop to think that by taking the cigarettes, I was hurting the guy who owned the commissary.

I met many prisoners on the job. One of them was James Dukes, a barn boss on his tier, sentenced to death for killing a Chicago police detective. His execution was scheduled for August 15, 1962.

Illinois counties with a population of a million or more could perform their own executions. The Cook County electric chair was located in the basement of the same building that housed my cellblock. I walked by this room every day with the commissary cart, on my way to the different tiers. I couldn't see the chair because it was behind a closed metal roll-up door to hide it from passersby. When an execution took place, the metal door was rolled up so that the chair was visible to witnesses in the small observation area. I imagined that the room became crowded on execution nights. There must be, I thought, around thirty people crowded into the room to watch a man die, a spectacle never as glamorous or as exciting as the scenes portrayed in movies.

There was a lot of talk about ending capital punishment during this era. A guy named Ciucci was scheduled to die soon, too. We conversed several times, though I'm not sure what we talked about. But I definitely remember the night he got electrocuted. Convicted of killing his wife and three small kids, he always maintained his innocence until right before execution when he confessed to killing his wife. He claimed he did it because she killed the kids.

Everyone knew if Ciucci, a white man, got the chair, then Dukes, a black cop killer, would definitely get it. Some news articles still mistakenly report that Ciucci was the last man executed in Chicago, but Dukes's execution was the last in the Cook County Jail. After his execution, State authorities dismantled the electric chair and stored it away with another from Joliet.

When Ciucci's time drew near, everyone in the jail expected

him to get a stay of execution because he'd had four trials before the conviction and a dozen appeals afterward. The stay didn't happen this time. Prison guards led him blindfolded through the cellblocks on the night of March 22, 1962, and placed him in the electric chair. At one minute past midnight, Warden Jack Johnson signaled three guards in another room who then pressed a button, sending 1900 volts of electricity into Ciucci.

We heard that the streets surrounding the jail were crowded with people, some who protested the death penalty and others because of a rumor that they'd see the jailhouse lights flicker during the execution. I also sat in my cell expecting to see the lights dim as they applied the juice, just as it did in the movies. But like the crowd on the street, I was disappointed.

When I rolled the commissary cart up to Dukes's tier the morning after the execution, he stood by himself with his head hung down as though in deep thought. He heard me rolling the cart up to and ran over to the bars. "Did they kill Ciucci?" he asked.

Not thinking, I answered, "Yeah, burned his ass last night."

Dukes had dark black skin, but when I mentioned Ciucci's fate, he I saw the color slowly drain from every visible part of his body. He turned a sickly yellow. He didn't move but remained frozen in place as I finished selling commissary items to the prisoners on his tier. Then I walked away.

I hadn't realized how news of Ciucci's execution would affect him or I wouldn't have told him. That memory of him changing color or will remain with me for the rest of my life. His fear destroyed my heroic image of dying in the electric chair that I'd held for so long.

Five months later, the State of Illinois took Dukes's life:

> THE LAST state execution in Illinois took place August 24, 1962 when cop killer James Duke was electrocuted in the basement of the Cook County Jail. The deep and abiding doubts about the morality of capital punishment can be seen in the recent statement of Warden Jack Johnson, the man who pulled the switch in Duke's electrocution.
>
> Johnson said, "I had a definite feeling it was wrong. There was a feeling of guilt. But I rationalized it. I said, 'Okay, society, this is what you wanted and I gave it to you. It must be right.'"
>
> —Gary Delsohn, *Illinois Issues,*
> Illinois Periodicals Online.

Even so, Illinois revived the death penalty by lethal injection in 1990, but again banned capital punishment in 2011.

* * * * *

I sold cigarettes to the guys who worked in prisoner intake. They, in turn, would sell them to new arrivals who had money but no cigarettes. I think cigarettes were twenty-five cents a pack then, and intake guys sold them for three to five dollars a pack. I made about forty dollars a day for my part. I gave the cash I accumulated to a guard I trusted, and he'd buy and send me a money order at the jail. That way I'd have some money when I got out.

After my sentencing, I started counting the days until my release. I paid the barn boss of the new tier to allow me to move into a single cell so I could be as comfortable as possible for the next six months. Meanwhile, I had to keep my mind occupied so I wouldn't go stir crazy. I got him to take the bed out and I slept on the floor. I started to draw a chain of tiny human figures on the cell walls. Before long, I had the steel walls and ceiling covered with little figures, and hung odds-and-ends from the ceiling.

"Come into my cell and I'll get your cigarettes," I told one of the black guys on the tier who sold me cooked chickens he'd snatch from the kitchen.

"Uh-uh, man, I ain't going in there." He stared at the junk hanging from the metal ceiling—burnt bread, voodoo-like dolls, string, and some colored ribbon.

I can't remember why I did this, but the other prisoners had a fear of going into my cell, too. I guess they figured I was some kind of witch. I was happy they felt that way, because I knew I wouldn't be hassled.

I also took a piece of string and pulled it through a cardboard box. When I pulled and released the string, it made a sound similar to a bass fiddle. I played it every night—and now imagine how irritating it must have been to everyone in earshot.

One day, I was allowed to go outside, the first time in a solid year of confinement (after six-months awaiting trial for the six-month sentence). It was great to breathe fresh air again. When I had to go back inside, the smell hit me—sweat, urine, and thousands of unwashed bodies. After living with the stink for a year, I had become desensitized to it. Even though I probably lived better than most inmates, Cook County Jail was still the most miserable place I had ever been, except for Middlesex County Training School.

Free Again

"You've got to go to Old Town when you get out," Mulligan said.

Mulligan was the reporter for the Cook County Jail newspaper who'd written that I was a karate expert when I'd first arrived there. He was a heroin addict, so I knew we'd never be friends even though we'd become chummy in the slammer.

"When we get out, I'm going to show you how to steal money orders," he said. "I've made a good living doing it."

After being in jail with killers, a little thievery didn't seem so bad. I was beginning to forget my vow to work and stay out of jail.

"Sounds great," I said. "Tell me how now—why wait?"

"No, no. When we get out I'll show you."

But when I headed for Chicago's Old Town after my release from the Cook County Jail in the spring of 1962, I never saw Mulligan on the street.

I rented an apartment close to LaSalle Street, two blocks from North Avenue at heart of the vibrant artists' enclave. Silvio, a guy I'd met in jail, visited daily. At night, we'd go to the Village Pump Bar near my apartment to drink, listen to music, and pick up girls. My brother Tony came to Chicago, and I let him live with me. One day, the landlord needed to get into my apartment to fix a leak and Tony, being contrary as usual, wouldn't let him in. The landlord evicted me.

About that time, Faye Dorfman, who I'd stayed in contact with, wanted me to go to work in her boys' camp again. I didn't want to but couldn't say no after she'd stuck by me. I later realized that she probably thought she did me a favor by giving me a job. It would have been better if I hadn't accepted. Faye had to sell the place because of the low enrollment that summer. I figured word got around that she'd hired an ex-con and another drunken cook. Maybe the Jewish community was aghast at the thought of sending their kids to a camp that hired people like me.

I never saw Al again because he'd been sentenced to prison. I wanted to thank him for his help, but he was so high profile that if an ex-con visited him or even wrote to him, it would be detrimental. After his release, he went to Las Vegas and purchased casinos for the pension fund. The fund owned quite a bit of Vegas in the early sixties. I knew if I went to see Al, he would have set me up with a gravy job in Vegas, but I was too embarrassed to try because I had lied to him about committing the crime that sent me to jail.

When the camping season ended and I returned to Chicago, I applied for a job with Yellow Transit, a large trucking company. There was a long line of applicants, but because I wore a white pressed shirt to the interview, they chose me over all the others. The white shirt was the only thing that made me different from the other job seekers, and I can't think of any other reason I stood out. Once hired, I had to pass a lie detector test.

I went into an office at the Yellow Freight Warehouse in Cicero, Illinois, where I'd go to work if I passed the test.

A guy in his thirties put a cuff on my arm, attached a few leads and said, "I'm going to ask you some test questions. I want you to purposely lie so I can get a base to work from."

"Okay."

I forget the exact questions. Maybe he held up a red card and asked, "Is this a black card?" and then hold up a black card and ask, "Is this a black card?" He asked opposing questions like that for about half an hour.

I thought about what Sully's wife had told me long before how to manage a lie detector test: "If they ask you a question and your answer will be a lie, think of a question you can answer truthfully. Like if they ask you if you've ever been arrested, think, did I ever beat my mother? Then when you say 'no,' it won't show up as a lie."

"Okay," the test monitor said. "Have you ever stolen from an employer?"

I thought, *Have I ever beaten my mother?* I truthfully answered, "No."

"Have you ever been convicted of a crime?"

Have I ever beaten my mother? "No."

This went on for a while. Then he asked, "Why is it you take so long to answer my questions?"

"I reviewed my memories so I'd be certain I told the truth."

He accepted my answer and I got the job unloading trailers at the Cicero terminal where they sorted freight going to different parts of the country. I soon regretted taking it. My co- workers were boring, and I certainly didn't fit in. Unloading boxes all night was boring, too. I felt bad that I took the job away from some poor guy with a family who needed it more than I did.

One night I ran into Vito, a guy I knew from Cook County Jail. A bunch of Italians who had been convicted of voting fraud came into jail with short sentences, acting like they owned the joint when I was almost finished with my sentence. I didn't like their attitude, but they were the ruling class, and my Italian name helped me get along with them. (Groups of prisoners of the same race or ethnicity hung out together inside the jail for mutual protection and common interests.)

Vito was one of the guys who hung out with us. Every morning, breakfast coffee was delivered to the tiers in a metal container with a lid on it. Vito sat on this container every morning to relieve his hemorrhoid pain. (This was the extent of any medical treatment in jail for that ailment.)

Vito said he ran a bar for the syndicate, and I believed him. One night after my release, I visited the bar. Vito had three good-looking girls sitting on his immense lap. He had blue-tinged lips and must have weighed four hundred pounds. I thought him ugly as sin, but he always had good-looking women hanging around him. Go-go girls were the rage then, and Vito had a couple of them dancing on the bar. Sometimes women customers wanted to demonstrate that they could dance, too. Often they were tipsy and fell off the bar to peals of laughter from the patrons and the real go-go girls.

Vito offered me a job driving hot cars to California and New York. That seemed a lot more glamorous than unloading trucks. The thought of returning to jail never entered my mind.

He drove me to O'Hare Airport, pointed to a Cadillac and said, "Go get it." He handed me a key. It didn't fit. I got out and a man who must have owned the car stood there looking at me.

Vito came by and picked me up. "Wrong car," he said.

"Where's the right car?"

"Don't worry about it. While you're waiting, you can go to the ball park and get ID tags from all the Cadillacs in the parking lot. Then I can print up registrations to match. I'll give you ten bucks for each one you get."

Back in the '60s, the auto ID tag was a little metal plate on the doorjamb that could be knocked off with a screwdriver. Vito told me I could probably get a hundred tags in one day.

I told Vito I needed some speed to stay awake while driving. We went to a bar off the Eisenhower Expressway to get some. He scored and handed me an envelope full of white crosses.

"Whatever you do," he said, "don't tell anybody you're using this shit."

The first car I drove to California was a brand new four-door Cadillac. At twenty-two, I certainly didn't fit the profile for an older man's car. I stopped at a diner and called Faye to tell her I was in Texas.

"I bet it has something to do with your job at Yellow Freight," she said.

I didn't say anything, and was glad I hadn't when I turned to see a Texas Trooper eavesdropping. He pulled me over as soon as I drove out of the parking lot.

"Where are you headed?"

I started thinking about how I wasn't supposed to leave Illinois because of my five-years probation.

"I'm delivering this car to California for a friend of mine who's graduating medical school. He's flying home after the ceremonies."

Much to my surprise, he believed me. (I'm still surprised by how cool I'd been under the circumstances. If that happened today, I'd be too nervous to say a word.)

I took some of Vito's Benzedrine to help me stay awake. After not sleeping for a few days, I started hallucinating again. As I drove under a bridge, I saw it falling on me. I ducked down while driving sixty miles an hour, lucky I didn't crash. The car started having transmission problems, though, and I had enough nerve to take it to a Cadillac dealer and complain. The service manager rode around the block with me and told me I'd make it to California, but that I should put the car in the shop for repairs when I arrived.

After the police stop in Texas, the drive became nerve-wracking. When I crossed the California border, I encountered a roadblock, supposedly an agricultural checkpoint to stop diseased fruit and vege-tables from entering the state. I got nervous because the checkpoint seemed like a legal way to give everyone the once-over. An officer told to me to pull over to the side and show my registration. I couldn't find it, and he was about to start searching the car when I finally found the one Vito had made in the glove box. The officer glanced at it and waved me on.

When I arrived in L.A., I called the number Vito had given me and said, "I've got a delivery from Chicago for you."

"Come on over," replied a voice on the other end.

I drove to the address, parked the Cadillac in the driveway, and rang the doorbell.

A big, good-looking guy opened the door and pumped my hand. "Hey, nice to meet ya. I'm Jim, and this is my wife, Sue. You want to spend the night here, or do you want me to drive you somewhere?"

Sue was attractive and friendly, and the house was nice, with a sunken living room and a swimming pool. But I declined the invitation. They weren't the kind of people I felt comfortable with. I thought them rubes who had probably purchased a hot car for the thrill of it. Like people I'd known back in Chicago and Boston who wanted to buy stolen merchandise so they could brag about it.

"You can drive me to the airport," I said, "but take another car. The one I'm dropping off has something wrong with the tranny."

"In that case, you tell your boss I'm deducting the cost of repairs from the price."

I did, and Vito got pissed at me for letting them know about the problem.

My next car was going to New York, a much easier drive on toll roads all the way. I met Vito there and gave him the car. We went out and ate at a steakhouse on Eighth Avenue where I had the best steak ever. Having money to spend made a weekend in New York a lot of fun. But strolling along Eighth Avenue brought back memories of people I had robbed on that street, and all the junkies, now dead, I used to know.

When Vito introduced me to some pretty Puerto Rican girls, my bad memories faded as we drank and partied all night. I flew back to Chicago the next day.

I visited Vito in his bar on Milwaukee Avenue. It was dark inside and I didn't recognize any of the guys spread out along the bar. Some of his mob friends were there, sitting around talking. Well, not really talking, but growling at each other as they all tried to look menacing. One of them even told another, "My son can kick your son's ass any day."

I busted out laughing, but shouldn't have. These guys were serious—so deadly serious that it was probably one of them who shot Vito in the head not long after.

After the mob killed Vito, I thought about Al Dorfman's tire getting shot out. I knew for certain that if I'd been driving, I wouldn't have lived long enough to meet Vito. But maybe his associates would get the idea that I knew too much, and decide I should get the same treatment. Not only didn't I fit in with Vito's friends, I didn't want to fit in. I may have been a criminal, but I never wanted to hurt anybody like these gangsters who played for keeps. And if I became one of them, I wouldn't have a choice when ordered to take someone out.

Memories of the Cook County Jail dogged me as another possible consequence for hanging around with those guys. The thought of getting sentenced to fifty, sixty or seventy years scared me. So I took a hike and started looking for a legit job.

Wimpy's and Beyond

At twenty-two, I didn't have many more skills than when I was sixteen and newly released from Middlesex County Training School. But I had learned to communicate a bit better, and so I answered an ad for an assistant manager at one of the four Wimpy's Grill hamburger restaurants in the downtown Chicago Loop.

I went to an office where I was scheduled for an interview with the regional manager himself. He appeared to be in his late twenties, an age I could relate to.

"Hi, I saw you need an assistant manager," I said when he asked me to tell him a little about myself. "I could fill that position if you promise not to show me any favoritism and let me advance on my own merit."

He didn't say anything, but he appeared a bit confused by my approach.

"I don't mean to imply that anyone would ever do that, but it seems that whenever I get a job, I'm soon advanced over people who have worked there longer than I have."

I saw his eyes light up with interest. He probably thought I was some kind of workaholic. I was a hard worker and usually did advance quickly when I worked, but I had never worked at any one job long enough to brag about it.

"Where have you worked that you were promoted?" he asked.

"Amalgamated Insurance Company, Yellow Freight, and Tecumseh Lodge. I ran the kitchen at the lodge, so I won't have a problem managing a small restaurant." I figured if I lied well enough, he
wouldn't check my references, and he didn't.

"You'll have to work six days a week," he said.

"No problem."

I started work the next day in a downtown Chicago Wimpy's. It
was more like a coffee shop with booths and waitresses than today's
fast-food hamburger joint. My starting salary was ninety dollars a
week. As assistant manager, I did general restaurant work, like help-
ing wait and clean tables. When the waitresses got busy, I handled
the takeout orders. I liked working in the city. Plenty of good-looking
women came into the restaurant, and I always flirted with them. As a
result, I received substantial tips.

I worked happily for a few weeks until a waitress said, "You got
some nerve, keeping our tips."

"What are you talking about?"

"You get a salary, we don't. Any tips you get should come to us."

I felt like a louse. What she said was true: I made a salary, they
didn't. I never knew it was customary to give all tips to the waitresses.
I always thought whoever got the tip, kept it. From then on, I didn't
take any tips.

One day Silvio stopped in the restaurant and watched me work
for a while.

"I see you have to hustle for ninety bucks a week."

"Yeah, but I like it here."

"How many days a week do you work?"

"Monday through Saturday," I said as I cleared dishes from the counter.

"You can make the same money working five days a week as a painter," Silvio said in a voice that implied I'd be an idiot not to quit and go to work as a painter with him.

I went to see the general manager who shook my hand as if I was an old friend.

"I'm sorry to tell you this," I said, "but I got drafted. I have to report for duty in two weeks, so I won't be coming to work any longer."

As usual, I made the wrong decision. I went to work painting, something I'd hated doing ever since I was forced to paint at Middlesex County Training School because the fumes made me sick.

* * * * *

Sam Keith owned a small painting business where he employed two or three painters during the busy season. Sam was Jewish and I looked a lot like him. Customers often asked if I was his son, and he'd act insulted. He was a nice guy, so I didn't get upset. I always wanted to ask him if maybe on his way to Europe he had stopped in Boston for some pleasure; we looked enough alike that this was a possibility.

Sam had played basketball in high school and had received a scholarship for it, but he'd gone into the Army instead. A disgusted look washed over his face whenever he talked about his time in the Army. He liberated some concentration camps, he said, but never went into detail.

Sam liked me because I was a hard worker and every day completed a lot of work. His business consisted mainly of painting apartments for real estate companies. Renters got a few rooms painted when they signed a new lease, but the porches, windows, and hallways on these buildings needed regular maintenance. Painting for Sam wasn't bad, as we did mostly exterior work and I loved being outside. One day we had to paint closets and I became so dizzy from the fumes that I could hardly drive home.

Another time we painted windows on Chicago's South Side. The neighborhood was changing from white to black during the Civil Rights era, and there was significant racial tension. I was on a ladder painting a third-floor window when Sam yelled up to me, "Climb through the window and unlock all the windows in that apartment!"

When we painted windows, we had to move the bottom sash above the top one in order to paint the crossbars, and then move them up and down after painting so they wouldn't stick as the paint dried. I went through the window and when I looked up, I heard a voice say, "Where you going?"

A black guy was sitting up in bed with a chrome-plated .45 automatic. When I saw that big-ass gun pointed right at my chest, I tensed up, expecting him to pull the trigger any second.

"I'm just going to unlock the windows so I can move them up and down and they won't get stuck," I blurted out.

He kept the gun trained on me until I climbed back out the window.

The weather changed after that incident, and Sam ran out of work. No one bothered to tell me that once the weather turned cold, there wouldn't be any work, and I didn't have the good sense to figure this out. Sam didn't pay unemployment insurance for seasonal work, so we couldn't collect any.

I'd bought an old Plymouth Coupe from a carpenter who worked for Sam. The winter was brutally cold, and the temperature didn't get above zero for days at a time. To get my car to start, I'd get a metal garbage can cover, pour charcoal briquettes on it and set them aflame. Once they burned brightly, I'd shove the lid under the crankcase of my car and go inside for an hour or so. When I came out, my car would be warm and start right up. But the Plymouth didn't have a heater in it. The lights used on roadwork then were the cannonball-sized oil lamps. I took one of these and kept it burning while I drove so I could warm my hands when they felt frozen. Those were some lean times.

* * * * *

Silvio moved into my apartment, and before long, my brother Tony stayed there, too. There was a multi-storied garage across the street. I went into the garage to see how much they charged for parking, hoping my car would start in the mornings if I parked inside. An attendant came over and seemed real friendly.

"Did you know this was the site of the Saint Valentine's Day Massacre?" he asked.

"No, I didn't."

"Yeah, and right up the street is the Biograph Theatre. That's where the Feds killed John Dillinger," he said.

The theatre was in walking distance, and I began to watch movies there. I could also walk to Lincoln Park and often visited the zoo and arboretum. When I walked through the door of the arboretum on freezing winter days, the warm sweet air embraced me. The plant enclosure was so large that it took half an hour to walk through it. By gazing at the greenery, I could imagine myself in Florida, or a jungle, or anywhere I desired. A stroll through the plants and flowers always lifted my spirits. Eventually, I put indoor plants in my apartment and bought a sunlamp so I could take my imaginary trips from home. One night I fell asleep under the sunlamp and suffered severe burns over my entire back.

The gloomy, freezing Chicago winters always depressed me. Tony, Silvio, and I couldn't find jobs that winter, and that was doubly disheartening. (I think we were all scared one of us might end up supporting the other two.) I didn't have many marketable skills since none of my previous jobs required many. My experience as an assistant cook at the boys' camp didn't qualify me for serious restaurant work, and I hadn't stayed long enough at Wimpy's to qualify for another managerial trainee position.

Tony had worked as a cook ever since his job at the state police barracks when he was a kid. Experienced cooks could always find jobs if they wanted one.

All Silvio knew how to do was paint. I began to toy with the idea of dabbling in crime again, but after reminding myself of how Vito got hit and that I was still in the midst of my five years' probation, dishonesty didn't appeal to me. For the first time in my life, I began to consider the consequences of breaking the law.

One day Silvio asked me, "You got a cigarette?"

"I was going to ask you the same thing."

I usually smoked three packs a day. Even though butts were only a quarter a pack, I had a hard time staying in smokes without any money coming in.

"Come on, I'll show you how to get some smokes when you're flat out," Silvio said.

He silently tiptoed to the apartment across from mine, to a small door used by the iceman in bygone days to deliver blocks of ice. He opened the door unnoticed, and snitched a few cigarettes from a pack on the kitchen counter.

"The woman always leaves her cigarettes here while she watches TV," said Silvio. "There are a dozen more apartments where I do the same thing. That way, I never run out of smokes."

We'd get dinner every now and then by knocking on our neighbor's doors and telling each one that we forgot to get an ingredient for dinner. That way we could borrow a can of tomato sauce from one, and a package of spaghetti from another.

One night Tony brought a hunk of cheese and some bread home. Silvio and I asked if he was going to share.

"Sure, I'll give you guys one sandwich each but that's it."

We watched as Tony cut two slices of cheese so thin they could have floated on air. Silvio and I laughed so hard that we never even ate the pieces of transparent cheese.

I finally got a job working in an all-night restaurant just so I could eat. Then, eventually, all three of us were hired to unload freight cars at Crooks Warehouse. I'll never forget the time when a couple of detectives stopped me and asked me where I worked.

"I work for Crooks," I told them, and one cop's face lit up. Evidently he thought I literally meant criminals and I was about to let him in on something!

Tony and I liked to work together while unloading freight cars. One day the car we had to unload was stacked to the roof with hundred-pound sacks of sugar. As hard as rocks, these paper bags were difficult to get a grip on and difficult to lift. A forklift driver made a circuit every fifteen minutes or so to drop off an empty skid and take away the full one.

Tony never cared for physical labor, so it was no surprise when he told me, "I'll give you half my pay if you do my share of the work." That meant I'd be making seven-fifty an hour instead of five dollars. I agreed and worked as fast as I could to have the skid loaded by time the driver came to remove it. I'm not sure how much I unloaded that day, but I emptied two freight cars, and I recall telling Tony, "I unloaded a million pounds today."

However many pounds I unloaded, there were way too many. That night my body shook all over from the exertion. The next day I told Tony he had to unload his share. He quit, and so did Silvio. I got fired soon after because I sat down to rest while I waited for a driver to remove a full skid.

Silvio and I went to R. H. Donnelly Company to look for work. They printed and distributed phone books for Chicago. I lied and said I had a high school education, so I got hired. Silvio didn't. My job was to review the paperwork of the guys who delivered the phone books. They were paid per book delivered and for the old ones they brought back. My boss, two recent college graduates, and I did this job daily. I'd process ten or twenty workers to every single one my co-workers did. Before long, every driver wanted to have me review their paperwork because I did it fast and, whenever possible, gave them extra credit.

Silvio quit looking for a job, and when rent time came around I crude- ly said, "I ain't f-ing you, so why do you expect me to pay your rent?"

He moved back to his mother's house, and told everyone he supported her. He gave her $25.00 a week for room and board, and she did his laundry. She was a kind Italian woman who shared the same birthday as me. I rented a room from her for awhile, and she fed me so well, I outgrew all my clothes in a matter of weeks.

As the weather turned again, I got a union job painting the new Chicago water filtration plant that was under construction. It was getting cold in November, but even though I had to work outside, I was happy to have a job with good pay. The business agent from the painters union came around, and the foreman told him he knew I wasn't in the union, but he couldn't find any union painters. I wondered if I'd get canned, but the business agent drove away and I continued working.

I had my first experience with walking on steel girders a few inches wide at the water filtration plant. Looking down was plenty scary. I discovered if I carried a long plank (what we called "stringers"—a piece of wood that reached from one steel beam to another), I could maintain my balance and easily walk beams that scared many other painters. I felt like a high-wire walker using a pole for balance. Eventually, I found I could also work construction sites with high-rise steel frames. My job was to walk the beams and paint red lead on the bolts that the ironworkers installed. (Today the ironworkers paint the bolts themselves.)

Silvio worked on the high-rise, too, but didn't like walking the high I-beams.

"I'm not risking my life," he said.

"Man, how do I get home, then?" I asked.

"Tell the foreman you're sick or something."

I went to the foreman. "I hurt my back carrying that heavy plank across the girders by myself."

"State regulations say you need to get it checked out," he said. "Here's the address for the clinic."

He handed me a card. When I went to the clinic, the doctor prescribed physical therapy in the form of back massages. I enjoyed these, and the girl who did the massages was cute, so I continued my therapy for as long as I could.

Love, Lust and Marriage

While working at the R. H. Donnelly Company, I surveyed the women working there and spotted an attractive girl named Brenda. She was nineteen, but looked much younger. Well-built and fresh looking, she also appeared to be pure and innocent.

I stepped on the elevator with her sister Jo, who also worked at Donnelly's. "You and your sister hardly look old enough to be working," I said.

"I may as well tell you right now, we've both got a kid," she warned, spitting the words out like a challenge.

I hardly believed this because she looked even younger and more innocent than Brenda, maybe thirteen or fourteen.

Despite the warning, I asked Brenda for a date. She accepted and gave me her address. That same night, I drove to her family's apartment at 76th and Halsted Streets.

It was a long drive from the North side of Chicago to a 7600 South address. The Dan Ryan Expressway had recently opened and it went through all-black neighborhoods on the South side. It seemed there were stories in the newspapers every day about white motorists who were attacked by gangs of blacks after their cars broke down. Many people were afraid to drive on the Expressway at the time. I, on the other hand, thought the news stories were blown out of proportion by the media (as many are today). During my time driving junky cars that often stalled out around Chicago, I found that the first to stop and offer help was always a black driver. Not only that, I survived over a year in the county jail with an 80% black population—a population that wanted much the same things as any white: freedom, a happy family, and a trouble-free life.

I'd recently purchased a 1953 Ford convertible, another junker, and it took all my spare money to keep it running. So I was prepared for it to break down on the highway but didn't let that stop me. I figured Brenda was worth the drive and any risk I might endure if the car broke down.

When I arrived at her apartment and rang the bell, Brenda proudly displayed her baby and said, "A trophy from my marriage." Debby, a chubby baby, reminded me of cherubs in classic paintings of heaven.

I should have sensed something awry when she referred to her baby as a trophy, but the comment went over my head. Maybe she should have sensed something about my character when it did. I'm sure if she'd known of my recent release from the county jail and my five years' probation, she never would have agreed to go out with me.

It turned out that not only did Jo have a baby, but her other sister, Elsie, had a baby, too. No husbands in sight; I should have turned and ran.

I didn't have a problem with Brenda having a baby. I liked children but never took guff from one. I treated them the same way as I'd been handled as a child. I'd administer a good kick to the butt to any smart-assed kid. I remembered how I acted toward adults, and I wasn't about to let children treat me with the same disrespect that I'd displayed toward older people.

Brenda led me into the living room.

"This is my mom," she said, gesturing to a nice-looking woman with red hair.

"Hi, I'm Josephine." She took my hand in hers and held it far too long. "Welcome to the family."

Josephine's speech and demeanor made it clear that she'd been drinking, so I ignored her comment and how she'd caressed my hand. She reminded me of the women I'd grown up around, drunk and flirtatious, only she was better looking than most Hano house-wives.

"I used to work as a singer for a radio station," she said, rattling on about her past in a raspy voice. "I'm going to my favorite fucking bar at 63rd and Halsted. Stop by and see me any time. I'm almost always there."

"Ma, you know how rough that neighborhood is?" Brenda asked.

Josephine waved a hand. "If anyone gives him a problem, I'll kick their ass. They don't call me the terror of 63rd Street for noth-ing, you know."

Her slurred speech became increasingly hard to understand, but the mean look that crossed her face confirmed the truth of her words. If Josephine's appearance matched her internal nature, she would have be the most terrifying monster I'd ever seen. I later learned she

323

burned her son's hand using the gas stove, straddled one of her daughters and beat her daily, and goaded her ex-husband to almost kill her boyfriend with a pipe just to see some excitement. Her reported list of sins could fill a book.

I didn't understand how someone could be as cruel as Josephine.

Not long after I met Brenda, I rented a truck and moved all her mother's belongings to another apartment. After working hard all day, Josephine said, "Thanks, *SUCKER!*"

I had the good sense to walk away. Normally I would have done something obnoxious to a person who took advantage of me and then insulted me like that, but she was Brenda's mother. I knew there would be repercussions if I acted out.

* * * * *

My boss at Donnelly's always bragged about his beautiful wife. One night I took Brenda out and ran into him and his wife in a restaurant. She was...well, not beautiful at all. I wondered later if she was beautiful in his mind.

Another night as Brenda and I walked on the Southwest side of Chicago, I ran into Sully, my old friend from Deer Island, at 26th and California Streets, near Cook County Jail—a highly unlikely coincidence. The last time we saw each other had been in New York.

We hugged one another like long lost brothers.

"When did you get to Chicago?" I asked.

"Been here a couple of years now. This is my wife, Teresa." Sully's new wife, a tall, good-looking Polish girl, smiled at me shyly.

"You live around here?" asked Sully.

"No, I have to report to my probation officer once a month," I said, pointing at the courthouse down the street. "What happened to New York?" I was really asking what happened to Patsy, his former wife.

"Patsy tried to get me arrested. She told the cops a bunch of stuff I had done. They came to the house and had their hands on me, but I broke free, jumped a few fences, and here I am."

I knew about the fences Sully had jumped. I climbed them one night to get to the back door when my girlfriend wouldn't open the front door for me. They were high wire fences laced with barbed wire to keep burglars out. In my mind, there was no way a normal cop would climb them to apprehend a suspect. It wasn't all that surprising that Sully had eluded the police.

We went into a bar to have a few beers and talk about old times. As usually happened when I brought a good-looking woman into a bar, some asshole would hit on her and try to take her away from me. So it was no surprise when three hillbillies strode over to where we stood.

The one in the center looked Theresa and Brenda over and said, "You girls want to dance?"

I tensed up, trying not to ball my hands into a fist. "Can't you see they're with us?" I said.

"Ain't asking you to dance. I'm asking the ladies."

"Yeah, and I'm telling you they don't want to."

As soon as I'd finished my last word, one ran at me with a pool stick in his hands.

Oh shit, here we go, I thought.

I instinctively grabbed the stick and pulled the attacker forward to throw him off balance. I ripped the stick from his hand and whacked him over the head with it. He fell to the floor unconscious. Sully fought with the second guy, and I went after the third with the pool stick. He ran around the pool table, and I chased him, poised to smash the pool stick into his head. He threw a pool ball and hit me above my left eye. It hurt like hell and stars exploded in my peripheral vision, but I continued to go after him. I passed by Sully, now struggling with the third hillbilly who I hit in the head with the pool cue. He dropped like a sack of shit. The guy I was chasing flew out the door before I could catch him.

When the cops came, they took me to city hospital right away because blood was dripping over the left side of my face from my split eyebrow.

When the emergency room doctor examined me, he said, "You're lucky. I've been sewing up people for a year now and I've gotten very good at suturing wounds." He spoke the truth, because I can hardly see the scar now.

After I was released from the emergency room, Brenda and I went to the apartment I'd recently rented for her on the Southside, and I went to sleep. I'd just purchased a '53 Ford convertible and spent most of my money restoring it to running condition. Her brother Gus lifted my keys while I slept and took it for a joy ride. He smashed it up and ran back to my apartment to tell me what happened. Though pissed at him, I didn't want him to go to jail, so I called the police and told them someone else stole my car.

They came to take a report, and right away noticed my stitches from the previous night. I still wore the bloodstained shirt. Obviously, they thought I'd driven my car, wrecked it, got hurt, and was now accusing someone else of crashing it.

They questioned Gus and he told them I knew he had wrecked my car before I called and had reported it stolen. Gus didn't get arrested, but I did, for making a false report.

With my five years' probation, this charge counted as a violation. I certainly didn't want to go back to the county jail, so I hired a lawyer. We went to a district court on the far south side of Chicago. My attorney engaged in an argument with the judge. The judge scowled, pointed his finger at me, and said in as mean a voice as he could muster, "You're going to jail."

"Why me? You're arguing with him, not me," I said, pointing at my lawyer.

"Next case," the judge said.

I fired the lawyer.

After a little research, I found there were five good criminal lawyers in Chicago referred to as "The Five B's" because their names began with the letter B. I chose the one named Brody. I couldn't really afford him, but I had to pay the price if I wanted to stay out of jail. At the mere mention of his name, I was able to get my case continued until a different judge sat on the bench. Once a new judge was seated, Brody appeared and the charges were dismissed. Brody told me that what I paid him didn't even buy the gas he used to drive his Cadillac all the way to the southernmost point of Chicago where the district court was located.

* * * * *

A few days after our bar fight, Sully and I returned to the same place to have a couple of beers. We were welcomed as conquering heroes. The bartender said, "Those guys you fought had been terrorizing the patrons of this bar for quite a while. Everybody was scared of them, and they were considered real tough guys."

"Guess they weren't so tough after all," I said. I credited beating them to my survival instinct, not toughness.

The owners of the bar also said that the syndicate backed their business. I believed them, because in those days, jukeboxes earned big money from bar patrons feeding them quarters almost around the clock. The mob would open a joint just to put a jukebox in.

The owners passed on the word that I had a job as an enforcer-collector if I wanted it. (I thought of my friend, Jimmy Bryant, and his childhood dream. He had always talked about how he'd beat people and wreck their houses if they didn't pay up.) I wasn't hard-hearted enough to work as an enforcer, so I declined the job.

* * * * *

My intention in dating Brenda was to get laid, not to get married. But before long she said those dreaded words: "I'm pregnant."

My first thought was, *The baby isn't mine. I must be the most convenient guy to blame.*

I suspected she still had sex with her ex-husband, and the one time Silvio and I went to her apartment late at night, we saw her in bed with another man. Plus, by the time she told me, I had quit seeing her. Brenda didn't want another baby, and my entire life had been so miserable that I'd never wanted to bring another life into the world, so I looked for a way out.

Abortion was illegal in 1963. I searched for someone to do the "job" but could only find a guy who said he'd perform an abortion using a coat hanger. The thought repulsed me, and I declined the offer without mentioning it to Brenda.

Brenda thought I should marry her. I agreed because I felt sorry for her. But every time we got near City Hall, where a marriage license and a justice of the peace awaited, I made unreasonable demands that she couldn't agree to: "Once we're married, you can't see your mother anymore," I would tell her.

I acted like an asshole, but I wasn't marrying material. And I sure as hell wasn't qualified to raise a kid.

Not long after my insane demands, Brenda got a job on a farm where she babysat and worked the fields. I believed her gone, permanently. I rationalized that I hadn't really fathered her new baby, so when she left, I felt happy. Selfish, inconsiderate, and blind to how the situation affected Brenda, I allowed my old survival instinct to prevail.

A few months passed, and I received a letter. The manager of the building where I lived liked me and confessed she thought about trashing it when she noticed another woman's name on the envelope, but she delivered it anyway. The letter was Brenda saying, "I must talk to you. Important!"

I drove out to the countryside where she lived on a small farm near Calumet City, Indiana. She was babysitting for a half-dozen kids when I arrived. I took them all to an ice cream parlor, and think it may have been the first time they'd gone because they became raucous with excitement.

Brenda told me how Cloyd, her ex-husband, had threatened to take custody of her daughter because of her pregnancy and his assertion that she couldn't properly care for Debby. She reached out to hold my hand, and I felt how calloused hers had become. My heart went out to her and Debby, but I still didn't believe the baby she carried was mine. Looking at her large stomach and little Debby, I just couldn't walk away from them and leave them to their fate. I agreed to marry her, and we soon went to City Hall to get our license.

"When people see my big belly, and little Debby standing with us while we're being married, they're going to think what a nice guy you are," Brenda said.

I felt like a nice guy, but the way she talked meant, *They're going to think you're a fool.*

Still, I didn't see any other option.

We married in August of 1963, and by October, I was unemployed again. I searched for a job every day, but I couldn't find one.

We didn't have any insurance or money to pay for a hospital birth, so Brenda connected with a home birthing organization. She assured me it was safer to give birth at home than in a hospital. I didn't know anything about it.

"Face it, you're a loser," I berated myself. "Find a way out of this mess."

Brenda's mother rented an apartment across the courtyard from us. When I walked through the neighborhood, I'd often hear her drunken voice shouting, "There he is, my favorite fucking son-in-law!" I'd cross the street and tried try to ignore her, but she made sure everyone in hearing range knew I was the object of her affection. One or both of Brenda's sisters often stayed with us. Whenever my sisters-in-law moved out, it seemed my brother Tony moved in.

I never learned how to say no. I always shared whatever I had with friends or family, and believed that was how it should be. Naïve, I didn't realize they were taking advantage of my good nature. After a few years of practically running a bed and breakfast for family members when I could barely pay my rent or feed myself, I learned to rent a hotel room when they cried about not having any place to stay. It eased my conscience and made it hard for them to mooch off me. Hell, one time I used my last twenty-five dollars to bail my brother Tony out of jail. The next morning he went to court, got the charge dismissed, and the bail money returned to him. I asked for it back.

"I can't give you this," he said. "It's all the money I've got."

My jaw hit the ground. My feelings for him were never the same after that, but I still let him pop in and out when he came to town broke.

Vietnam... Almost

The marriage was doomed from the start because we immediately began to take our frustrations out on one another.

Brenda claimed that a wife's place was in the home.

"Fuck that," I said. "If I can work, you can, too."

That got her pissed off, so she started telling me that my shoulders weren't wide enough, or that my dick wasn't long enough. Because of all the time I spent in reform schools and jails, I didn't have much sexual experience. I didn't know if all women's pussies got stretched out after having a kid or not, but I had to agree with Brenda, my dick wasn't big enough to fit her. This was long before penis enhancements—not that I could have afforded one if they were available. Anyway, I never had such a low opinion of myself or my physique, and I became self-conscious and defensive.

My opinion of Brenda wasn't much kinder than her opinion of me. The next time Silvio came by to have a few beers, I got up my nerve to ask him about female anatomy.

"Man, I don't know what to do. Fucking Brenda is like sticking my dick in a manhole."

He laughed so hard I thought he was choking. "Told you not to marry her."

"So what can a woman do to tighten up after she has a kid?"

"All the hookers use alum to tighten up," he said. "If it works for them, it should work for your wife."

"Where do you buy that shit at?"

"Any big supermarket. Look in the seasoning aisle, you know, around the salt & pepper. It's spelled A-L-U-M. Tell Brenda to put a teaspoonful in a douche and follow that with a douche of warm water. It doesn't burn and it's painless."

"How do you know, have you tried it?"

"Fuck you, Joe. I know because my brother had a bad case of hemorrhoids and he used alum to shrink them."

So, I went shopping. When I arrived home, I gave Brenda a container of alum.

"Here," I said. "Use this to shrink up your manhole."

Her mouth dropped open and she stared at me like I was crazy.

"Look," I said, "it ain't me that's small; your vagina is stretched out of shape."

"You bastard," she said and threw alum at me.

If we'd had a healthier relationship, we could have discussed the issue and agreed upon a solution, but we enjoyed taking our insecurities out on one another.

Money was also a problem. I hardly had any for cigarettes, which in my mind were more important than food. I did stop drinking, though. I wouldn't spend the little money I could hustle up on booze and let Debby or Brenda go hungry. But I did get the urge to jump in my car and just drive away. Chicago was a terrible place to spend winters, especially with a car that had a leaky radiator. I couldn't afford to keep putting antifreeze into it and had to drain what water didn't leak out at night, then refill it the next day. I actually had water freeze while pouring it into the radiator one day when it was 40 below zero. Scientists say moving water won't freeze, but I disagree.

I also had to contend with Brenda's ex-husband coming by to pick up his daughter every weekend. He was a little guy compared to me—a hillbilly from somewhere down south. He told me he divorced Brenda so he could go out and party. It used to burn me up to see Brenda always making sure she looked her best every time he came by. I didn't think for a minute that he cared that much for his daughter; he came to see Brenda. But I couldn't deprive Debby of seeing her father, even though I was jealous as hell. Funny how that works—being possessive, I mean. I didn't give a shit about Brenda, but the thought of her fucking somebody else set me to boiling.

* * * * *

Like many Americans in 1963, I watched the television news reports stating that if Vietnam fell to communism, all the countries in Southeast Asia would fall like dominoes. In those days, I believed all the bullshit on television and was ready to go to Vietnam to kill "those dirty commies." I would have done a hell of a good job of it, too. All my years of incarceration had taught me to hold my emotions in check and do what I had to do. I wasn't patriotic, but the thought of getting away appealed to me. In the back of my mind, I formulated ways I could make money in Vietnam. Hell, if I could

335

make $40 a day while locked up in the county jail, I knew I'd find a way to hustle over there.

My old cut-and-run instinct kicked in again. On December 22, 1963, I went to an Army recruiting station locate near Montrose and Broadway in Chicago. At that time, if you could walk and talk, the Army gladly signed you up as cannon fodder. I figured my criminal record wouldn't prevent me from enlisting, as it had several times before.

The recruiting sergeant cheerily spewed his bullshit. "The Army is a great life. In twenty years you can retire and live anywhere you want," he said. "Just fill out these papers and you'll be ready to go in a day."

"I've got a wife and a baby about to be born."

"No problem. We take care of your dependents." He promised me the Army would see that Brenda received food stamps and a check deducted from my Army pay. If I hadn't mentioned Brenda, my conscience wouldn't have let me sleep. And if I didn't have that damn conscience, I would have been a real lifetime criminal instead of doing all the drunk punk stuff I did.

All I had to do was sign on the dotted line, and I'd be free to go. Relieved by this information, I planned to enlist after Christmas. I knew I'd be a good soldier because I'd engaged in street fights my entire life, and I was ready to maim and kill anyone I was ordered to—and probably a few I wasn't. I didn't think I'd be scared in a fire-fight. Cops had shot at me, and I counted the bullets, waiting for them to empty their guns so I could go up against them hand-to-hand. I was always more afraid of losing a fight than of getting killed.

Lee Harvey Oswald had assassinated John F. Kennedy the previous month, and Lyndon Johnson had stepped up to become president. Once I read that he liked to go skinny-dipping with other men and mistakenly thought he must be queer. Of a contradictory personality, Johnson helped many with his Great Society programs, while at the same time treating those close to him shoddily. But he was going to be my commander-in-chief, and I convinced myself that I couldn't think too badly of him.

I went home to tell Brenda about my enlistment, but before I could tell her anything, she went into labor. All along, Brenda had assured me the baby would be a boy. I'd planned to name him Antonio, after my father. In our furnished apartment on the 4400 block of Broadway in Chicago, I watched as Brenda lay in bed, surrounded by two visiting nurses and a doctor. She looked at me with hate in her eyes as she labored.

"It's all your fault, you bastard!" she screamed.

I calmly listened as she ran through her entire repertoire of swear words, some I'd never heard before. Her suffering was obvious, and there wasn't much I could do to comfort her other than stand by while she castigated me for being a man, for fucking her, for getting her pregnant, for any problem she could imagine.

She had my sympathy, but I finally let her hateful words ruffle me a bit as she lay on our bed with her legs in the air while a nurse told her to breathe in and out, and a doctor stuck his fingers in her vagina like the baby was lost and he needed to find it. I had no idea about anything that went on during a birth—the extreme pain, the screaming, the mess, or the medical procedure. I knew absolutely nothing about childbirth until this moment. I'd sat with my dad when my brother Andy was born, but that situation was antiseptic compared to this. The bloody mess I gazed at on my bed was beyond my comprehension.

When the baby's head started to crown, it had a full head of hair, but I didn't know this. It appeared to me that the bloody mess was the baby's exposed brain, because the long hair soaked in gore looked similar to pictures of brains in science books.

Suddenly, the baby's head seemed to be stuck halfway out. The doctor pushed his fingers past the head and into Brenda's vagina, hooking two fingers under the baby's arm and gently pulling it into this world: a slippery, wet baby with matted hair and a big cry.

The doctor held the baby by the legs for all to see—not a boy at all, but a girl.

I believed her to be my daughter, because when the doctor held her by the legs I could see she had a unique rib cage, just like mine—as if I have an extra rib, like my brothers, too.

Ambushed by love, it didn't matter at all to me that I'd fathered a girl. Once I saw she was indeed mine, that bloody, gory little thing magically changed into a beautiful, squalling baby girl who altered my life forever.

Love for her overwhelmed me. I decided I wasn't going to Vietnam, back to jail, or anywhere else. I wanted to stay home with my daughter. I didn't know how I'd support her, but I'd find a way.

It was a good thing I hadn't signed the enlistment papers. I would have had to go to Vietnam before seeing the little girl who saved me from murdering people.

Epilogue

"Can I name her Josephine, after my mother?" Brenda asked.

I stupidly agreed. At that moment, I forgot how much I disliked my mother-in-law and her name. She wasn't a very nice person, and later, the name grated every time I said it.

Poor Josephine! She only had a dresser drawer for a cradle. There had been no baby shower or anything given to us for the baby to wear. Out of work, I struggled to come up with rent money every week, so new baby stuff and food were scarce. But I took any job I could get to survive without turning to crime.

Finally, as a father, I fit in. I happily walked the floor all night with the baby, and at other times drove her around so she wouldn't cry. For the first time in my life, I loved someone unconditionally. I knew I had a hard road ahead to support a wife, two daughters, and myself. I didn't know how I'd manage, but somehow I would.

Soon after the baby was born, a nurse who came to check on her told me I should apply for welfare. The word made me cringe, and my pride wouldn't let me accept it. I needed help at the time and should have taken it. I'm now glad I didn't, even though I struggled.

Around this time, I ran into Vince, a guy I'd met in Cook County Jail. He showed me his latest scam. He split a one-dollar bill with a razor blade, and then he'd split a twenty-dollar bill and paste the one and the twenty together so he then had forty dollars instead of twenty-one. He passed the bills with the twenty side up, and no one ever flipped these over. (That's probably the reason why clerks now look at both sides to see if a bill is counterfeit.) I succeeded in splitting a one and a twenty, but decided against passing it. I knew it was a federal offense and didn't want to go back to jail.

I managed by working jobs I despised, but I reminded myself how much better freedom is than living under lock and key, and I persevered.

If I got locked up again, there would be no one to look after my kids other than my wife, who I couldn't count on for anything because she didn't like to work and cared more for herself than the kids. We split up in 1970, and after trading the girls back and forth for a few years, they mostly grew up with me. It turned out to be tough life for the kids, but not as difficult as my own childhood.

After Josephine—"Gogi"—was born in 1963, I worked as a painter. I joined the International Brotherhood of Painters in 1966. I'm a member of the union to this day.

Gogi gave me three granddaughters and two grandsons, who so far have given me four great-granddaughters. My adopted daughter Debby gave me two granddaughters, and my second daughter Eva, born in 1967, has given me two grandsons. My son Joe, born in 1974, has a two-year-old son and newborn twin girls.

My daughters turned out to be good parents, and I'm proud of all my grandchildren. When I see them, I know that all the stuff I went through in my childhood and later with my kids was well worth the trouble. Though my marriages ended in divorce, my dream of having a happy family finally manifested in my relationships with my kids, grandkids, and great- grandkids.

Though my origins were humble—perhaps less than humble by many people's standards—I'm truly thankful for the life I've created. Common sense and my work ethic finally won out: I've stayed out of jail for fifty years.

During my married life, I went to trade school and learned to be a draftsman. I took welding classes, and then air conditioning and heating classes, but I remained a painter for financial reasons. In 1974, I acquired an assistant stockbroker's license. I also acquired a real estate license in Illinois that same year. A few years later, I obtained a contractor's license in California.

In 2006 at the age of 66, I took an interest in writing and entered a creative writing program at Yavapai College in Prescott, Arizona. I graduated with a certificate in 2009. This creative outlet finally allowed me to channel all the anger and impulsivity that caused me to admire criminals and commit crimes. I fervently hope my readers are inspired to improve their lives as a result of my newfound ability to share my experiences through the written word.

I also enjoy art, and I took a sculpting class in 2008. I filled my yard in central Arizona with sculptures I created from rebar and cement, and filled my home with paintings and sketches.

In 2011, at age 71, I ran my first marathon.

Because of my dedication to exercise, writing, sculpting, I remain open to new ideas and new activities. When I turned 75 I made out a bucket list. The year is coming to an end and so far, I've flown a WWII biplane, gone skydiving and hang gliding, kayaked over a 20-foot-high waterfall, rafted down Colorado white water, gone on numerous kayaking and hiking trips, and twice rode the zip line at Out of Africa. (Loved it both times.) Guess even as an old man, I remain a thrill-seeker.

I've become an inspiration to my kids, who see that the "golden years" can truly be golden.

About the Author

Born in 1940, Joe DiBuduo grew up poor in Boston. He led a troubled childhood and spent time in reform and training schools. As an adult, he spent time in the house of corrections. A turn of fate led him to California and then Chicago, where he married and had children. For the next thirty years he worked as a construction painter in many states, heading wherever the jobs could be found.

He earned his GED at age 30, and a certificate in Creative Writing from Yavapai College at age 69. Books include collections of flash fiction and "flash-fiction poetry," a children's picture book, a young adult novel, the novel *Cryonic Man,* and *A Penis Manalog,* a mixed-genre narrative inspired by Eve Ensler's *Vagina Monologues.* His story, "The Night Café," won a New Short Fiction Award from *Jerry Jazz Musician.*

DiBuduo is now retired and lives in Prescott, Arizona. Anger used to be a daily part of his life until he began to write. Now if something upsets him, he writes about it.

Suggested Reading

Abominable Firebug.com
http://www.abominablefirebug.com/Roslindale.html (Accessed 28 February, 2012).

Cormier, George. *Triumph Over Truancy.* Smashwords, 2011.

Delsohn, Gary. *Illinois Issues.* Illinois Periodicals Online,
< http://www.lib.niu.edu/1977/ii770303.html>, 4 March, 1977, p. 3.

Devlin, Mark D. *Stubborn Child.* New York: Macmillan, 1985.
Johnson, Richard B. *Abominable Firebug.* iUniverse, Inc., 2006.
Massis, Julie. "Good, bad of reform school recalled." Boston Globe Online, July 19, 2009.
http://www.boston.com/news/local/articles/2009/07/19/boys_reform_school_in_shirley_brings_bot h_good_bad_memories/ (Accessed 28 February, 2012).

New York Times Book Review. *Stubborn Child.* Mark Devlin. Atheneum, 1985.
http://www.nytimes.com/1985/07/05/books/books-of-the-times-098679.html (Accessed 28
February, 2012).

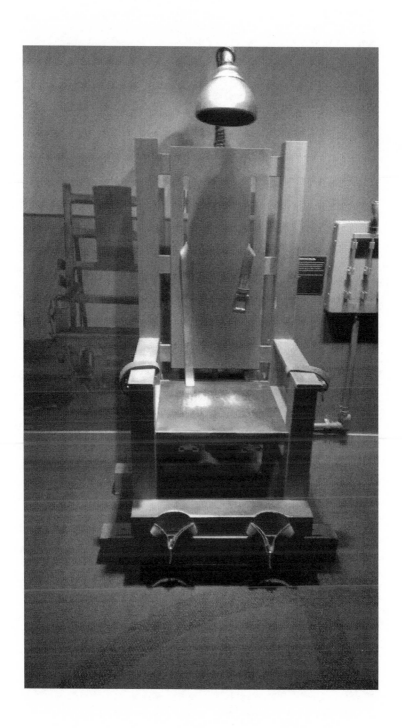

COPYRIGHTED MATERIAL

© 2015 copyright by Joe DiBuduo

First edition. All rights reserved.

ISBN: 978-0-9831956-8-9

Printed in the United States of America. No part of this book
may be used or reproduced in any manner whatsoever without
written permission from the publisher, except in the case of
brief quotations embodied in critical articles and reviews. For
information please email: questions@ jadedibispress.com

Published by Jaded Ibis Press, *sustainable literature by digital
means*™ an imprint of Jaded Ibis Productions, LLC, Seattle,
Washington USA.

Cover design by Debra Di Blasi.